The first skirmish was with language itself, that most powerful servant of guilt and shame and traditional authority. Lewd to many persons was an indecent dream, an unmentionable crudescence of dirty delights and distasteful desire. We referred to ourselves as "lewd," the LEWD Commune, LEWD persons. We sought to contrast the fact of our being with the fear of a word. The deliberate representation of ourselves as LEWD was a significant factor in the detoxification of a word —a word which, like porno or obscene, has the power to close a mind as well as pucker a mouth. Whether we were actually lewd ceased to be crucial, as the stigmatizing power of the word languished in our presence.

— from the introduction

LEWD

The Inquisition of Seth and Carolyn

BEING A REAL AND TRUE ACCOUNT OF THE ASSERTION OF THE PEOPLE'S ANCIENT AND JUST LIBERTIES IN THE TRIAL OF SETH MANY AND CAROLYN PECK AGAINST THE MOST ARBITRARY PROCEDURE OF THE COURT AND ITS MINIONS

Introduction by Seth Many

with illustrations by Carolyn Peck & Co.(mmune)

BEACON PRESS *BOSTON*

Library of Congress catalog card number: 72-75541
International Standard Book Number: 0-8070-0521-5
Beacon Press books are published under the auspices
of the Unitarian Universalist Association
Published simultaneously in Canada by Saunders of Toronto, Ltd.

Printed in the United States of America.

A limited edition of the memorable LEWD memorandum of law, proclaiming the legality of Mother Nature is available, price on request, from the LEWD Library, 197 Lake View Avenue, Cambridge, Mass.

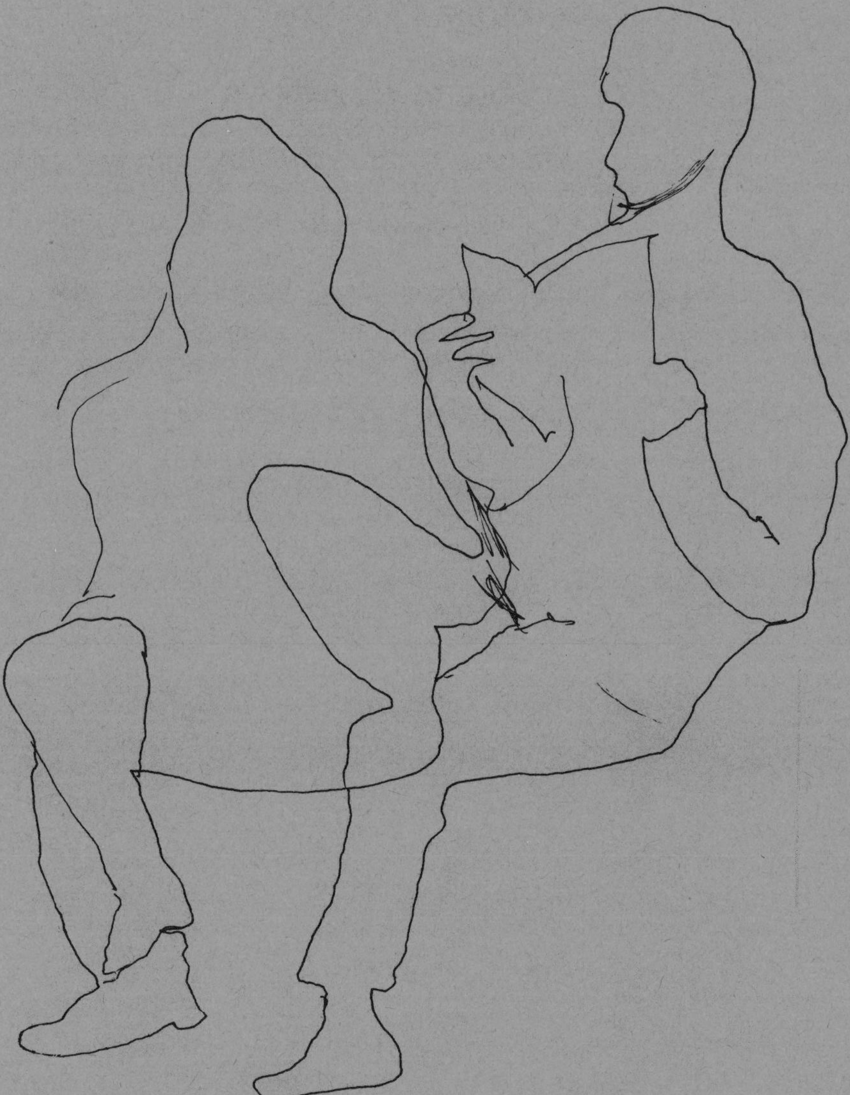

ACKNOWLEDGMENT

A grateful LEWD acknowledgment to the unsagging labors of editor Ray Bentley, designer Dick Bartlett, and the many busy Beacon Buccaneers that this naked Inquisition might reach the printed page.

CONTENTS & DISCONTENTS

COMMONWEALTH OF MASSACHUSETTS

MIDDLESEX, TO WIT:

To the Third District Court of Eastern Middlesex, holden at Cambridge for the Transaction of Criminal Business, within the County of Middlesex,

Edward D. McNulty

of Cambridge in said County, in behalf of the Commonwealth of Massachusetts, on the ninth day of March, in the year of our Lord one thousand nine hundred and seventy, on oath complains that

John Doe whose other and true name is to said complainant unknown, truly Seth E. Many, and

Jane Doe whose other and true name is to said complainant unknown, truly Carolyn R. Peck

on or about March 9, 1970
was guilty of open and gross lewdness and lascivious behavior in the presence of Edward D. McNulty

against the peace of the said Commonwealth and the form of the statute in such case made and provided,

____
Edward D. McNulty

COMMONWEALTH OF MASSACHUSETTS

MIDDLESEX CAMBRIDGE DISTRICT COURT

COMMONWEALTH OF MASSACHUSETTS

v.

SETH E. MANY AND CAROLYN R. PECK

Now comes the Defendant in the above entitled action and moves that the Commonwealth be ordered to file a statement of further particulars. Specifically:

1. Where did each alleged act of open and gross lewdness occur?

2. At which time of day did each alleged act of open and gross lewdness occur?

3. Where was complainant at the time of each alleged act of open and gross lewdness?

4. Describe in detail each alleged act of open and gross lewdness?

5. Did Defendant speak to complainant at any of the above times? If so, state what he said.

6. Did Defendant gesture to complainant at any of the above times? If so, describe the gesture.

7. Did Defendant in any other way show awareness of complainant's presence at any of the above stated times? If so, state how.

8. When did the acts of lewd and lascivious cohabitation upon which the complaint is based occur?

9. Where did the acts of lewd and lascivious cohabitation occur?

10. State specifically the alleged acts of defendant which constitute lewd and lascivious cohabitation.

____

Seth E. Many

COMMONWEALTH OF MASSACHUSETTS

MIDDLESEX CAMBRIDGE DISTRICT COURT

COMMONWEALTH OF MASSACHUSETTS

v.

SETH E. MANY AND CAROLYN R. PECK

Now comes the Commonwealth in the above entitled action and files the following answers to the defendants' Bill of Particulars.

1. The Commonwealth refuses to further specify in that the complaint sets forth the grounds.

2. The Commonwealth refuses to further specify in that the complaint sets forth the grounds.

3. The complainant is the Commonwealth. No further specification required.

4. The Commonwealth refuses to further specify in that the complaint sets forth the grounds.

5. The complainant is the Commonwealth. No further specification required.

6. The complainant is the Commonwealth. No further specification required.

7. The Commonwealth refuses to further specify in that the complaint sets forth the grounds.

8. The Commonwealth refuses to further specify in that the complaint sets forth the grounds.

9. Upon the premises of 197 Lakeview Ave., Cambridge.

10. The Commonwealth refuses to further specify in that the complaint sets forth the grounds.

Edward D. McNulty
For the Commonwealth

INTRODUCTION

THE LEWD THING did not begin in high places, in Government Halls, in the dim reaches of the Pentagon or CIA, or even in the Municipal Palaces of local government. Nor was it a deep and low conspiracy involving outside provocateurs designed to confront and disgrace the leaders of our country. Instead, it all began at home, on a quiet middle class street in Cambridge, Massachusetts, a district somewhat over-represented in the psychiatric wards and police stations of the city, but otherwise respectably undistinguished.

Never a cause célèbre, the LEWD thing gained a local reputation as somewhat weird, but largely irrelevant. With few exceptions it was spurned as non-newsworthy by establishment, radical, and reactionary alike. From left to center to right it was one of the innumerable curios of Today, a conversational cocktail, a snicker over the morning coffee.

Yet the LEWD affair, in its modest origins, was a prototypical confrontation of American liberal theory and Amerikan illiberal fact, a confrontation of religious and secular mythologies, a conflict of democratic vs. authoritarian traditions, a tediously personal yet profoundly universal recapitulation of the struggle of awareness for open expression.

In all there was none of that tragedy and drama present which grips those confronted by the inexorable and inevitable weight of poverty, illness, war, or implacable and devastating authority. At each point in the prosecution a "way out" was possible: a simple promise to don our clothes; a move to more hospitable loci; an established lawyer to supply the necessary reassurance. At first a problem in isometrics, the development of tensions carefully guarded by civility, a local dispute, LEWD became an isotonic exercise in controlled challenge, a challenge to the existing colonial system of authority that negates reason and self-regulation in its Religious Quest for absolute social control.

In January 1970, the Cambridge Commune, 5 persons deeply self committed to the Usness of being — sharing, hoping, sleeping, failing, laughing — purchased a home on Lakeview Avenue, an old home with many possibilities for change, formerly occupied by the managers of Butcher's Wax. No wax museum now, it soon witnessed naked events which raised ancient but respectable fear and hostility in a significant part

of the neighborhood. For the persons in that Commune believed that the naked sexual self could be a portion of the richness of being together. Seth and Carolyn, sensing also the ways in which we deprive ourselves of an honest and open relationship to the sun and air and earth around us, took satisfaction in being *in* the alltogether on their porch and roof.

Some of the younger neighbors, catching wind of this irregularity next door, snatched the opportunity to test the values of their conventional parents by raising a great commotion when we became visible. This was what they had learned; that the naked body is shameful, that it must be covered in certain particulars in certain ways in certain places. In general, the society they came from (and ours also) had repeatedly refused them admittance to the "mystery of the body," shamelessly maintaining their ignorance while imbibing them with its necessity. Sex: undescribable, unvisible, untouchable, and illegal.

The several parents who took up this challenge from their own and owned young, found their values to be flaccid in and of themselves. So they called in the police to re-erect them. This they did reflexly, as the distinction between morality and power, a distinction which commanded the separation of church from state, had long been mystified in middle America, and was never a fact in the theocratic polity of Massachusetts. Their quest for a solution in the power of the Commonwealth was moved both by their impotent morality and the need to regain that time when rules were unconsciously followed. A reassertion of spiritual authority on the basis of muscular superiority. Brawn over soul.

These tactics we had met before. The only support that so many social values have today is that of bribery and coercion. The only reason for their acceptance and the only justification for their existence is force. Rules, such as the LEWD prohibition or those governing the marriage state, are believed to have moral validity where they have only political viability. We decided to fight for our lives.

Our enemy was more than a mere naked prohibition. In the streets, in the media, in the courts it was a battle against the hundreds of unconscious rituals and barely conscious rules that serve to immobilize and deprive the common man and woman of substantial freedom. It was a battle against superstition and ignorance as well as unconscionable and uncredible authority.

The first skirmish was with language itself, that most powerful servant of guilt and shame and traditional authority. Lewd to many persons was an indecent dream, an unmentionable crudescence of dirty delights and distasteful desire. We referred to ourselves as "lewd," the LEWD Commune, LEWD persons. We sought to contrast the fact of our being with the fear of a word. The deliberate representation of ourselves as LEWD was a significant factor in the detoxification of a word — a word which, like porno or obscene, has the power to close a mind as well as pucker a mouth. Whether we were actually lewd ceased to be crucial, as the stigmatizing power of the word languished in our presence.

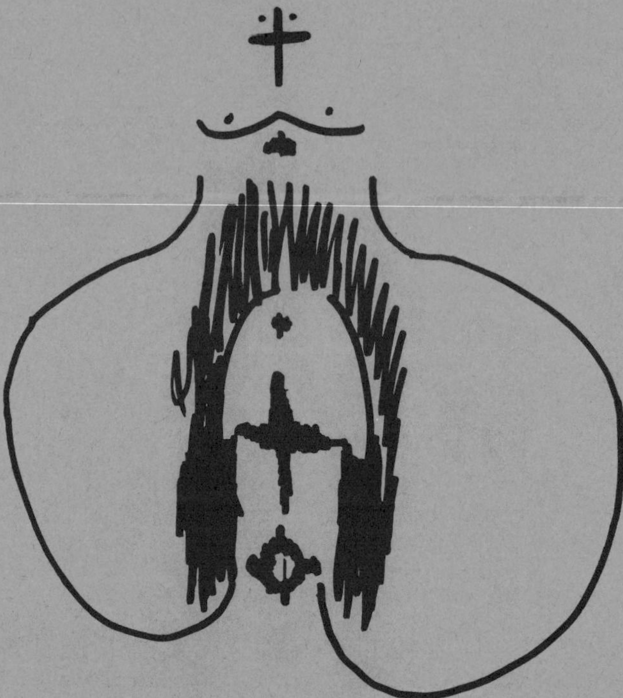

Like Black, LEWD began to connote not shame, but pride. Pride in the acceptance of an inescapable involuntary designation which held out a challenge to irresponsible authority. A meaning now quite different from the qualities with which it was originally invested. In the course of this acceptance, we rediscovered the tradition of LEWD, which was a pitched struggle between the laity, the vulgar people, the common man with the clergy of vested interest. LEWD served as a reminder of the dialectical and rhetorical nature of labels, the use of labels to gain mastery over fellow man. And over one's own unexamined, creepy-crawly self.

The multiple repressive-oppressive aspects of language were not confined to "lewd" and its indecent relatives. In the anti-personal, authoritarian language of the courts we found and attempted to neutralize the corrosive effects of such common usage as: (1) Jane and John Doe to refer to real persons, namely, Carolyn and me; (2) "private parts" to refer to the allegedly forbidden sights, the pubes, the cock, the cunt; (3) "Mr.," "Miss," "Dr.," etc, all of which confer a privileged status both in court and out. In order to relieve the especially pernicious power of "Dr.," in the 9 months leading to our jury trial I became "Dr. E." — legendary enemy of all those who wage war on sex (a quack and charlatan by appearance)

— and Carolyn became that social knockout, "Whammo!" Our professional training presented us with a special authority that was both liability and opportunity. At times our understanding of the situation led us to an ironic acceptance of titles and honorifics, aware of their peculiar authority, yet unable to avoid their application. This was especially the case in court, where the rules of the game were more severe and injured sensibility more capable of arbitrary revenge. At those times our project of linguistic detoxification faltered through immediate fear.

Our understanding of language induced us to honesty, indeed provocation in our public meetings. We called a cock a cock, a cunt a cunt, etc. Inevitably this alienated large numbers of almost supporters who require a more or less regurgitive feeding of a "value" language, i.e. a language which conveys a specific morality. Once at a festival on the Charles River I mentioned the word "chick" with mild contextual irony, and was immediately called down by a female language militant. On the Cambridge Common, the use of the word "fuck" to describe sexual congress gained

me the wrath of love freaks and puritans alike. In all, such cases were infrequent, and people responded positively to the use of here and now words which crystallized and empathically induced our common situation of expressive bondage. Thus the open use of language, in the context of fear and threatening arrest, helped to dramatize the ways in which society was engaged in a power-manipulative game under the pretext of maintaining a public interest in personal morality.

From the beginning we eschewed language which exalted a professional and elitist understanding of our problem (though I succumbed to the temptation at our first District Court trial to testify as an expert witness in my own defense). Both psychiatric and legal terminologies served to enrich our understanding and communication with other persons, but were not used to develop privileged communications (e.g. with judges, other lawyers, physicians, psychiatrists, etc.) which are typically exclusive and exclusionary in character, and delay the development of equal opportunity for everyman. We divested ourselves of the typical role protections implicit in our situation. We refused privileges we understood to be extended by virtue of our status, and we early decided against the use of professional witnesses and expertise in our trial as contrary to our hope for a legal system comprehensible to and employable by the people.

But if language and status were both danger and possibility, so too were all appearances. The power which government had over our peaceful bodies, our sexuality, our communal way of life became a dual edged sword when exposed to public sentiment and related to a universal predicament. When our house was inspected by the fire department for violations shortly after our arrest, when I was refused my driver's license for six months and threatened with the need for a psychiatric examination, when the police harassed a benefit auction sale at the request of "concerned" neighbors; then the symbols of entrapment became explicit and allowed us to relate our situation to oppressed persons everywhere.

To the extent that the system of oppression is together, centralized, and based on obvious and superficial discriminations, e.g. skin color, length of hair, etc.; then the sword falls semi-automatically and can be reversed, turned back on the authority that wields it. In these times the knowledge of centralized authority is commonplace, n.b. the interlocking systems of FBI-local police-fire dept.-welfare dept.-psychiatric hospital-campus cops, etc. The ease with which authority may be mobilized against the individual citizen or group is no paranoia, but common experience to the black, the long-hair/beard, the ex-convict, or mental patient, etc. As examples of this pervasive, discriminative misuse of authority multiply among the middle class itself, a realignment, not of peripheral priorities, but of central meanings, takes place. Merely choosing a new shield and a new motto is insufficient. To opt for the protection of already established power is no less than to identify with colonial habits of distrust and competitive struggle and to side with an instinct for oppression. To accept non-privileged status may be to volunteer for oppression, but it is also a chance to become part of the democratic organization of society.

As institutional harassment of our lives multiplied and identified us as oppressed, we simply faced a fact that millions have denied. That one can struggle. Can choose to assert control over one's life, even when the context is the enemies' palace or concentration camp. The process of course is both freedom and slavery. But it is a process which seeks to enjoin slavery, not to justify and enjoy it at the expense of others.

Yet as the battle took us further from home; in the streets, in the Motor Vehicle Registry, in the Police Station, and in the Courts, we recognized the growing difficulty of carrying on the battle in such a way as to recognize ourselves. Each environment registered its impact and created in us the desire for compromise, retreat, "peace, now!" At such times overreaction and attack often seemed the only alternative to hypocrisy and shame. When Ralph, one fine day in the Cambridge Common, invited us all to join him in naked communion, I stripped, but out of no joy in the sun or the air or the gathering of people. Then it was a political act; to be naked was a challenge to the surrounding power. Could I allow a brother's appeal to meet my hollow fear, my shallow motivation? He was carrying our words, the word, into real space, and asking us to join him. Not a challenge but an act of faith. I joined him. The crowd surrounded us in a kind of silent conspiracy, covering our nakedness with their own clothed bodies, avoiding the confrontation that all expected would bring on further mindless tyranny.

In the courts especially, our battle to be ourselves met a kind of monomania, an impersonal fanaticism in the person of court bureaucrats from judge to bailiff. No less than an Imperial Salon, it was characterized by courtly dress and codes of dress, a rigid attention to styles and fashions that transcended legitimate concern with actual disturbance or substantive justice. A kind of attention to the Prerogatives of the Court that stipulated the singular Reign of Unquestioned Authority. When a dog ran through the courtroom, Judge Viola of the District Court ordered the courtroom closed to any further spectators. In a Superior Court hearing on our Motions to Dismiss, spectators were forbidden from sitting (non-obstructively) on the floor in a hall without benches, or on the Courthouse steps, and were forbidden (unless from "recognized" media) from taking notes in the Courtroom. In our Superior Court trial with Judge Ford, he ejected Chuck of Trout Fishing because he refused to stand when the

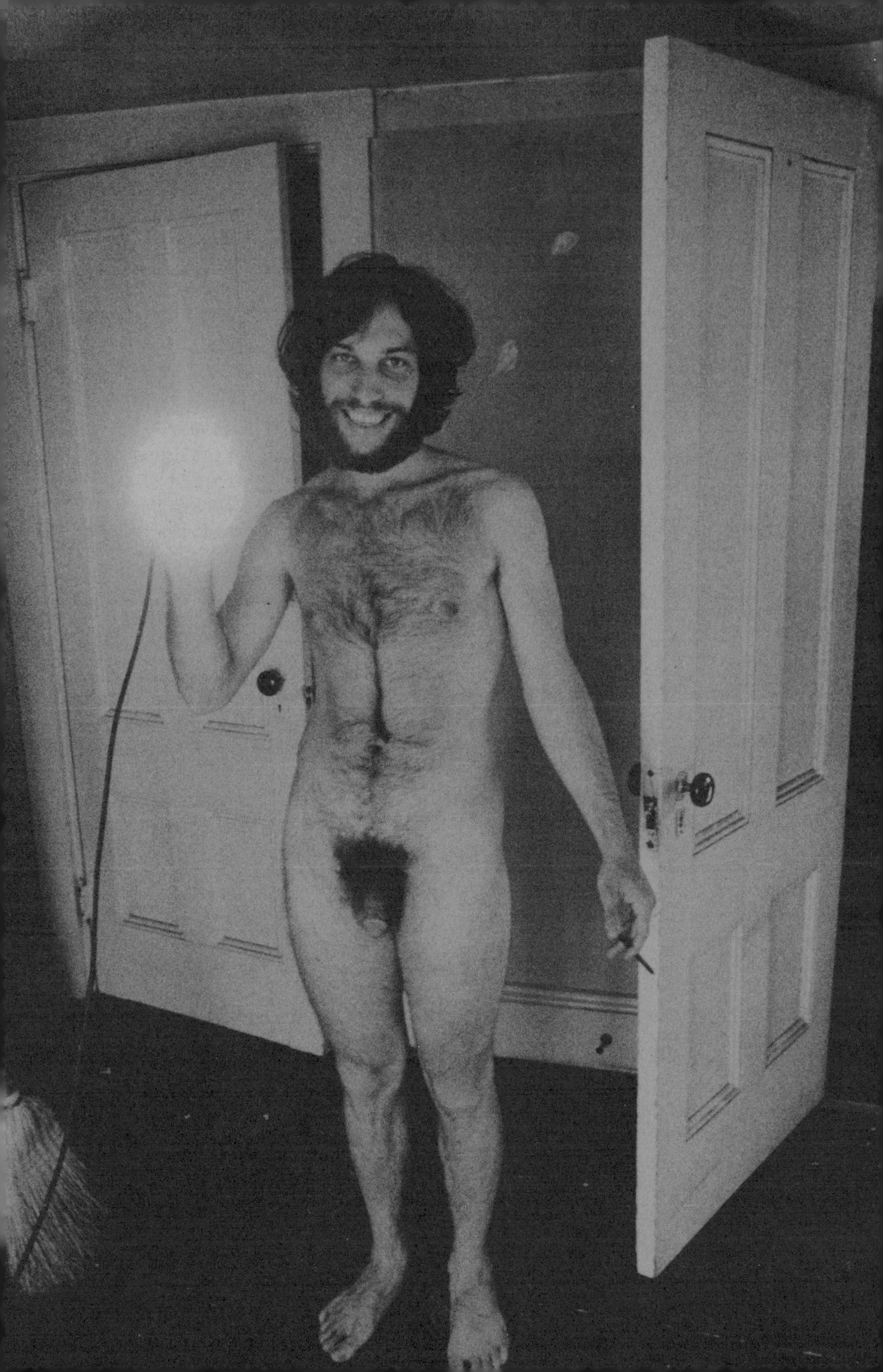

judge entered. The same judge had me thrown out of the Courthouse where I was peacefully awaiting the resumption of our own trial. The judge persistently took account of the emotional responses of spectators at the trial long before any could be characterized as disruptive. In all this attention to style there was the sense of a preventive schema designed to arrest disorder at its very roots, i.e. at the heart of life itself. Thus any variation from the preordained ritual was perceived by the Court (Judge and Officials) as a threat to the organic life of the Court itself. This was nothing but an exaggeration of the fear which society has of moral change, a fear that the system is so unstable that one change will bring the whole crashing down.

This is not to suggest that individual officers or the judge himself did not demonstrate a flexibility consistent with human diversity. A dress code regulation demanding that all persons in court appear in coat/necktie or dress was waived during the proceedings, not at any request of ours. Perhaps this was a judicious attempt to avoid a cause célèbre at the very onset of the trial. If so, it only emphasized the arbitrary regulation which attracted so much attention thereafter. In our experience, the Courts would do well to actively eschew those prerogatives which are relevant only to Imperial, not Due, Process. Thus they might be subsumed under a general standard of operation for public agencies which qualifies interference by the necessity of a showing of harm, or real danger. While such a showing may be disputable, it would at least remove the foolish and fraudulent ceremony from its present position of import. Such a standard would serve to eliminate those rules, robes, and rituals which only demonstrate but do not excuse the Titticut Follies of our Courts.

Judiciary attention to the inconsequents of trial style are important in more than one sense. They serve to deprive defendants of the fair and open trial to which they are entitled by allowing the judge vast exclusionary powers, such as exclusion from a public courthouse, from a courtroom because someone is wearing a hat (a Quaker, perhaps?), an open shirt, etc. Dress and appearance rules are the prime mechanism for the maintenance of repressive (i.e. unconscious) authority, and thus were a major focus of our concern, since we had been brought to court because of the most enveloping dress rule of them all, the masking of the genitals.

In the movement from Unconscious to Conscious, from Mystery to Reason, the first fortress to be captured is that of control over bodily function and physical appearance. Looks are more than skin deep. They are the stamp and stigmata, the standing and the status of society. Until we assume our own unique appearances, our identities will remain at best divided between public and private, at worst completely devoid of individual or inter-State commerce.

II

It would take an actual living presence to assimilate the non-verbal information: the posturings, the sounds, the attitudes and expressions, the smells of the court during our enforced holiday there. The record for you remains inalterably incomplete. What the words you will read demonstrate is always a concern for the direction, the *business* of the Court. They exhibit its well charted channels, its broad expanse of shallows, and a few of its shoals.

This was just one harbor into which a number of vessels were drawn, some by chance, some by choice, some at tow, but most for commerce; to carry on the business of the day. The transcript is but a limited ledger of that commerce. Just what meanings the trial had in the lives of those concerned is a tale still in the telling. Our own lives there as codefendants

— there knowingly, but only at the coercive bequest of the Commonwealth, were directed towards an exploration of the ways out, ways that might somehow complement our Being there. We asked no surrogate representative; neither law nor lawyer could be for us what we could not be.

The trial is a social game for the reconciliation of conflict with order. As a real game, it can only be meaningful if it is conducted by real players, for and by the participants to the conflict. It is a mechanism of coerced, enforced, non-violent confrontation. It succeeds largely, like government itself, because its authority is not in dispute. It fails for many reasons: for bad faith, for overextension, and especially today, because the confrontation does not take place between the opposing interests, nor does it take place on any grounds of equality. Instead the real trial, an adversarial process, is displaced in favor of a schizoid dramatization wherein the major players are social surrogates for the principals; wherein legal functionaries who are professional actors/actresses expect and demand a passive audience at their performance.

In this latter-day kind of drama, everything occurs at a distance, and the heart of the conflict, an insoluble problem between divergent interests is never revealed by those interests themselves. The meanings of the trial thus remain statically and ritually social and only barely and superficially correspond to the real society that has engendered the value disparity of the contending parties.

Fortunately this was not the case in our trial. It *was* the Commonwealth of Massachusetts v. Carolyn and Seth. That it was the Commonwealth, rather than just our unhappy neighbors can be seen written in the history of this colony of Puritan values and puritanical enforcement of morality. The theocratic and elitist character of the LEWD charge could have no progenitor other than a Supreme Authority, in this day, the State itself.

Our trial, as with the more blatant governmentally inspired "conspiracy trials" was painted by the Commonwealth as a challenge to State authority, the Law itself. And in the sense that our prosecution was at the hands of the State it could be only that. For the interpretation of law is, these days, scarcely a matter of individual ability, let alone concern. Yet the challenge to the LEWD prohibition was but an element in our defense necessitated by the institutional separation of law and fact. In the first instance we disputed the law itself and the authority of the State to promulgate such regulation. But as to the jury trial we asserted our innocence in the eyes of the law. Such was not a challenge, but a capitulation to the legal process of the State. We took our case before the only legally constituted authority with respect to the facts of an alleged crime, i.e. a jury "of the people."

During the proceedings against us, a nine month rite de passage, we uncovered a multitude of legal sins. Despite the U.S. Constitution's guarantee of a trial by jury in felony proceedings (ours was a felony with the opportunity of up to six years in jail for each of us), we found that in Massachusetts, one must be *convicted* first in lower (District) court to get a *jury* trial in Superior Court. Despite the Constitution's guarantee of a speedy trial, ours took place some nine months after our initial arrest.[1] Despite the Constitutional guarantee of a fair and open trial, ours took place in an arbitrarily (though perhaps not unkindly) governed feudal fiefdom in which the judge turned openness and fairness into a farcical maintenance of priestly custom. We were *allowed* to represent ourselves, over the Commonwealth's objection, only after our competence had been called into question and the burden of proof turned against us. We were forced in both District and Superior Courts to shoulder the expenses of a

[1]The D.A. reassured us that we were indeed fortunate as many persons were still in jail awaiting trial for over a year!

court record which should be available, as a matter of course, for any concerned citizen to review.

The right to a jury of our peers was yet another myth which we exploded. The issue was not merely the inability of our defense to raise those questions which were central to prejudice in our case, questions such as those put to the Judge himself which would raise the issue of a profound spiritual conflict of interest. Nor were we merely concerned with the audacity of the jury selection process which permitted the Commonwealth to exercise substantial discrimination in the composition of the original jury pool. Rather, our primary concern was with a systematic jury selection process which ruled out approximately one-half the population *before* possible jurors were even contacted. This one-half of the population represented the "have-nots," those without the legal status of both "citizen" and "voter" (registered). It represented predominantly that in-

credibly disenfranchised group of persons we refer to as "kids" and the transients, low classes, ex-convicts, mental patients, etc.

A jury of one's peers implies a standard of both social and legal equality. Our jury system, based as it actually is on gross age chauvinism and social immobility (voting-residency requirements), is a regressive standard which operates against all groups which are not middle aged and middle class. Beyond this relatively simple problem of a jury base that is too narrow, too exclusive, is the more fundamental problem of what constitutes a "peer" in a community of diverse range and value. In the classless society there are *no* "peers." In a one class society there are *only* "peers." America as a whole remains heterogeneous, a mixed bag. And while certain (or perhaps most) "communities" have a kind of class uniformity, this is certainly not the case in larger urban or urban-suburban complexes like our own Cambridge-Middlesex County. Thus because justice is not merely legal, but more fundamentally social and derived from a set of agreed upon values, the current peer jury system inadequately protects the possibility of substantive justice for the young, the minority group, or the individual.

One answer to this dilemma regarding social justice is to allow juries to be formed from a sample of the population which defendants presume to represent their community (e.g. the black community, the radical community, etc.). Such a manifest "politicizing" of the jury would do much to eliminate the substantial inequity of the current system, which only rationalizes, but does not eliminate, the middle class politics of contemporary juries. Then and only then would political prisoners stand the chance of a fair shake.

The alternative is to open the jury system, once and for all, to everyone. While this solution does not avoid the obvious dangers of certain age, status, class, etc. overrepresentation, it at least reduces the overt level of social hypocrisy involved in asserting a "jury of one's peers." It thus allows us to reflect on the way in which a jury system itself is less than an answer to the problem of adequate social justice for those whose values and life expressions diverge from the central core of respectability.

The Judge himself represents no less a problem for the alleged criminal. Heretofore, the issue of judicial "conflict of interest" has been restricted to primary genetic relationships or economic investments. Clearly, psychological "investments," which are at the basis of all "conflict of interest" may be expressed in a variety of ways. The stock that a person (Judge) holds in a corporate undertaking may be of much less import than the stock he takes in some religious or political enterprise. We asked that Judge Ford disqualify himself on the basis of an inferred central religious identification (Christian/Jew) because the core of the Judeo-Christian ideology is an anti-sexual, anti-naked, anti-lewd view of humanity. His religious identification (which he refused to reveal) may actually be less important than his political or social affiliations. We did not know. But we did understand that conflict of interest is not merely a question of stock investments and business friendships. The concentration of the "conflict of interest" debates on these particulars demonstrates only the poverty of thought with which justice has been invested.

III

How is it then, that we were found not guilty? Simple enough. Our beings represented no real threat to the predominantly middle class values of our jurors. On the contrary, I suppose we represented a kind of semi-secret aspiration of the liberal bourgeoisie which includes sexual freedom and body liberation, the honest representation of self, and ultimately, an attempt to understand and render authority reasonable, but not to do away with it. In a kind of triumph for do-it-yourselfism, we became what the middle classes yearn for: a sexual, satisfied, self-respecting, self-regulating being. A being that has adequate food, shelter, health, and education; a being that is determinedly but civilly engaged in the struggle for personal freedom.

The essential freedom that the middle class lacks is the freedom to feel. This is most clear if we start from the inside, contact our own bodies, and then reach out for others. From every direction, cerebral north to swinger south, pagan east to esalen west — the greatest, fattest, most over-educated middle class in the world seeks its greatest victory in the rediscovery, the uncovering of the body: sensual, sexual, salivating, twitching, and touching. The aspiration begins with the demand for privacy, the right to be left alone, untouched by public demand. The right to have dreams, the right to cover oneself in and with those dreams, the right to masturbate, to discover oneself. The right to put on, take off, doff and don whatever the whim. The right to be foolish, fopish, proud, or prurient. The right to view dirty pictures in private.

Such rights become quickly sterile. The right to be alone becomes a rite of loneliness. The Individual reaches out for others. And in reaching, seeks to touch and share, to express that pleasure in sense and self formerly confined to one body, one's own. Seeking now to relate. To become a person in relation to others. A social animal, freely relating, voluntarily exploring, touching, feeling. Not a social sacrifice. Not a dead body to be used for the economic reasons of Church or State. But an individual animal, a new species, reaching out of the dark of legitimate privacy into the light of a new together day.

Yes. The Jurors were part of this middle american transvaluation, a cross cultural neo-pagan pollination, without which radical and reactionary alike would have no anchor, no scapegoat. And without which the liberation movements — the gay, the now, the kids, the women — would have been only cerebro-synaptic events, moving bodies enervated only at the Center for Social Control. A transvaluation raised in the rich soil of a now irrelevant privacy and isolation, fomented by an economy of abundance, and triggered by the inherent laxity vector of repressive desublimation — a transvaluation to gain what money can't buy, the integration of the most local autonomy, body autonomy in private, with the most luxuriant possibility, the voluntary uninhibited sharing of sensation with others.

But if the jurors found us "not guilty" because we were part of their aspirations for freedom, in what way did our trial speak to that mass of persons in this world huddling, sickening, and starving from birth? People still seeking the minimal requisites for life: shelter, health, and nurture? Only, if at all, in its recognition of and demand for the sensate social focus of freedom. Our trial tenaciously proclaimed that freedom is *real*; that it is concerned with action and social behavior and real bodies, not with rituals, spiritual ephemerae or the good life after death. Our concern was with the freedom of body and spirit to act in concert. With conscience as expressed in deed. From Nietzsche to W. Reich to the great mass of persons now literally groping together for the wisdom of the total body, the popular history of these times is to be written in the reintegration of soil and soul, body and mind, object and subject, individual and society, in evocative ways of sharing and flowing, rather than domination and control.

There are many stories that this is not, except in small part. It is not the tale of our commune; of lonely, angry, or friendly neighbors; of courageous friends; of our explorations of the media or the soapbox; of our supporting ventures and peradventures (LEWD memorabilia: penis candles, silk-screen middle-finger/fist T-shirts); or of the multiple ideas that never made it (a soft drink with live sperm, a LEWDstock Nation on an off-shore island, the naked liberation of that offensively fenced-in Jewel-of-Cambridge, Fresh Pond). But we did what we had energy for. What was necessary. What felt good. Read this and touch . . . feel . . . Be . . .

LEWD

— Seth (Dr. E.)
Cambridge LEWD Commune, 1971

[What follows is an abridged version of the actual court transcript of the trial of Seth Many and Carolyn Peck, held in Superior Court, Cambridge, Massachusetts, from January 6 to January 12, 1971.]

WE TRUST
IN GOD

HEARING ON MOTIONS — JANUARY 6, 1971

THE CLERK: 87990 and 1: Jane Doe, alias Carolyn R. Peck; John Doe, alias Seth E. Many.

May it please the Court, this case has been sent from the First Session to the Third Session for trial. It has been brought to my attention that each of the defendants are here pro se, without counsel, and it is my understanding that they wish to pursue a motion to dismiss which has previously been ruled upon without prejudice.

THE COURT: Carolyn R. Peck?

DEFENDANT PECK: Yes.

THE COURT: You heard the Clerk announce that you wish to appear pro se, for yourself, is that so?

DEFENDANT PECK: Yes.

THE COURT: Our record must show a knowing and intelligent waiver of counsel, and without knowing anything about you whatsoever, I would urge you, as I urge all defendants in these conditions, to engage counsel. Now, what is your background?

DEFENDANT PECK: Well, my background is basically that I believe the Massachusetts Constitution which says a man should have the right to defend himself.

THE COURT: Excuse me. You have a constitutional right to defend yourself; no one quarrels with that.

DEFENDANT PECK: But that's related to what I'm going to say: I think the whole criminal process should be geared so that an ordinary citizen can work his way through it without having to rely on a group of experts called lawyers to help him make very important decisions affecting his life.

THE COURT: Until that utopian plateau is reached, you do have a very intricate form of trials and procedures in which members of the Bar of Massachusetts are willing and able to represent you.

I just want to make sure you are competent to represent yourself, so you have the right to a trial that will be meaningful. I want to find out something about your background and experience, to make that determination, or whether I should appoint someone to represent you notwithstanding your desire to ——

DEFENDANT PECK: I would never accept an appointment.

THE COURT: Before you get to that point, I want to hear something about your background and experience.

DEFENDANT PECK: I'm really reluctant to do that, because I think that part of my claim is going to be as an ordinary citizen and not because I have special abilities or special training. I want the procedure to be geared for an ordinary person. If I have to be that ordinary person to make that point, I'm willing to be that.

THE COURT: Will you tell me, please, in general — I don't care at this point about the nature of the complaint against you, whatsoever; I just want to know something about you and your background, experience, and education, to make a judgment on this question of attorneys. You may end up having it the way you want, but I have to make that decision. So will you please tell me in a very brief way your background?

DEFENDANT PECK: Well, I graduated from college and from law school——

THE COURT: Which law school?

DEFENDANT PECK: University of Pennsylvania. In 1967. I'm a member of the New York Bar. I am not a member of the Massachusetts Bar.

THE COURT: I would say you are eminently qualified to take your own case, except for your lack of knowledge — which is no criticism of you — of, perhaps, the Massachusetts procedure. But go ahead.

DEFENDANT PECK: I admit to a great lack of knowledge, even after talking to people here — they say that it's very intricate. So part of what we're trying to do is even ask your assistance so that myself and ordinary people can work their way through the system.

THE COURT: That gets involved with what the judicial function is, which is not the issue at the moment.

DEFENDANT PECK: It may become it in this trial, so I would like to even make that point now.

THE COURT: In due course. The first order of business: I will permit you to waive counsel. We have a form which is required so the record will show that you have done that. You may sit down in the meantime, Mr. Many. Is that your name, Mr. Many?

DEFENDANT MANY: "Seth" is all right, Seth Many.

THE COURT: Mr. Many, you may sit down.

DEFENDANT MANY: If you prefer that I sit, I would prefer you to use "Doctor," but it doesn't matter.

THE COURT: Well, makes no matter, meaning or difference to me if you stand or be seated. Will you please be seated?

First of all, Miss Peck, if you are going to defend yourself — Mr. Officer, will you please turn that defendant's counsel table around at right angles to where it is? Let's put it in the usual place where the lawyers sit. If you want to move it over to my left. *(Table moved)*

THE COURT: Now, Miss Peck, you may step within the bar enclosure. I want you to sign this. I am going to permit you to sign this form.

DEFENDANT PECK: One small point: All through it's been Jane Doe, alias Carolyn Peck. I would prefer it be entitled in my name. It implies that I was not ——

THE COURT: One thing at a time, please.

DEFENDANT PECK: But I have to sign it as "Jane Doe, truly Carolyn R. Peck." I prefer to sign ——

THE COURT: You can sign it any way you want.

Will you call the next defendant?

THE CLERK: Yes, sir.

87991: John Doe, alias Seth E. Many.

THE COURT: Mr. Many, you have heard my ——

DEFENDANT MANY: "Doctor," sir. I don't believe in titles, but if you insist on addressing me, I prefer "Doctor."

THE COURT: Well, you're a doctor of what?

DEFENDANT MANY: Of medicine.

THE COURT: Well, I want you both to understand the first thing I know about these cases is when they are called in court. You're a Doctor of Medicine, of course we'll call you "Doctor."

Dr. Many, you have heard my interrogation of Miss Peck on this matter of counsel. Do you also wish to represent yourself in these proceedings?

DEFENDANT MANY: That's true.

THE COURT: Will you tell me, as she did, something, just briefly, about your background, for that limited purpose?

DEFENDANT MANY: I was born in 1939 under the sign of Sagittarius. My sun is in Jupiter, and my moon is in Leo.

THE COURT: Apart from that — those areas are not admitted to practice in this jurisdiction — will you tell us, please, your education and background?

DEFENDANT MANY: My educational background consists of kindergarten in Brookside Elementary School; grammar school in Mendham, New Jersey; high school in Morristown, New Jersey; college at Swarthmore College in Pennsylvania; medical school at the University of Pennsylvania, in Pennsylvania. Internship at Albany Medical Center, in Albany, New York, and psychiatric residency in Syracuse, New York.

THE COURT: Now, Dr. Many, have you given full consideration to this desire on your part to represent yourself?

DEFENDANT MANY: Yes, sir.

THE COURT: Do you have funds with which to employ counsel, if you so chose?

DEFENDANT MANY: No, sir.

THE COURT: And notwithstanding that, you wish to represent yourself?

DEFENDANT MANY: That is correct, sir.

THE COURT: Without in any way criticizing your intelligence — quite the contrary — but you understand that the legal procedure is a specialty, just like the practice of medicine and psychiatry, and unless a person is experienced in this field, it's very difficult to operate and to make sure your rights are protected. Have you given full consideration to all of that?

DEFENDANT MANY: I understand and appreciate your attempt to help me in this matter.

THE COURT: You have a constitutional right, as we all know ——

DEFENDANT MANY: I think it's more than a right. I think it extends beyond a right. I think it's a virtual necessity for citizens to begin to represent themselves for what they are.

THE COURT: Well, my advice to you — which you need not take — would be, as I say to every defendant in your position, to have counsel employed to represent you, or engaged by themselves to represent them, only because they can do a better job because of their knowledge of procedure, but nevertheless, you are within your rights to defend yourself. I am going to have this form sent down, Dr. Many, which is the same one, same form that Miss Peck had.

THE CLERK: May he also come within the enclosure?

THE COURT: You may step within the enclosure, Mr. — Dr. Many.

THE CLERK: May it please the Court, I believe the Court Officer wishes to speak to you. *(Court officer confers with the Court; then goes to the rear of the courtroom and tells someone to stand.)*

THE CLERK: Refuses to stand.

THE COURT: Well, Mr. Officer, I understand we have a spectator who refused to stand when the Court came in and now refuses to stand and make himself known. You have my authority to eject him from the courtroom and not be permitted to enter again. Just a minute, please.

(Man leaves the courtroom)

THE COURT: Mr. Officer, you may advise that man that he is welcome to come in again at any time as long as he is willing to go along with procedures in the court.

Yes, Doctor?

DEFENDANT MANY: I would like to raise a question as to whether he has not, in fact, exercised his conscientious right to come here as a citizen, in peace. He has hurt no one.

THE COURT: That is not open to you. I will not hear you on it. You may proceed with your case.

(The Clerk gives a paper to the defendant Many)

DEFENDANT MANY: Raise the same objection to John Doe, whoever he may be.

THE COURT: You may sign that any way you choose.

(Defendant Many signs a paper)

THE COURT: You may represent yourself as counsel. I want to say to both of these defendants that if at any time during these proceedings you change your mind, which I urge you to do, you may engage counsel to represent you.

THE CLERK: May it please the Court, it is my understanding, though I have not talked to either defendant, that they at this time wish to renew motions to dismiss which were originally filed on September 25, 1970, and were heard on October 1 , 1970, before Mr. Justice Collins.

DEFENDANT PECK: We also have several additional motions that have to do with jury and other matters.

THE COURT: Do you have copies for the district attorney?

DEFENDANT PECK: Yes.

THE COURT: Have you seen these?

MR. MILLS: Your Honor, there is some confusion. We have two separate motions to dismiss.

THE COURT: Have you made your name known to these defendants so they will know who you are?

MR. MILLS: I am the Assistant District Attorney.

THE COURT: Would you like to tell them your name, because I don't have it.

MR. MILLS: David Mills, Assistant District Attorney.

THE COURT: I have no desire to be counsel for either the defendants or the Commonwealth, but nevertheless I have to endorse this "Filed late by" — it's not timely, but I will endorse it, "Filed late by consent of Court."

DEFENDANT MANY: Will you tell me what that means, sir?

THE COURT: It means you have no right to file the motion at this time.

DEFENDANT MANY: When did it have to be filed?

THE COURT: It's immaterial, because you are being allowed to file it by leave of Court.

DEFENDANT MANY: I see.

THE COURT: That is one of the many reasons why you should have your own lawyer.

I will hear the moving party. Who wishes to present it, Miss Peck or Dr. Many?

DEFENDANT PECK: Yes.

THE COURT: *(To Defendant Many)* Be seated.

Is it Miss Peck? I want to get it right.

DEFENDANT PECK: Yes. We have already argued it orally once, so I will

be very brief and touch the highlights that I think are important for the actual trial. Essentially, the argument is that the statute is vague, that on its face the term "open and gross lewdness and lascivious behavior" offers very little meaning in terms of concrete actions.

As the cases have been construed in Massachusetts decisions, it doesn't provide ordinary citizens with very much guidance if they wish to guide their behavior to be legal. So that terms like "open," which implies "public," and has been defined in the dictionary as "public," has been construed to also apply to such places as private homes or a public toilet that was unoccupied by other members of the public, except somebody who was peeking in, apparently. And that, also, the cases don't provide much guidance because the courts are reluctant to discuss the facts fully because they are embarrassed, that the courts' attitude actually reflects their basic notions about sexuality, about the body, and that this isn't legislation for acts that are harmful — which goes back to the third point, which raises the question of due process and other possible constitutional rights that are infringed upon by this statute.

The basic important claim for the proceeding of the trial is that this statute lacks any finding of legitimate state interest or harmfulness to either individuals of the state or to any legitimate interest the state might protect through legislation.

There have never been any legislative hearings or findings that these acts lead to harmfulness. In fact, a lot of data raises serious doubts about whether legislation of this sort actually does do anything to improve our society. There is a claim to be made, in fact, for openness; instead of legislating against openness, legislating in favor of openness.

THE COURT: You're talking now as a matter of — you must distinguish whether you're talking public policy, which is a legislative matter, or whether we're talking constitutionally. Are you still talking about constitutional ——

DEFENDANT PECK: I think the fact that there is no legislative policy and no justification for legislative policy behind this statute raises an issue of constitutional proportions of due process, and particularly where our statute regulates private conduct, conduct in persons' homes, conduct that reflects attitudes people have, that goes to their basic beliefs and how they choose to live their lives and relate to the world around them. These are things the Constitution serves to protect, and the state can't, without showing some legitimate interest and some danger to itself or to its citizenry, act and legislate and punish people by putting them in jail.

The other important claim is related to the waiver of counsel. That is ——

THE COURT: Excuse me. Do I understand your first point to be you claim lack of sufficient standards?

DEFENDANT PECK: Within the statute itself. It's vague, it's void for vagueness, which is a constitutional doctrine that has been applied in other common-law offenses like breach of the peace, where the courts have found the statute so vague it allows law-enforcement agencies wide discretion, and they often enforce the law discriminatorily, against minorities. Often this was in terms of Black people in the South. They were accused of breach of the peace, or the civil-rights workers were. And finally the courts looked at that and decided one of the problems with a broad statute is it can be just applied against people the state or police officers or a neighborhood doesn't like, for whatever reasons.

This, again, is important for our defense and for some of the facts we hope to develop during the trial.

The other claim was about the procedure, that in exercising our constitutional — now I'm talking about the Massachusetts Constitution — constitutional right to defend ourselves, in order for that to be meaningful, the whole process has to be understandable to an ordinary citizen. So far, it is presented as a morass, and the possibilities of a further morass on appeal, raise difficulties for anyone who wishes to defend himself simply and honestly, and to present himself to his peers; and I think the concepts of justice, in order to operate at all, have to be very simple and very human, and I think the structure we have today is not.

THE COURT: I'm not certain how this relates to your motion to dismiss. Is there some connection?

DEFENDANT PECK: Yes, in that already — I hope this motion to dismiss looks backwards to what we have already been through — that is, through the procedure in district court, where we didn't have a jury trial, where motions were made, where evidence was heard, perhaps prejudicial to us, perhaps erroneously admitted, and it's never looked at by a superior court. Because this is a trial de novo, it means you don't even know what went on in the district court. Persons could have perjured themselves; they could now perjure themselves. There is no way for the Court to protect its interest in justice, which, I think, is what the Court has an interest in, if it's operating properly. It means that we've already been subjected to a trial that could have led to our conviction, we could have been serving sentences — lots of people are, and probably about 90 percent of the cases in district court aren't appealed, so that people are serving sentences in a process that's never examined by a higher court, that's without a record, where all sorts of prejudicial matters can come in and operate and people are in jail because of that.

That's something that concerns — should concern, I think, the whole state, concerns us as people who have gone through it, who hired a stenographer to try to preserve some of our rights, to try to limit the kind of testimony that could go in by presenting it in an appellate court, but we were prevented from doing that.

Also, just the whole process of getting finally to trial — I think we have been to the Superior Court four times. If we ever were arraigned, I'm not sure what it was, whether it was called an arraignment — it came after an argument of a motion. There were times when we weren't notified of something. And these are things that can confuse and make it difficult to prepare ourselves and create an emotional hardship on clients and on the people who go through — delete the clients.

(Defendant Peck confers with Defendant Many)

DEFENDANT PECK: Oh, and then the complaints: The complaints don't specify the place of the offense. They only say the name of the crime — open and gross lewdness and lascivious behavior.

THE COURT: Just a minute. I'm going to look at those again. Go ahead, please.

DEFENDANT PECK: The complaints accuse us of open and gross lewdness and lascivious behavior on March 9. They don't specify what acts the Commonwealth intends to rely on, to prove the conclusory terms of the statute.* The complaint doesn't state where the alleged crime took place — it could have been anywhere. Perhaps we might have an alibi if the place were specified.

It doesn't — it fails to specify the intent, which I think is required as a matter of constitutional law, in any statute that is penal and that is vague. This has been held to be so in the Supreme Court decisions involving obscenity, which is an offense closely akin to open and gross lewdness and lascivious behavior, since it involves sexual and moral standards.

Also, this is the same complaint with which we were charged in the district court. Even though it said "On March 9," the district court allowed in evidence for subsequent days, which was improper, which might have been what he based his conviction on, which would mean there would be no reason — if his procedures were looked at by a higher court — it would mean there would be no reason for us to be here — that the whole case shouldn't be here, and we wouldn't be taking up the energy, time and expense of trying something. And that's just another problem which the district court never examined.

And both the Massachusetts Constitution and the United States Constitution provide that anyone accused shall know the nature and cause of the accusation. I don't think that you could be said to know the nature of it from such a charge as open and gross lewdness and lascivious behavior. As we have talked to people about what has happened to us, I think almost everyone, including lawyers and ordinary people, have wondered what that was, and I don't think it is known to an ordinary citizen, or, in fact, is knowable to an ordinary citizen, and that the complaint should, therefore, be dismissed at this point because it fails to specify the matters to be tried.

THE COURT: Anything to add, Miss Peck? Is that it?

DEFENDANT PECK: Oh, I'm finished.

THE COURT: Dr. Many, anything you care to add?

DEFENDANT MANY: Yes, your Honor. I would like to add that these claims relate both to the state Constitution and also to the Federal Constitution, operating through the Fourteenth Amendment, the due-process clause, so I don't think that's clarified.

*Valid criminal laws must be based on specified acts rather than suggestive words or vague interpretations. — C.P.

I think my brother, Carolyn, has also failed to consider the way in which this particular crime puts us both in double jeopardy and represents cruel and unusual punishment. The crime of open and gross lewdness in the State of Massachusetts is a felony punishable by up to three years in the state penitentiary. However, there are at least two other crimes on the books that seem to represent the same acts and are not distinguished or distinguishable in statutory terms, and those are lewd, lascivious and wanton behavior, and lewdness in public and indecency. It's purely an arbitrary matter which crime is chosen to be prosecuted — arbitrary in the sense that it depends upon the political and cultural values of those people who are prosecuting the crime. Therefore, it's an arbitrary procedure, and it's also cruel and unusual punishment. No matter whether we win or lose here, we can go back home and be prosecuted for precisely the same acts and the same behavior in terms that are outlined in the statutes.

THE COURT: I don't follow that last part, Dr. Many. What do you mean by that?

DEFENDANT MANY: We can be prosecuted because of the very vagueness of the statute, which fails to specify the terms, whether you call it open and gross lewdness and lascivious behavior or lewd and wanton behavior, or public indecency and lewdness. The case law suggests that these have been variously applied with no discrimination or distinction between them, that they each carry their own burden of penalty and punishment, and each of them represents in its own way the same precise acts that are capable of being interpreted, for whatever purposes, with different punishments granted for each of these so-called acts.

So what I'm claiming is that this puts us in a position of being harassed and prosecuted under several laws which, because of their vagueness, refer to similar activities.

I am also claiming that three years for being a naked person is not just an absurdity, but it's also a cruel and unusual punishment.

Now, I would like to argue, basically — and this represents the body of my argument — that the law represents an establishment of religion, in terms clearly laid out by the First Amendment to the Constitution.

I would also like to argue, secondarily, that the law serves to restrict the area of religious freedom and expression. This statute, Chapter 272, Section 16, comes to us under the title of "Offenses against Chastity, Decency, Morality and Good Order."

Now, simple perusal of the laws will suggest that the content of each of these concepts is religious both in historical genesis and in contemporary application. In fact, chastity itself, by *Webster's Dictionary*,

means purity; and for those of you who recall that we are living in the Commonwealth of Massachusetts, the term "purity" reflects and suggests the reason for which certain persons came to this country, and that was to find purity, and they were called Puritans, and there were two branches of Puritans. In 1620, the Plymouth Colony established itself under the Mayflower Compact, which gave an oath of allegiance to God, and devoted themselves to establishing Christianity in the new land.

In 1630, the other branch of Puritans, the Congregationalists, split off from the mother church in England in order, once again, to do away with levity, ritual, obscenity, heresy, that they felt was established in the mother church, and they came here to embody their religious ideals in the law of the land. They came here to establish a church that was the state.

Now, a reading of the laws as they existed at that time — 1641 — the Congregationalists wrote a body of law called The Rights of Man, in which they punished by a capital sentence, the sentence of death, such crimes as heresy, witchcraft, blasphemy, sodomy, bestiality, adultery — these were the crimes.

Now, they contained within them the corpus of my argument, because the connections between religion and chastity, the connections between sexual activity and heresy, were anti-religious behavior, were well known and assumed by those Puritans.

The Constitution, the Constitution of Massachusetts embodies the claims of the Congregationalists. In 1780, when the Constitution was ratified — this is the Constitution of Massachusetts — there were two Articles, Article 2 and Article 3, which clearly substantiate the claim that not only was there connection between church and state, but that the state was the church.

Now, in the early Puritan times, the only persons who could hold office were Puritans; the only persons who could vote were male Puritans; and the only persons who were to have the rights and respect of the laws were Puritans. We can look to the banishment of Roger Williams to our brother colony, Rhode Island; Anne Hutchinson's banishment; we can look to the death sentence served on four Quakers in the Boston Common in the two years 1649 to 1651; we can look at the death sentence given to two adulterers in 1644, to substantiate the plain and patently anti-sexual religious bias of the law.

Now, it is true that in 1832, the third section, the third Article of the Massachusetts Constitution was amended to include not just Congregationalists, but to include all Christian sects — that is, to give equal protection of the Massachusetts law to those who professed and practiced Christianity.

Now, it's no accident that in 1917 or 1913, the Massachusetts Legislature passed a law guaranteeing free religious expression to all persons. Yet it was 11 years later that the courts ruled that in their opinion, religious freedom meant that Jews as well as Christians were allowed to come under that Article, that Amendment to the Constitution.

And all these arguments are more clearly detailed and outlined in my brief.

However, it is also clear that these religious proscriptions against the state interfering with either a person's religious behavior or the establishment of a church religion, it's clear that these were not applied to persons who were not Christians, who professed alternative religions that didn't have a Judeo-Christian background. And, again, I refer you to my brief for substantiation of this particular point.

Now, I have made the claim that this law as it's currently applied today does not represent necessarily a strict Congregational or Puritan viewpoint. For that, they would have had our heads. But what I am claiming is that the law today represents the establishment of Judeo-Christian religion, and I make that claim both from the history of Judaism, which looks to the Old Testament and Genesis for its insight and its wisdom, and it looks to the story of Adam and Eve, and it looks to the shamefulness of the naked body, when Eve chose to pluck the fruit from the Tree of Knowledge, and it shows that God came down and punished Eve for doing this thing, punished her by the sentence of pain and suffering — whenever her sexual being was involved, pain and suffering were to be the concomitant. And Adam, too, was punished to sweat and toil for this sin. The sin, the plucking of [the fruit from] the Tree of Knowledge, was rapidly followed by the development of fear and shame on the part of Adam and Eve.

Now, Judaism has taken this story and exalted it and put it into their own laws, and both the law of Moses, Leviticus and Deuteronomy — books in the Old Testament — again detail the language. The anti-sexual character of that particular religion was manifest. Leviticus punishes masturbation by years of penance. Homosexuality is a crime punishable by death.

Now, these laws are still carried out. For the Jew, the naked body represented the most shameful, disgraceful part of man — the naked body — when that body was an expression of sexuality. In fact, the crime for adultery on the part of the woman was to strip her publicly and thrust her into the public eye, where she could be publicly shamed.

Now, Judaism flowed into Christianity. As Judaism developed, it developed ascetic and monastic ideals — that is, more and more the religion tended towards anti-sexuality.

Christianity, in its organized form, picked up this aspect of Judaism. You recall that the early Christians were Jews. They practiced as Jews. It was only when they were driven out of the mother church — the father church, rather — when they were driven out, that they established themselves as a separate body, yet they carried over the insight and inspiration of the Old Testament into their own teachings. So we have Justinian, in the Sixth Century, punishing homosexuality and other sexual acts with the death sentence. And we have the establishment in Christian doctrine by Augustine, the doctrine of concupiscence, or original sin, which was already present in Judaic doctrine. This doctrine meant that all of us, each one of us, you and me, is born into original sin.

Now, some of the comments of the early Church Fathers are very

interesting. They represent themselves as openly anti-sexual. They come down particularly hard on the heads of women for having any sex whatsoever. They suggest that the Devil himself is embodied in a woman, which may or may not be the case by your own lights; but what is very clear is that this doctrine was never repudiated by what we today call the Christian Church, nor was the doctrine of original sin in the Old Testament teachings, in the law of Moses, repudiated by the Judaic faith, by the Hebrew faith.

And so, as the religions worked themselves out and Calvinism became an accepted form, we had to translate the Catholic Inquisition into the Calvinistic diatribe and punishment against witches — and, again, witches were sexual beings; witches were punished if they had too many nipples. If they had nipples over their body, that was an evidence of the fact that a person was a witch. Millions of witches were murdered for heresy. In our own Commonwealth, in Salem, most of you are familiar with the fact that witches were put to death on the most dubious of evidence.

Now, let me say that this was not precisely the case in England, that anti-sexuality was considerably ——

THE COURT: We are only dealing with the law of Massachusetts.

DEFENDANT MANY: I would like to mention that the law of Massachusetts itself involves the ecclesiastical law of England in the common and statutory law of Massachusetts — that is, what was punished in the churches and for which people gave and did do penance was punished in the courts in England during the Puritan Revolution, when Cromwell had ascendancy — that was around 1650. So now we see again this very interesting conjunction of church and state when the Puritans gained ascendance.

Now, what has happened in America today is that all of this has become invisible to us, and that is because we have surrounded ourselves with people who by and large believe in the Judeo-Christian ethic, and who support it in all their actions, and who are afraid to deny or question it. And this posture, which reflects the heritage and tradition of Judaism and Christianity, represents an establishment of religion, and that is no more clearly the case than in Massachusetts, where one can with no trouble at all follow all the history of association of church and state and see it reflected in all the laws. Now, the law ——

THE COURT: Excuse me. Let me ask you a question. In other words, as I understand your argument now, you are going farther than the statute — you say not only is this law unconstitutional, but it operates in an area where the state should not be permitted to operate; is that ——

DEFENDANT MANY: Precisely.

THE COURT: All right. Go ahead.

DEFENDANT MANY: The state should not be permitted to establish religion in one form over another, and this is precisely what has happened today. There are many forms of religion — paganism, Buddhism, parts of Zen — which did not deny the human body. They don't consider it wicked or sinful or disgraceful. It is part, to them, of nature, and part of life, and part of existence.

Now, our code, our Judeo-Christian code, reifies these attitudes I have talked about, these anti-sexual attitudes in the law. Now, I mentioned how chastity means purity. It's very interesting that "lewd" means anti-clerical, or belonging to the laity. It means, and it meant in its inception, those people who did not affirm and carry the beliefs of clergymen — and that is, indeed, the essence of the word "lewd." So you now see that in its application, the law against lewdness was, in fact, applied to people who were profane, who were blasphemous — that is, people who acted and operated against the established church. In Sedley v. King, in 1633, Sir Charles Sedley stood out in the balcony of his bawdyhouse and poured urine over the assembled mob, and they broke down the doors, and he was found guilty of breach of the peace.

Now, that law became the basis for the common American obscenity doctrine. It became the basis for the development of the English law pertaining to open and gross lewdness, because here we have the conjunction, very clearly, of two events — one, a breach of the peace, a mob rioting, and an assault taking place; they have these things conjoined with blasphemy or heresy, which was sexual in nature, because Sir Charles Sedley also stripped on that balcony. Now, this particular act of being in the nude was abstracted from this case and used in further cases to prosecute written materials on the basis of obscene libel.

So here we have the beginnings of American obscenity laws, but also clearly the beginnings and the current form represent the Judeo-Christian ethic.

And finally, in Emerson v. Arkansas, in 1958 ——

THE COURT: Let me know what page you are looking at.

DEFENDANT MANY: Page 21. I will mention that the United States Supreme Court invalidated a state prohibition against the teaching of the doctrine of evolution on the grounds that that prohibition constituted an establishment of religion.

Now, if the doctrine of original sin or the genesis of man through the rib of Adam or whatever, constitutes a religious doctrine, so, too, do the laws that we are faced with today — offenses against chastity, decency, morality and good order, and, in particular, the law against lewdness which we are faced with, open and gross lewdness and lascivious behavior.

Now, I would also like to argue the free-exercise clause of the Constitution, and I will deal with this quite simply:

We have heretofore argued the establishment clause: We suggest that the state cannot establish a religion, an official religion, but we haven't argued that persons also have a right to the free exercise of religion.

In U.S. v. Seeger, the Supreme Court found that a person, even though he may not express his belief in the usual terms, may not express a belief about a supreme being, may express his own deeply committed belief in such a way that it occupies a place in his life, a place in his life that is comparable to that of a person expressing it in religious language.

THE COURT: Are you talking about the draft cases?

DEFENDANT MANY: Yes, that is the draft case.

THE COURT: All right.

DEFENDANT MANY: And a further extension of those cases has suggested that, in fact, the terms in which a person states his belief are not crucial, because each of us is subjected to different education, different upbringing, a different language — in a word, it is not the terms that count, but the place that belief occupies in a person's life — that is, his commitment to that belief, his understanding of that belief, etc.

Now, what I am suggesting is that that state statute against open and gross lewdness is a prohibition against our constitutional right to the free exercise of our conscientiously and deeply held beliefs, beliefs that are religious in nature; therefore, that this statute should be invalidated on that basis.

THE COURT: Have you finished, Doctor?

DEFENDANT MANY: I have finished my argument on the laws in support of the motion to dismiss. I have some further motions which I have made because of my convictions in this respect.

THE COURT: I have to deal with them one at a time. I am going to take a short recess, and then I will hear the Commonwealth on this particular motion.

(*Recessed at 3:02 p.m.*)

(*Court reconvened at 3:15 p.m.*)

THE COURT: Eject that spectator! He will not be permitted back in this courtroom. If he wants to go to jail, we'll oblige him. He is not to be permitted back in on the penalty of being jailed.

That, for the record, is the man who frequently and habitually refuses to stand, in defiance of the Court.

(*A man is removed from the courtroom*)

THE COURT: Now, I will hear from the Commonwealth on the motion.

MR. MILLS: Your Honor, at the outset, the motion of the defendants, or both defendants' motions are objected to in whole, and there are some specific areas we would like to be heard on.

As to the defendants' objection that the complaints lack specificity, the remedy, I think, is not a motion to dismiss, but through an appropriately drafted bill of particulars.

As to the defendants' comments that there is no specific allegation of intent within the complaint under 272, Section 16, I think that it is appropriate for the legislature to draft rules of conduct when they are directed toward activity, and that it is a proper inference for the Court as well as for jurors to draw that activity, when it is not unconscious or subconscious, be something which is intended by a human being to do [sic].

As far as the objection of Dr. Many that this particular procedure constitutes a threat of double jeopardy to him, I think that his claim is untimely now, and actually is misplaced in this particular proceeding. If there were a subsequent proceeding against Dr. Many, which is purely hypothetical, then I think his claim of double jeopardy would be appropriate. I think under the circumstances ——

THE COURT: Excuse me, Mr. Mills. In the brief filed by Miss Peck, she has another aspect of double jeopardy which she has raised. The claim is made that the trial in this court, having been tried in the district court, is in itself double jeopardy, quite apart from any future prosecutions, from any future conduct.

MR. MILLS: Yes; this particular proceeding is an appeal from the finding of the district court, and double jeopardy connotes the involuntary action of the defendant and a voluntary action of the state; and both Miss Peck and Dr. Many are here of their own choosing upon appeal to the Superior Court, and, therefore, the Commonwealth finds no merit in that contention.

THE COURT: Well, it's all interesting and novel, what they say: They were forced to have their trial, as I understand, in the district court in order to avail themselves of their constitutional right to a jury trial in this court.

MR. MILLS: Well, then, I think the claim, although perhaps then being valid, although I don't mean to suggest that, is without prejudice to them, because they have in the end exactly what they wanted *ab initio,* and so they have no prejudice.

THE COURT: Go ahead.

MR. MILLS: As far as Dr. Many's remarks as to the cruel and unusual punishment, his argument was eloquent. I tried to follow as much of it as I could, and I think the substance is that because there are other crimes in the General Laws which in substance may be indistinguishable from this one, it makes the punishment for the particular crime specified in Section 16 of General Laws, 272, to be cruel and unusual. I don't follow the argument, and I think it is without merit.

If his cruel and unusual argument is simply as to the maximum penalty of three years, we don't see that there is any merit in this — three years. The penalty, first of all, hasn't been imposed, and second of all, I think that ——

THE COURT: Let me ask you at the outset — the jury isn't here — this is going to be a jury trial, is it not, Miss Peck and Dr. Many?

DEFENDANT PECK: Yes.

THE COURT: Then I will ask a question which I would not if it were jury-waived: What are the factual allegations? I'm not accepting that as truth, but what are the factual allegations of this case? Is the alleged open and gross conduct in the interior of a dwelling or outside in the open, or what? I know nothing about the case.

MR. MILLS: The actual place of the alleged activity, as far as I know of it at this point, your Honor, is on a sunporch, enclosed ——

DEFENDANT PECK: I object to his allegation without offering evidence of it.

THE COURT: This is to enable me to understand the nature of the charges here. It's not before the jury. It's the offer of the Commonwealth as to what it hopes to prove. It is not evidence, not evidence at all.

MR. MILLS: By way of apology to the Court and Miss Peck, prior to noontime today I didn't know her case or this particular case at all even existed.

THE COURT: I didn't, either. So go ahead.

MR. MILLS: From the brief discussion I had with the police, and from the ever-so-brief opportunity I have had to read the police report, I believe the activity which is the basis of the complaint took place upon a sunporch attached to a building.

THE COURT: An open sunporch, enclosed sunporch — or do you know?

MR. MILLS: Closed, I believe, in the respect that there was glass or plastic on the window — and this is only — I'm just guessing, from photographs.

THE COURT: That gives me the general idea of what the case is all about. But go ahead.

MR. MILLS: Although I would love to be philosophical and eloquent — I haven't spent four months on this — but Dr. Many's argument against

the constitutionality of the statute, first as an establishment of ——

THE COURT: Excuse me. Let me ask one further question which may sound elementary, but do I gather that this is a case of alleged nudity on the sunporch of a private dwelling occupied somewhere in Cambridge?

MR. MILLS: If your Honor please, it is a case of open and gross lewdness in Cambridge.

THE COURT: But what is the conduct that the Commonwealth alleges that constitutes open and gross lewdness?

MR. MILLS: With all respect, first, I wish that that were presented by a bill of particulars, because then I could more properly answer it, and ——

THE COURT: Usually that comes from the defendants.

DEFENDANT MANY: We requested a bill of particulars at the district court and were denied.

THE COURT: I'm just getting a bird's-eye view of this case, that's all. If you don't know, that's all right.

MR. MILLS: I don't think I really know, Judge.

THE COURT: All right. Go ahead.

MR. MILLS: As to the establishment of religion, Dr. Many's argument that this particular law comes from the Judeo-Christian tradition and therefore is unconstitutional ties in logically, I think, with his correlative statement that all of the law of the Commonwealth derives in some part from the Judeo-Christian tradition, so, to be completely logical, then, his argument must be that all of the law of the Commonwealth is unconstitutional, because it derives from Judeo-Christian tradition, which really is absurd. And as to this particular portion of the law, which is 272, Section 16, although anything having to do with the control or behavior of citizens of the Commonwealth, because it in some way comes from the legislature, and the legislatures, at least in the greater percent, are regular human beings from the society, we have laws deriving from the feelings of people, and if the feelings of people have in millenniums past been touched by some ethic tradition, I don't think it's possible to expect anything from them that has not in some way been touched by their own belief and ethics.

To call this particular law, any more than any other law in the Commonwealth, unconstitutional because so derived, I think is an argument which, although scholastically logical, would be practically indefensible to uphold.

And therefore, on behalf of the Commonwealth, the entire motion is opposed.

THE COURT: What about the argument that the open and gross lewdness and lascivious behavior is prohibited, constitutionally prohibited as a

vague standard?

MR. MILLS: Well, I think with a little practice ——

THE COURT: I'm just asking.

MR. MILLS: With a little practice, I could cite 14 or 16 Commonwealth cases, your Honor, and the one that comes to mind, or the particular standard of law which comes to mind is that persons of ordinary understanding must be able to know and understand what a statute means. I never use myself as an example. I suppose in some measure it is a matter of taste and degree.

Based upon the cases that have been decided in the last ten years by the Supreme Judicial Court on vagueness and on the vagueness doctrine, I don't think that this particular statute could be called void for vagueness, particularly in view of the extended history of the social implications of this law as expressed by Dr. Many. If it has a background so profound and so deep and so universally imbedded in the society, then I don't know how members of the society could fail to understand it.

THE COURT: Now, I am going to take this motion to dismiss under advisement.

The defendants said they had some other motions for me to consider.

(*Defendant Peck hands two documents to the Clerk, who hands them to the Court*)

THE COURT: The first motion is to have the trial conducted pursuant to Massachusetts General Laws, Chapter 278, Sections 33A through 33G inclusive.

It is my custom to defer action on such a motion until the end of the trial, in which case I will hear parties and make a ruling at that time.

THE CLERK: May it be filed?

THE COURT: Oh, yes, it may be filed. Certainly.

I also have a motion to be permitted to examine jurors. Do you have a copy of that motion, gentlemen?

MR. MILLS: Yes, your Honor.

THE COURT: Well, first of all, I am going to say, without argument, it is not our practice in this Commonwealth, although it is in most states elsewhere, to permit parties or their counsel to interrogate the jurors directly, but the Clerk does interrogate the jurors and oftentimes we will propound additional questions which have been suggested by the defendant in the particular case.

Let me read these now, if I may.

DEFENDANT PECK: My reading of the statutory law suggested that there was authority to allow the counsel to fully examine the jurors.

THE COURT: It can be done, but it's a matter of discretion; but I will look at this. My practice, however, is for me or the Clerk to do it, but I don't necessarily limit the questions to those the statute requires.

Let me see what I have here.

DEFENDANT PECK: A lot of the suggestions are related to the arguments we have made about the motion, to try to get at some of the thoughts, possible prejudices.

THE COURT: Let me say this: Generally, in such a case as this, it is my practice and the practice of most of my colleagues to bring home to the jurors the nature of the case, and if any of them would be offended by the case or would feel because of the nature of it that they couldn't be fair and impartial jurors, to make that fact known, and we would excuse them. Let me hear you on your motions, please, Miss Peck.

DEFENDANT PECK: I would like to be permitted to examine the jurors to determine the possible prejudice or bias or interest they might have in the case beyond the statutory questions, because in many respects, I view this trial as a cultural trial. I feel like I come from a different cultural tradition that could be viewed with bias by people of a different cultural tradition than mine.

The questions are framed to try to determine if the jurors would have prejudice against different cultural traditions, maybe in ways that they don't even recognize — things like whether they think "Hair" should have been closed down permanently in Boston, regardless of, perhaps, of what the law held; if they had a prejudice against nudity, against any kind of display of the human body; the Commission on Pornography, to see if they are up to date with things that — with studies that have been made about pornography, about sexual behavior in America.

There are many who dislike the changes that America is going through, and this is to try to find out if those people might have a hidden dislike or distaste that they wouldn't know they had, even by a questioning that didn't go into this in any depth.

This also tries to direct attention to possible religious origins of their prejudice which would interfere with their making a fair judgment, such as Question No. 18, the Biblical doctrine that the naked body is shameful and must be hidden. If they have such a view, I think they couldn't hear a case that involved evidence about people who didn't feel ashamed about their naked bodies — they wouldn't be able to accept that as true. They wouldn't be the impartial jurors they should be.

It also reflects some of the possible prejudice against people with long hair or beards that both of us have and a lot of our friends have.

Question No. 24: "Do you think something ought to be done about the hippies in Cambridge?"

From things such as mass raids that have gone on, I know there is a lot of prejudice in this community. It is in some sense a divided community. We hope to have jurors who aren't on one side or the other, or at least can fairly show themselves to be.

THE COURT: Of course, these jurors, as you know, are chosen from the entire County, and not just from Cambridge.

DEFENDANT PECK: Yes. Many County residents come into Cambridge, I'm sure, to shop. They are familiar with what's going on. They read the local newspapers.

The question about seeing the movie "Woodstock" is hopefully to get people who have some exposure to what is happening in the world, so that we don't have people who are totally unfamiliar with the issues of the day and with the changing standards and if they saw the movie, they might have a better understanding of what we're about and what a lot of the changes are about.

Question 28, mentioning, for instance, Country Joe & the Fish: Somebody who has no familiarity with rock music might also have a hard time understanding the cultural values we represent and our way of life represents.

Question No. 29 also involves basic philosophies about the state and religious laws of the state and how much the state should be punishing diverse ways of acting and whether they accept established forms ——

THE COURT: Let me ask you this: Is this a case essentially where it's alleged these two defendants have walked around in the nude on a sunporch? Is that basically the allegation? I'm not asking for an admission, just the allegations of the case.

DEFENDANT PECK: Yes.

THE COURT: Is that just about it, Mr. Mills?

MR. MILLS: Is that question directed to the Commonwealth?

THE COURT: Whoever can answer it.

MR. MILLS: Perhaps Miss Peck could best answer.

THE COURT: Was that the allegation in district court?

DEFENDANT PECK: Well, as Seth said, we asked for a bill of particulars in the district court and we got the answer that the Commonwealth doesn't have to tell you anything.

THE COURT: My point is ——

DEFENDANT PECK: I'll tell you what: I have a transcript from the district court.

THE COURT: I don't want to see the transcript. I want to know something about the case in a general way, so I can intelligently ask questions of these jurors without waiting for the Commonwealth's opening. Just a general statement.

DEFENDANT PECK: I will make a brief statement.

We live in a commune on Lakeview Avenue in Cambridge. We moved in there on January 1. It is essentially a middle-class neighborhood — well, it's a very diverse neighborhood. It has people with a lot of different values in it. But we openly express to people that we are a commune. Very often we walk around naked in our home. That is our normal way of being. It's nothing extraordinary for us. And we built a sunporch which is in the back of the house, and we work out there and sun out there, naked.

THE COURT: I gather this is an enclosed sunporch, as the district attorney mentioned?

DEFENDANT PECK: It had glass and plastic on it. Those are — or just plastic.

THE COURT: I take it, a roof?

DEFENDANT PECK: Yes. A porch, enclosed.

MR. MILLS: Your Honor, if Dr. Many and Miss Peck would want to stipulate, I have a one-paragraph police report and two photographs which I would be very happy to show to the Court, and ——

DEFENDANT PECK: No, we are ——

THE COURT: I don't need that. Just in order to be able to ask the jurors about their possible bias or prejudice, I need to know something about the nature of the case.

DEFENDANT MANY: I think perhaps, with due respect, some of our neighbors call us Communists because we suggest that we live in a commune. Other neighbors say there's a nudist colony down the street. So, like these are some of the factors.

THE COURT: Those things are not in issue in this trial. Well, go ahead, Miss Peck, please.

DEFENDANT PECK: Question No. 32, which asks if they think the only purpose of sex is reproduction, also gets at something that is essential to the differences that we have — that is, that sexuality isn't something that is a bad thing or a shameful thing, and if somebody would view it that way, they won't be able to view even something like the naked body or something that isn't openly sexual or not even necessarily sexual without judging him, judging him without prejudice.

And similarly, Question No. 40 was just to try to make sure that they would be able to apply the law without prejudice in matters that involve obscenity, where there is a lot of prejudice and bias.

MR. MILLS: Your Honor, as to this motion, it is opposed in toto, and we would just like to comment that the jury guarantee of both the law of

the Commonwealth and the Federal Constitution is a jury of one's peers, and that does not mean in any case a jury chosen or selected by the defendant.

To go a little bit further, if this particular motion were allowed by the Court, and either you or the defendants were allowed to pose these questions to prospective jurors and to make a selection of jurors based upon these questions, they would, in effect, be depriving themselves of what the Constitution guarantees, which is a jury of their peers, chosen from the Commonwealth as a whole, and the questions propounded here would so restrict the jury as to deprive them of precisely what the Commonwealth guarantees to them.

Thank you, your Honor.

THE COURT: Not to overlook you, Dr. Many, did you want to be heard on this motion?

DEFENDANT MANY: Yes.

THE COURT: I meant to hear you first, then, before the Commonwealth. Go ahead, Doctor.

DEFENDANT MANY: Not only have we been interrogated by the Probation Department, but it is alleged that the Probation Department interrogates prospective jurors. We believe that there is substantial bias already introduced into the system of gaining jurors. We understand that jurors from 21 to 25 are characteristically excluded, even though by law and statute they may be included in the jury.

We understand that there is prior conference on the question of who the jurors will be, from which group they will be selected, and that includes the district attorney but not the defense.

THE COURT: Doctor, where do you suggest this conference takes place — at what level?

DEFENDANT MANY: There are several different levels. We have been advised that the Probation Department and the Police Department have the ability and in certain cases do examine persons before they are chosen as jurors, from the jury list. We have also been told that the D.A. has a part in the selection of any particular list from which jurors will be chosen. And we believe that if the prosecution is ——

THE COURT: I don't follow you. We only have one jury list in this county or any county. Do you suggest that there's more than one list?

DEFENDANT MANY: I suggest that that list has already been substantially limited by the kind of interrogation process that takes place.

How is it chosen, for example? Is it chosen simply from a list of voters taken at random? What is the process? I mean, on all these things we are not absolutely familiar, but we do have substantial reason to believe that bias already exists in this process. And what we are trying to do is correct the very naked bias that's introduced. If there are any jurors under 30, I will personally be surprised. Yet over 50 percent of our population in America consists of people under the age of 27.

THE COURT: What you are suggesting in these motions is that the venire has been chosen contrary to the statute, Doctor?

DEFENDANT MANY: I suggest, yes, that there are traditions that have been established in the selection of the jury that go beyond any statutory construction.

THE COURT: Take the statute for a moment: Do you suggest the statute has been violated by somebody or anybody?

DEFENDANT MANY: I am not making any allegations as to that.

THE COURT: Go ahead, please.

DEFENDANT MANY: I think the arguments here basically center around the kind of education which persons have been exposed to, and the kind of religious ethics to which they subscribe, so that in a sense many of these questions are representative of that; and I will not go into it more closely except to say that history and the way history is written today presents an extraordinarily biased view of the nature of man, and anyone who has a wider understanding or has experience with alternative forms of perception and seeing things recognizes this as the truth.

I am done as far as oral arguments. I think it's very important that we be permitted the opportunity to examine jurors. I believe that there is substantial bias within the procedure in which you have routinely suggested that you don't allow counsel to — counsel or clients to examine the jury. I think that is a very poor process.

THE COURT: Nevertheless, that is my ruling in this case. Regardless of how I rule otherwise on your motion, you will not be permitted to examine the jurors either personally or through counsel, nor will the district attorney.

DEFENDANT MANY: I would like to take exception to that.

THE COURT: Certainly.

DEFENDANT MANY: I also have a further motion to present to your Honor.

THE COURT: Just a minute. Anything further to be said on this particular motion?

MR. MILLS: From the Commonwealth, your Honor?

THE COURT: Yes.

MR. MILLS: Nothing further, except that we have permission through you to address Mr. Many and tell him that he is wrong as far as the district attorney's office, and I have no more knowledge than I think he has about any other manner of selecting the venire in Middlesex County.

THE COURT: I will add this one thing: I think if anybody has any information which would suggest that there has been any improper method in

selecting jurors in any way, that it should be submitted to the Court for consideration. Now, Dr. Many, do you have another motion?

(*Defendant Many hands a document to the Clerk who gives it to the Court*)

THE COURT: These questions are addressed to me, Doctor?

DEFENDANT MANY: That's correct, your Honor.

THE COURT: I hope you have in mind that the function of the Court in a jury trial is that the jurors decide the facts and the value of the facts, and the Judge runs the trial according to the laws of evidence and procedure and instructs the jurors as to the law to be applied, from which instructions all parties have the right, except the Commonwealth, have the right to take exceptions and to appeal.

But, nevertheless, I will read your motion.

(*Pause*)

THE COURT: I will hear you on your motion.

DEFENDANT MANY: We have requested that we be permitted — that I be permitted — this motion is made in my name alone — to examine the Judge for conflict of interest.

You have just suggested that you decide on the questions of law. Indeed, that is the tradition. Now, in the Roth decision, which governs cases dealing with obscenity, it's very clear that the jury, as a matter of law, has a right to decide both upon the facts and the application of the law to the case. This was a finding by the Supreme Court.

It's our contention that the facts are not differentiable from the law in this particular case, and that, indeed, conflict of interest is very profound when it is at the heart of such examinations.

Now, let me suggest that whereas we recognize —

THE COURT: Excuse me. Want to give me an example as to that last statement?

DEFENDANT MANY: The statement is that conflict of interest represents and is at the heart of cases of this sort. I think any reading of the confusion which surrounds the Supreme Court decisions with respect to obscenity can lead one to conclude that there is a great deal of bias and prejudice and disagreement and diverse opinion within the Court itself.

Now, my claim is that this stems from an unrecognized conflict of interest in these cases. Whereas we, as a country, have been willing to recognize conflict of interest on the basis of economics — if a judge holds stock in a corporation and he rules on a corporate problem, then he may well have conflict of interest — we have not been willing to recognize that there may be conflict of interest above and beyond mere economics, that there may be conflict of interest based upon the nature of the law and the nature of the judge's beliefs and creed, which are, indeed, much more powerful than the mere holding of stock in a corporation.

In effect, I am suggesting that if you hold stock in a creed or in a faith, and if that faith is such that it's embodied in the law, then you might well examine yourself with respect to conflict of interest.

And so my position is that ——

THE COURT: You mean I might have a bias in favor of the law?

DEFENDANT MANY: Not just in favor of the law, your Honor, but a bias in favor of a particular law that represents an establishment of religion. That's the conflict of interest we're looking at.

In accord with my argument that, in fact, this law does represent an establishment of religion, you in your role as judge may well be a manifestation of that establishment, even though you don't recognize it, per se. And ——

THE COURT: Excuse me. I'm trying to follow your argument. Suppose, then, on the question of the constitutionality of the law, I should rule against you: Do you not have a right to appeal to another court on this matter?

DEFENDANT MANY: The fact that we have a right to appeal in all these motions, I believe, has not substantially changed the fact that it's important for us to raise these motions at every level where they may be ruled upon.

THE COURT: You sound just like a lawyer now.

DEFENDANT MANY: I'm sorry about that.

THE COURT: I mean that as a compliment, not as an insult. It's quite true.

DEFENDANT MANY: Now, I have asked the questions — the questions in

here are designed in accord with the motion to dismiss that I filed, are designed to elicit very simply and without any confusion whether or not you subscribe to a body, an ethical code known as the Judeo-Christian ethic; and so, in accord with this, I requested that you yourself and in your own heart ask yourself these questions — whether or not you can undertake this case successfully without conflict or bias or prejudice in this particular respect.

Thank you.

THE COURT: The Commonwealth care to be heard?

MR. MILLS: The motion is opposed, your Honor.

THE COURT: This is the first time I have been called upon to pass judgment on myself. It's not easy.

Well, I will put it this way: I deny the motion. I find no reason to disqualify myself. And I note the defendant's exception to my ruling — both defendants, if they care to have it.

THE CLERK: The motion was only posed by one defendant.

THE COURT: All right.

DEFENDANT MANY: I take exception — is that required?

THE COURT: Yes, it is, under our practice.

Now, gentlemen, do you have any other motions to present?

DEFENDANT MANY: No.

DEFENDANT PECK: No.

THE COURT: We will recess now.

(*Court recessed at 3:45 p.m.*)

FRIDAY, JANUARY 8, 1971

THE CLERK: 87990 and 1: Carolyn R. Peck, Seth E. Many. Motions.

THE COURT: First motion I'm dealing with — there are two motions by each defendant to dismiss the proceedings. Each of those motions are denied.

MISS PECK: We'll take exception.

THE COURT: Exceptions of the defendants are noted to my actions in this regard.

The next motion is defendants' joint motion to be permitted to examine jurors. That motion is denied. Defendants' exceptions are noted. Anything further to be said before we impanel the jury?

MISS PECK: I understood that there was a list of panel with their addresses.

THE CLERK: There will be.

THE COURT: Yes, you will be provided with one of those.

MISS PECK: And also when Seth discussed the selection of the jurors, he mentioned there might be some questioning by the police officer and by the Probation Officer, and I had read that in the book about jury selection in Massachusetts. If there is any such questionnaire, we would like to see it and the results as it pertains to this particular jury.

THE COURT: Mr. District Attorney, do you have a questionnaire? Is there in existence a questionnaire returned from the jurors that you have knowledge of or possession of?

MR. MILLS: No, your Honor, no knowledge. No possession by the District Attorney's office.

THE COURT: All right. In that event, the motion is denied, if it is a motion. Anything further, lady, gentleman?

MR. MANY: Sir, I didn't understand. Did you cover all our motions to dismiss in your comments about the first two?

THE COURT: Yes. One motion before Judge Collins, as to vague and ambiguous — to clear the record, I deny that motion and note your exceptions to it, each of you. Then I have a second substitute motion you filed the other day, and I am denying that as well, and I noted your exceptions to that.

MR. MANY: I see. Thank you.

THE COURT: I have also denied your motions with respect to interrogation of jurors and noted your exceptions to that. As far as I know, that takes care of all of your motions.

MR. MANY: There was a motion for yourself, your Honor.

THE CLERK: That's ruled on.

THE COURT: That was denied. Well, I thought I did it the other day. I will deny it now, the motion to disqualify the Court or examine the Court, and note your exceptions to that motion.

THE CLERK: That motion was ruled on, your Honor, on Wednesday, and denied, with the exceptions noted.

THE COURT: Now, this business of picking the jury, we will have to clear the courtroom, to pick these jurors. That's up to the Sheriff's Department to take care of that.

MISS PECK: Can I ask a question about procedure? Could we have, make a challenge as each juror is called up, or do we wait until 12 are impanelled and then take our challenges?

THE COURT: I will let Mr. Clerk, Mr. Ewell, advise you right now what that is. I don't want to take the role of your advocate. That's why I urged you before and urge you now to hire a lawyer. I am not your lawyer. Mr. Ewell, you may advise the defendants of the number of challenges they have.

THE CLERK: You will be entitled to three challenges on each — each of you will be entitled to three challenges.

THE COURT: Two complaints.

THE CLERK: Yes, one on each. Forty jurors will be enough?

THE COURT: Yes.

THE CLERK: I'll send to the jury pool, which contains, I hope, approximately 100 jurors. From that 100 jurors, a request has been made for 40 jurors. They will be seated in the back of the courtroom. Their names by card will be drawn by lot. Twelve jurors will be seated. At that time the Commonwealth will be asked if they are content. If the Commonwealth is content, I will then turn to you, Miss Peck, and ask if you wish to challenge. You are entitled to three challenges without cause, and as many others as you have good cause to challenge.

When you decide you are content, when you have indicated to the

Court that you are content, I will then turn to Mr. Many, Dr. Many, and ask him if he is content. The same procedure will be followed in each case.

THE COURT: You probably could add, Mr. Ewell, about challenges for cause.

THE CLERK: Yes, sir.

THE COURT: Unlimited.

THE CLERK: It's unlimited for cause.

THE COURT: We will take a recess, and bring in the jury.

THE CLERK: Jury, Mr. Officer.

(Recessed at 12:08 p.m.)

(After the recess, 12:37 p.m.)

THE COURT: I am going to suspend this case until 2 o'clock and the jurors will please return directly to the — the jurors who will be selected for the jury panel, return directly to this courtroom rather than go back to the jury pool.

MISS PECK: There's a row of seats vacant now, and I would like to request that people who want to come to see the trial be allowed to sit there.

And I also note that there's one of the prosecution witnesses who is in, sitting not in places designated for the spectators, and it seems to me unfair, because our people have been excluded.

THE COURT: If that is a motion, the motion will be denied. Your case, the Commonwealth against Many and Peck, will be continued to 2 p.m.

MISS PECK: May I take exception to the denial of our motion?

MR. MANY: May I take exception as well?

THE COURT: Yes.

Recess.

(Court recessed at 12:40 p.m.)

WITNESSES FOR THE PROSECUTION

(The court convened at 2:08 p.m.)

THE CLERK: All parties ready?

MR. MILLS: Yes.

DR. MANY: Your Honor, I would like to take strong exception to a procedure under which I was assaulted and ejected from the Court House.

THE COURT: Are you talking about this case?

DR. MANY: I believe I am, yes. A procedure under which I was assaulted and dragged from the Court House, allegedly under your hand, by your bailiff.

THE COURT: You will be silent and be seated.

Proceed, Mr. Clerk.

THE CLERK: Yes, sir.

87990 and 1: Jane Doe, alias Carolyn R. Peck; John Doe, alias Seth E. Many, you are each now placed at the bar for trial, and these good people whom I shall call are to pass between the Commonwealth and you upon your trial. If you shall object to any of them, you will do so as their names are called and before they are sworn.

You each have the right to object to any three of them without giving any reason therefor, and as many others as you have good cause to challenge.

Be seated, please.

Jurors will make answer as their names and numbers are called and take their place on the panel as directed by the officers.

(Twelve jurors are called and take their places in the jury box.)

THE CLERK: Members of the jury, these are criminal actions wherein the Commonwealth, through Edward D. McNulty, a police officer in Cambridge, as complainant, the Commonwealth alleges on March 9, 1970, that Jane Doe, whose other name and truly — whose other and true name is said to be truly Carolyn R. Peck, on or about March 9, 1970, was guilty of open and gross lewdness and lascivious behavior in the

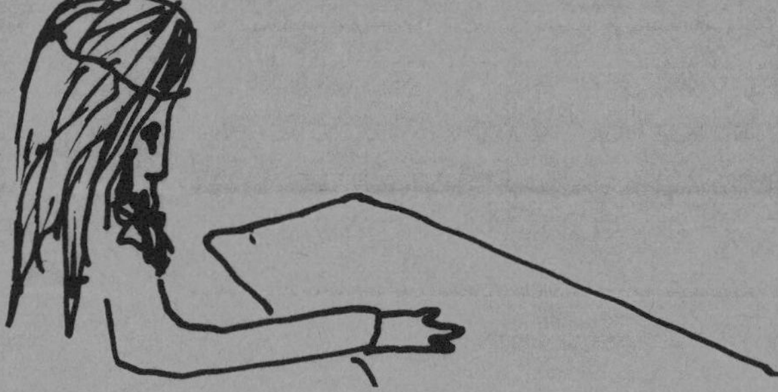

presence of Edward D. McNulty.

The Commonwealth further alleges that the defendant Seth E. Many, on or about March 9, 1970, was guilty of open and gross lewdness and lascivious behavior in the presence of Edward D. McNulty.

If there is any member of this panel who is in any way related to or acquainted with the defendants or the complainant or has any claim against the defendants or the complainant, or has any interest in this case, or has formed or expressed an opinion relative to the guilt or innocence of these defendants, or is sensible of any bias or prejudice for or against these defendants or the complainant, you will make it known to the Court at this time.

THE COURT: I want to add to this — what I have to say now is for the benefit of all the jurors who may be selected, as well as those in the box: This case, as you have heard, involves allegations that these defendants were engaged in conduct described or alleged to be open, lewd and lascivious.

I am advised that there will be evidence or testimony, that is to say, having to do with this charge, which also has to do with an alleged display of naked bodies in circumstances which the Commonwealth alleges to have been lewd and lascivious.

I say this because if any members of this jury who have already been selected or those who may be selected find the nature of such a case is offensive to their sensibilities so that it would prevent them from being fair and impartial, then they should make that fact known, and we would also excuse them for that reason, because we want to be sure that in all these cases that the jurors have no bias or prejudice in respect of any defendant and particularly the defendants in this case by reason of the nature of the allegations against them.

I hear nothing.

Go ahead.

THE CLERK: O.K. Jurors stand indifferent.

Is the Commonwealth content?

MR. MILLS: The Commonwealth is content.

THE CLERK: The defendant Carolyn R. Peck?

Want to step forward?

DEFENDANT PECK: First I would like to make a general objection. I don't think the panel as chosen, even regardless of the process, is representative of the age of the voters of the Commonwealth ——

THE COURT: That issue, Madam, or Miss, rather, is not before you now. We are dealing with this particular case. You now have an opportunity, if you desire, to exercise your challenges to those who have been impanelled.

DEFENDANT PECK: I will do that, but I also object generally to the composition of the panel, and take exception to the process and to the choice of these jurors.

THE COURT: Exception is noted. Do you have any challenges? Just make them known to the Clerk, please.*

(Defendants Peck and Many make challenges known to the clerk, and other jurors are called until both the defendants and the Commonwealth rest.)

THE COURT: Yes, Doctor?

DEFENDANT MANY: As my brother† Peck did, I would like to take exception to the composition of the jury; on the face of it, I believe that it's discriminatory and does not represent the jury of our peers.

THE COURT: Exception is noted. I will appoint Mr. Reeves as Foreman. He may remain in the seat in which he now finds himself.

THE CLERK: The Court appoints No. 120, Vernon D. Reeves, as Foreman of this panel. That is the juror down in this corner here. The jurors will please rise and raise their right hands.

(Jury sworn)

THE COURT: Now, Mr. Foreman, ladies and gentlemen, we are about to take the afternoon recess at this time, so we can let the other jurors go back to their room and rearrange the courtroom. We will be back with you shortly.

Recess.

(Court recessed at 2:55 p.m.)

(Court reconvened at 3:15 p.m.)

DEFENDANT PECK: Your Honor, I would like at this time to make a motion to adjourn until Monday on the grounds that a lot of people who had come to hear the trial were told that there would be no evidence admitted today, and therefore they went home. They weren't allowed to wait in the corridors, and it was cold outside.

The basis of this is our constitutional right to a public jury trial, and we assert that we want it to be public. We want the people who had

*Defendants' attempts to question jurors to determine prejudice were thwarted under the rules of The Court. The challenges that were made were based on name, occupation, and address — the only information provided other than direct observation. We could and did make "reasonable inferences" as to age and sex, and less reasonable inferences as to a wide variety of factors known to bear on sex attitudes. e.g. religion, education, ethnic identity, etc. — C. P.

†The use of the word "brother" was intended to underline the implicit sexism of male domination in the legal profession. — S. M.

expressed an interest to come and had taken the trouble to come to court to be able to hear.

THE COURT: Miss Peck, the door is open — the doors. Motion is denied. We will proceed.

DEFENDANT PECK: May I take exception?

THE COURT: Certainly.

DEFENDANT MANY: I take exception, also.

THE COURT: Certainly.

THE CLERK: Members of the jury, you will harken to two complaints made against these defendants before the Third District Court of Eastern Middlesex, Commonwealth of Massachusetts, Middlesex, to wit, to the Third District Court of Eastern Middlesex, holden at Cambridge for the transaction of criminal business, within the County of Middlesex:

Edward D. McNulty of Cambridge in said county, on behalf of the Commonwealth of Massachusetts, on the ninth day of March in the year of Our Lord one thousand nine hundred seventy, on oath complains that John Doe, whose other and true name is said to be truly Seth E. Many, on or about March 9, 1970, was guilty of open and gross lewdness and lascivious behavior in the presence of Edward D. McNulty, against the peace of said Commonwealth and the form of the statute in such case made and provided.

Edward D. McNulty, complainant.

(The Clerk then reads the same complaint against Carolyn R. Peck.)

To these complaints, members of the jury, the defendants have pleaded that they are not guilty, and for trial thereof have placed themselves before the country, which country you are. You are now sworn to try the issues. If they are guilty, you will say so. If they are not guilty, you will say so and no more.

Members of the jury, you will harken to the evidence.

Mr. District Attorney?

THE COURT: You may be seated, gentlemen, ladies.

MR. MILLS: Your Honor, prior to the opening will the Court entertain an oral motion by the Commonwealth?

THE COURT: Without saying too much in front of the jury, can you indicate what the nature of the motion is?

MR. MILLS: Yes. About counsel, and the defendants being represented by counsel.

(The Clerk confers with the Court)

THE COURT: I will accept your representation. Let me have your motion.

MR. MILLS: That the defendants be required by the Court to retain counsel for the purposes of this trial, and if not for their substantive defense, at least for the limited purpose of advising them as to Massachusetts trial procedure, so that this case will not go on an inordinate amount of time, and so that the record and their rights will be adequately preserved and presented.

THE COURT: Well, I've been through that on the pre-trial procedure, and they have elected to represent themselves. Have you changed your mind in that regard, Miss Peck and Dr. Many?

DEFENDANT PECK: No, I have not.

THE COURT: Dr. Many?

DEFENDANT MANY: No.

THE COURT: Do you wish, still wish to represent yourselves?

MR. MILLS: May it be denied without prejudice, to be renewed at a later time during the course of this trial?

THE COURT: No, I will deny it, because the matter is for them to decide, and not for the District Attorney.

MR. MILLS: Thank you. May I proceed, your Honor?

THE COURT: Yes.

MR. MILLS: Good afternoon, ladies and gentlemen of the jury:

This is a criminal action wherein it is alleged that the defendants were intentionally engaged in activity which is violative of a statute which has been enacted by our legislature of the Commonwealth, the Great & General Court.

The particular activity will be described by witnesses who viewed it, and it is in terms of the statute referred to as open and gross lewdness. And the witnesses for the Commonwealth will describe to you what activities and what things they saw at a certain address in Cambridge on, I believe, Lakeview or Lakeside Avenue. The street will be given to you by the witnesses. The places will be described by the witnesses as they come to the witness stand.

We will be concerned mainly with one particular day, and that is March 9 of 1970; and because this is a crime as defined by the Supreme Judicial Court of the Commonwealth, a crime which involves intention, the Commonwealth will offer to prove that the particular activity which will be described and related as it occurred upon March 9 happened on at least one or two other occasions, and this evidence will be offered to show the intent of the defendants and to show that they knew what they were doing. And there is, of course, no necessity for the Commonwealth to show or prove or attempt to show why they were doing it.

The witnesses for the Commonwealth will be, first, police witnesses who will testify as to their observations of 197 Lakeview Street on March 9, 1970; and there will be certain civilian witnesses who will

present evidence to you on the stand, orally, as to what occurred subsequent to March 9, 1970, and what occurred on or about March 1, 1970.

As to the exact definition of the statute and what type of facts the Commonwealth must present by way of evidence on the stand, the Judge at the close of this trial will instruct you in the law as to this matter, and you will take, then, the testimony of the Commonwealth witnesses as to fact, believing the portions that you wish to believe, disbelieving or paying attention, as your own minds choose, and apply the law then as the Judge will so instruct you.

Thank you.

May the Commonwealth witnesses be sworn, your Honor?

THE COURT: Mr. District Attorney, my suggestion is that your opening statement at least ought to summarize the facts which the Commonwealth intends to prove, to support the charges against these defendants.

MR. MILLS: Yes, your Honor.

Police Officers from the City of Cambridge will testify before you that on March 9, 1970, they were in the neighborhood of 197 Lakeview Avenue or Lakeview Street in Cambridge, and that while there, they observed the defendants nude and exposing their bodies in a porch or some other kind of area that is known and numbered as No. 197 Lakeview Street in Cambridge.

The civilian witness — one police witness will tell you that two or three days prior to March 9, 1970, he called at the particular address and attempted to inform the inhabitants there that complaints had been made.

There will be civilian witnesses who will, for purposes of showing the intention of the parties, testify that at least Dr. Many, one of the co-defendants, exposed his body on the roof-top of No. 197 Lakeview on March 1, 1970; and one civilian witness will tell you that a few days subsequent to March 9 — whether or not she knows the specific date, I don't know, but at a time subsequent to March 9, 1970, she again observed Dr. Many with a relatively limited amount of clothing on his body, again on the roof of No. 197 Lakeview.

And that will be the Commonwealth's case, your Honor.

THE COURT: Would you like to specify for us the date, time and place of the alleged offense covered by this complaint?

MR. MILLS: The date of this particular offense is March 9, 1970. The time, as far as I know, your Honor, is approximately 10 o'clock in the morning. That's as far as the date and time. The place is Lakeview Avenue in Cambridge, more specifically, 197 Lakeview.

THE COURT: Swear the witnesses in one at a time.

THE CLERK: The first witness, please.

MR. MILLS: First witness, Mr. McNulty, please.

DEFENDANT MANY: Your Honor, if it please the Court, I would like to make an opening statement.

THE COURT: Yes, Dr. Many?

DEFENDANT MANY: If it please the Court, I would like to make an opening statement with respect to the facts that we hope to demonstrate.

THE COURT: Well, the time for you to do that, Doctor, is at the conclusion of the Commonwealth's case. You then have that opportunity to make an opening of the defendant's case, not at this stage of the proceedings.

DEFENDANT MANY: I take exception, your Honor.

THE COURT: All right, Mr. Witness, if you will take the stand.

EDWARD D. McNULTY
(*Sworn*)

DIRECT EXAMINATION BY MR. MILLS

Q: Mr. McNulty, Will you tell us your name and occupation and your station of duty?

A: My name is Edward D. McNulty, police officer in the City of Cambridge, attached to Crime Prevention Bureau.

Q: Are you a detective in the department?

A: Yes, I am.

Q: How long have you been employed with the Cambridge Police Department?

A: Twenty-one years.

Q: Now, Detective McNulty, did you have occasion to be in the area of 197 Lakeview Avenue in Cambridge on March 9, 1970?

A: I did.

Q: What time of day were you in that neighborhood?

A: I received a call from my lieutenant to go to 197 Lakeview Avenue about 9 — 10:30 on the morning of March 9.

Q: And did you go to the neighborhood?

A: I did.

Q: Do you know what time you arrived, and can you tell us the exact street address where you did arrive?

A: I arrived at 187 Lakeview Avenue approximately 10:35 A.M.

Q: And were you in a uniform?

A: No, I was not.

Q: Were you instructed to go there by your superior officer or whoever is in charge of the Cambridge police?

A: I was.

Q: When you went to 187 Lakeview, what part of that particular dwelling house or whatever it is did you go to?

A: The second floor, the residence of John and Carole Gentile.

Q: And on the second floor, where on the second floor? Is that an interior room, exterior?

A: Exterior room, facing the house on the street, on the rear left, a child's bedroom.

MR. MILLS: May we use the blackboard, your Honor?

THE COURT: Yes.

Q: Detective, would you please come to the blackboard?

Q: And I would ask you, sir, to draw what you consider to be a fair representation of that portion of Lakeview Avenue which will adequately show the location of Nos. 187, 197, the houses in between; and will you make your diagram so that the size of the houses are in relative proportion to their actual sizes, if you can?

A: I'll try. (*Witness starts to draw*) This is 187. This is 197.

Q: Now, while you were at No. 187 — you were there as a policeman — who else was with you?

A: John Killion.

Q: Who is he, sir?

A: Cambridge police officer. He was my partner at the time. Sergeant John Galligan, Detective Joseph Amoroso, Carole Gentile and John Gentile.

Q: And while you were there, you were in a rear bedroom, did you say?

A: Yes, sir.

Q: Did you make any observations concerning No. 197 Lakeview Avenue?

A: Yes, sir. We were at No. 187, in a room situated like that. *(Drawing)* There was a window here on this side. From that window, I could see the porch attached to 197 that at the time was covered with some sort of plastic sheet — not sheet plastic, but roll plastic that ordinarily is stapled into place; and from this position here a very plain view was afforded to us of that back porch.

Q: And did you, from No. 187 Lakeview, have occasion to view the defendants at some area of 197 Lakeview Avenue?

A: Yes, sir.

Q: Were they clothed at the time?

A: They were not, sir.

Q: Could you describe to the Court and the jury what you noted about their behavior, their activity, their demeanor, characteristics — anything that you noticed in particular about the defendants?

A: We were there for approximately an hour, maybe a little less. And during the period of time we were there, almost all the time, Dr. Many was on the porch. He seemed to have some type of work project that he was endeavoring in.

During this period of time the defendant Peck entered the house at various times and came back out. She was probably out there three or four times.

Both of them at all times while they were on the porch were in the nude completely.

MR. MILLS: Your Honor, I am going to ask to offer these. Shall I show them to the defendants?

(Photographs shown to the defendants)

THE COURT: I don't want to see them yet, until you establish a foundation for them.

Q: Detective McNulty, I will show you two pictures that are marked on the back with identification as to when they were taken and the date they were taken, and I ask you, first, to look at the rear of the photograph. Are you familiar with the photographs?

A: Yes, I am, sir.

Q: Were they taken by some member of your department?

A: Taken by Detective Colleran.

Q: Were they taken in the course of duty? Was he assigned to take them?

A: I had called for him.

Q: Were you present when he took the pictures?

A: I was.

Q: And I ask you now to turn both pictures over and look at them. I ask you if those pictures are a fair representation of the area of No. 197 Lakeview Avenue that you saw on March 9, 1970, at approximately 11 o'clock in the morning?

A: They are, sir.

Q: And are the persons shown there the same persons who are defendants in this courtroom today?

A: They are, sir.
THE COURT: Are you offering the photographs?
MR. MILLS: Yes, your Honor.
DEFENDANT PECK: I object.
THE COURT: Let me look at them, first.
Does Dr. Many also object? I want to be sure.
DEFENDANT MANY: Yes. That's ——
THE COURT: Objections are overruled.
DEFENDANT MANY: Sir, but sir, you didn't hear the objection.
THE COURT: I know. Under Rule 71 of the Superior Court, arguments on objections are not permitted unless I ask for them. I seldom ask for them. The objections are overruled and the exhibits may be marked.
DEFENDANT PECK: I take exception.
DEFENDANT MANY: Take exception.
THE COURT: The defendants' exceptions to my ruling are noted.

(Two photographs received in evidence and marked EXHIBIT 1 and EXHIBIT 2)

MR. MILLS: May they be passed to the jury, your Honor?
THE COURT: They may.

(Photographs given to the Foreman)

Q: Detective, from the time you arrived until the pictures were taken and you left, how much time elapsed?
A: I would say close to an hour.
Q: And in the course of that hour, how many times did Miss Peck come into view, go back into the house, come into view, if you know?
A: I would say three or four, to the best of my recollection. Sometimes she was there for two or three minutes, other times she would just come out and go back in.
Q: And during the course of that entire hour, was Dr. Many also, always, to your knowledge, in the same location?
A: Yes, he was.
Q: And were you on the first floor or the second floor of No. 187?
A: Second floor.
Q: Were you at any time that day on the first floor?
A: No, sir.
Q: Were you at any time that day in any other house in that area?
A: No, sir.
MR. MILLS: No further questions. Your witness.

THE COURT: Miss Peck, you may ask first, if you will.

CROSS-EXAMINATION BY THE DEFENDANT PECK

Q: Before you had gone to the house at 187, after having received a call, did you have any prior information about the occupants at 197 Lakeview Avenue?
A: I don't believe I had.
Q: Before you went to 187, had you discussed with Mr. Gentile problems that he had been having or anything to do with this case?
A: No, I had not.
Q: When you arrived at 187, did you notice whether there was a porch at the rear of 187 on the second floor?
A: When I arrived, no.
Q: You didn't notice whether there was a porch or not?
A: No, I didn't.
Q: Now, you have testified that there were five people in the house at 187, is that correct?
With you — John Killion, John Galligan, Detective Amoroso and Mr. and Mrs. Gentile?
A: And myself.
Q: So that's six people. Were all of you at the window in this bedroom?
A: No.
Q: How large is the bedroom?
A: I would say 12 by 14 or thereabouts.
Q: Were all of you in the bedroom?
A: At various times.
Q: And were all of you looking out the window at various times to see — to look into 197?
A: I would say yes.
Q: And did you discuss what you had seen among yourselves?
A: Yes.
Q: Was there laughter?
A: Not to my knowledge.
Q: You also mentioned — oh, is there a back yard at No. 187?
A: Very small.
Q: Would you add it on to your drawing, approximately?
A: *(Witness goes to the board)* That would be the property line, as best I remember it.
Q: Do you know if there is a fence on the property line?
A: No, I don't recall.

Q: You mentioned that it seemed that the defendants were engaged in a work project. Could you describe the work project?
A: I didn't say the defendants. I said Dr. Many.
Q: Would you describe the work project that Dr. Many was engaged in?
A: I really don't know. From time to time, if I recall correctly, he had tools and was in, as I faced the porch, the rear right side of the porch.
Q: Do you know how large — will you testify how large the porch was that you were observing?
A: I would say it's 12 feet long and approximately four feet wide.
Q: And is it at the rear of the house?
A: Yes.
Q: Does it look onto a lawn of the property?
A: I believe it does.
Q: Is it on the second floor?
A: Yes, it is.
Q: When I came out onto the porch, did you observe what I did?
A: Yes.
Q: Would you describe what?
A: You seemed to be engaged in conversation with Dr. Many.
Q: Did I exchange words with you?
A: No, ma'am.
Q: Did I in any way wave to you or make any other normal communication with my body towards you?
A: No.
Q: Did you do so towards me? Did you rap on the window?
A: No, no.

Q: To your knowledge, did any of the other people while they were looking out the window rap on the window or call out?

A: No.

Q: When you looked at me, were you repulsed by what you saw?

MR. MILLS: I pray your Honor's judgment.

THE COURT: Sustained.

Q: Did it arouse your lust?

MR. MILLS: I pray your Honor's judgment.

DEFENDANT PECK: These are the relevant legal —

THE COURT: Wait a minute. Under Rule 71, which I have, we don't have argument. I'm thinking about it.

DEFENDANT PECK: Let me take exception to the first ——

THE COURT: Your exception to my first ruling is noted. I'm thinking about the second objection. . . .

With respect to the second objection, as to whether the witness's lust was aroused, the objection is sustained.

DEFENDANT MANY: I take exception to that.

DEFENDANT PECK: I take exception.

Q: Did I make any sexual overtures to you?

A: No.

MR. MILLS: I pray your Honor's judgment.

THE COURT: That is relevant. I will allow that question. Objection overruled.

Q: Did I make any sexual overtures to you?

A: No, ma'am.

Q: Did what you saw cause you to be upset?

A: No, ma'am.

Q: Did it harm you?

A: No, ma'am.

Q: Could you describe what your reaction was to what you saw?

THE COURT: I think we are getting far afield, now. We're not going to use a subjective test as to the witness's reaction. I am going to exclude this line of inquiry as to his personal subjective reaction as to what he may have seen.

DEFENDANT PECK: I wish to submit that when the legal standard itself is fairly vague, that —

THE COURT: Miss Peck, as I said, I am not hearing argument on objections, and I am ruling that that line of questioning is immaterial, and I note your exception to my ruling.

DEFENDANT MANY: I take exception.

THE COURT: I note your exception, as well, Dr. Many. You may have him describe what he observed, what he saw.

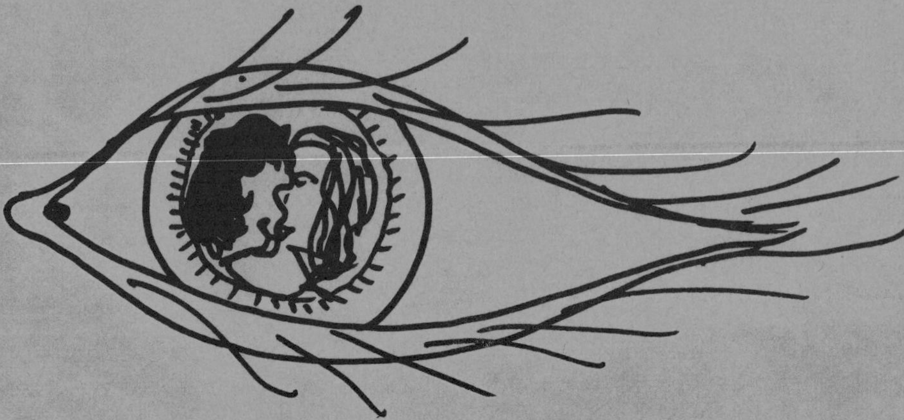

Q: Would you describe for the Court more fully what you observed when I — when you observed me?

A: You were engaged in conversation with Dr. Many.

Q: Would you tell me what you saw?

A: You?

Q: What did you see about me? Would you describe the "me" that you saw?

A: You with no clothes on.

Q: Well, what parts of me did you see that made you feel that you should arrest me.

MR. MILLS: I pray your Honor's judgment.

There has been no testimony of an arrest.

THE COURT: We don't want the subjective state of mind of the police officer as to arrest. He may state what he saw physically and what parts of her body, I think she means. What parts of her body did you see, Officer?

THE WITNESS: I think everything except from her ankles down, your Honor.

THE COURT: Front, back, sideways?

THE WITNESS: Yes.

THE COURT: The entire naked body except for the ankles?

THE WITNESS: Front, back, sideways.

THE COURT: All right.

Q: I would like to ask you why you are reluctant to name the things that you saw that you found objectionable.

MR. MILLS: I pray your Honor's judgment.

THE COURT: Objection is sustained.

Q: Have you ever read *Playboy* magazine?

MR. MILLS: I pray your Honor's judgment.

THE COURT: That is objectionable and frivolous, and the objection is sustained.

DEFENDANT PECK: I take exception.

DEFENDANT MANY: I take exception.

THE COURT: All right. The witness is not on trial; the defendants are on trial. What this gentleman saw or said he saw is for the jury to determine.

Of course, you may go into that. But what his standards, his subjective reactions are, is not material, is not in issue in this court.

Q: Will you tell me what type of lens was used?

THE COURT: Miss Peck, I think you might take exception to my ruling on ——

DEFENDANT PECK: I take an exception.

DEFENDANT MANY: Me, too.

Q: Would you tell me what type of lens was used on the camera which took the photographs that you displayed to the jury?

MR. MILLS: Objection, your Honor.

THE COURT: Objection overruled. He may answer.

THE WITNESS: I have no idea.

Q: Do you know whether it was a telephoto lens?

A: I believe it was.

Q: You believe it was?

A: I believe it was, yes.

Q: Is it your opinion that a telephoto lens reflects what the eye can see at the same distance?

MR. MILLS: I pray your Honor's judgment.

THE COURT: Sustained.

DEFENDANT MANY: Exception.

Q: Let me show you this photograph again.

THE COURT: Wait a minute. We generally have one interrogation at a time. Miss Peck has to do her own excepting to my rulings. It's not proper for you to do it. She can do it. You will have your opportunity when you ask questions. Go ahead.

Q: Was this what your naked eye could see, two houses away from 197, in the rear bedroom window, with five, six other people?

MR. MILLS: I pray your Honor's judgment and ask the question be clarified.

THE COURT: Referring to Exhibits 1 and 2?

DEFENDANT PECK: Yes. This is Exhibit 2 that I'm looking at now.

THE COURT: You may have your question.

A: Yes. In clearer detail, though.

Q: What was in clearer detail — the photo or the eye?

A: What I saw.

Q: Oh, you could see better than the telephoto lens?

A: Yes.

Q: Would you state where the railing — what the railing covers in this photograph?

A: I don't understand.

Q: Could you state what the railing covers — what part of the anatomy the railing covers of the two figures on the porch?

A: The rear end.

Q: Now, was this a fair depiction of what you could see from the rear bedroom window?

MR. MILLS: I pray your Honor's judgment. That has been answered.

THE COURT: Well, she may have her question.

A: I will have to take an — I don't think this picture was taken from the rear bedroom window. I think it was taken from the bathroom window.

Q: So this was taken from where you couldn't see at all? I mean, did you take any view from the bathroom window to 197?

A: Yes. I was present when Detective Colleran took the picture.

Q: So you also viewed from that window, as well as from ——

A: Yes.

Q: Is this what you would see from that window?

A: From the bathroom window, yes.

Q: Now, would you testify as to what it covers on the figures — the railing: What part of the anatomy the railing covers?

A: The rear end.

Q: If I had been turned to the front, what would it have covered?

A: The front.

MR. MILLS: I pray your Honor's judgment.

THE COURT: You may answer. You have answered.

Q: Could you be more explicit about "the front end"? I assume my front end would be the whole — from the top to the toes, and it seems very relevant which part of this was actually being covered by the railing from your view.

A: I would say that that would cover from your navel to the hip joint.

Q: Now, was I at any time when you were viewing me from the bathroom window, was I facing you?

A: I would say yes.

THE COURT: Let me see if I can ask this directly: Officer, as you looked towards this porch, did you see any of the private parts of this female defendant?

THE WITNESS: Yes, your Honor.

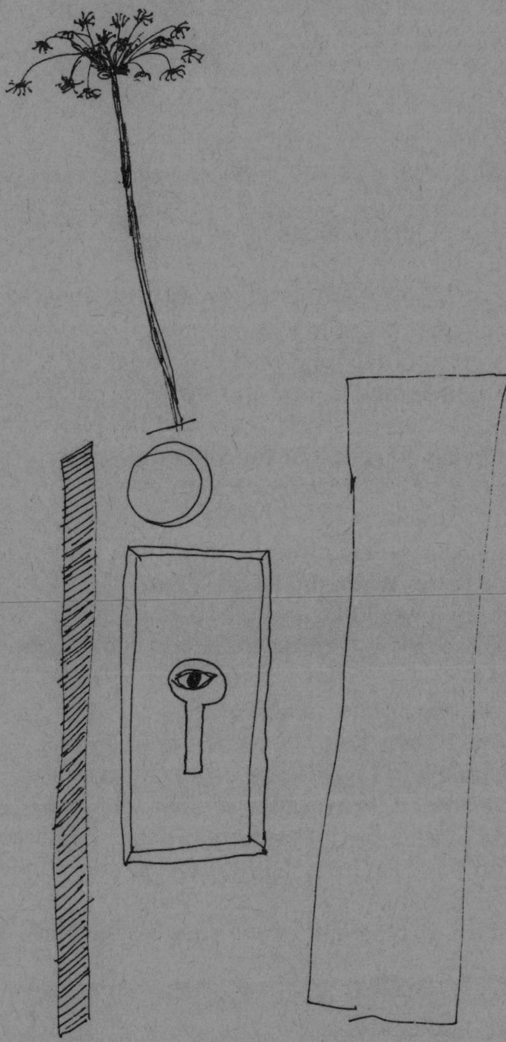

THE COURT: Could you see them with the rail in front of them — or was it not obscuring your vision?

THE WITNESS: Sometimes the rail would obscure it, sometimes it wouldn't.

Q: How long did you spend looking out the window?

A: I have no idea of the total time. I stated that I was there for a period of around an hour, and at various times I was in the bathroom, in the bedroom. I think at one time I requested the photographer to go outdoors to see if he could get pictures from outdoors.

Q: What was the photographer's name?

A: Edward Colleran.

Q: You hadn't mentioned him the first time when you testified as to who had gone there. When did he arrive at 187?

A: I would say it would be around 10:55.

Q: So altogether there were seven people looking out the window at various times?

A: No — yes, at various times, yes.

Q: For a total of how long?

A: Mrs. Gentile left, I would say, around quarter of 11. Detective Colleran got there around, between ten minutes of and five minutes of 11.

Q: And how much time did you actually spend at the window, looking out?

A: I have no way of stating that. I didn't keep a stop-watch on myself.

Q: Would you estimate?

A: I would say maybe half of the time I was there. Maybe more, maybe less.

Q: Was there somebody at the window at all times?

A: I really couldn't say.

THE COURT: Just a minute, please. It's time for us to suspend. You may step down, Mr. Witness.

THE WITNESS: Thank you. *(Witness steps down)*

THE COURT: Mr. Foreman, ladies and gentlemen, we are going to suspend this case until 10 o'clock on Monday next. It is my duty to inform you, as I do in every case, that you are not to discuss this case with anyone, including the members of your own jury panel, and you are not to make up your mind about the case or any part of it, certainly not arrive at a conclusion as to the guilt or innocence of the defendants, until after all the evidence is in, until counsel and the parties have had an opportunity to argue, and until the Court has had an opportunity to charge you on the law as it applies to the case.

Recess.

(Court adjourned at 4:10 p.m.)

MONDAY, JANUARY 11, 1971

DEFENDANT PECK: May we approach the bench?

THE COURT: If it's something you think the jury should not hear, I would be glad to excuse them.

DEFENDANT PECK: It was a matter of exceptions being taken. If Seth has to wait until he questions to take exception, it means he will have to go through some of the same questions, and we spoke about some procedure if my exceptions could also be made for him, as we go along.

THE COURT: All right. You may do that.

DEFENDANT MANY: And vice versa?

DEFENDANT PECK: And vice versa.

THE COURT: So we can understand, the record will show that in each case, exception will be taken by either defendant, it is the exception of both defendants.

DEFENDANT PECK: Thank you.

Want to come forward, please?

EDWARD McNULTY (*Resumed*)

CROSS-EXAMINATION BY THE DEFENDANT PECK, CONTINUED

Q: Would you approach your drawing and put in the window in the bathroom in 187 where some of the pictures were taken from? Could you draw it in?

(Witness goes to the board and draws)

Q: So it is the room adjacent to the bedroom, is that correct?

A: Yes.

Q: Okay. You can resume the stand.

Q: Now, I also asked you whether there was a porch on 187. Do you recall whether there was a porch on the second floor of 187?

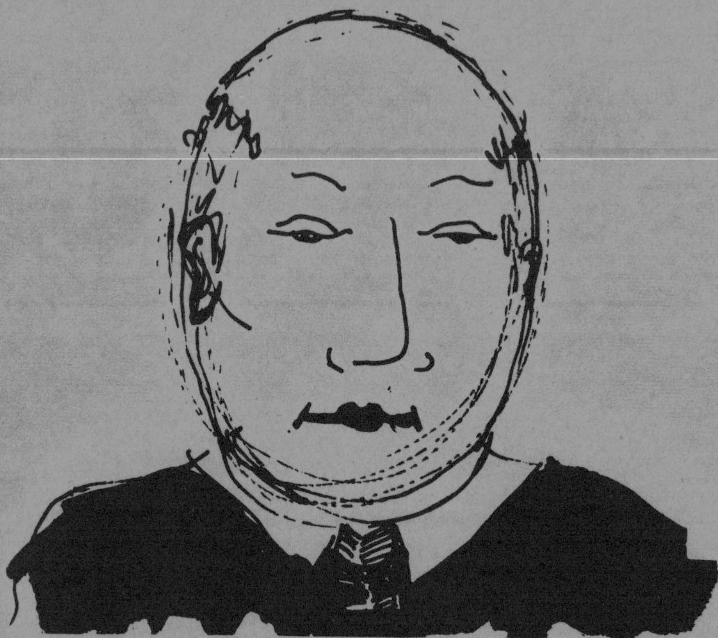

A: You asked me if I recalled it at the time, and at the time I had no knowledge of the porch being there.

Q: Have you since viewed the house?

A: Yes.

Q: You have. And is there a porch there?

A: Yes.

Q: And does it have windows that face 197?

A: Yes.

Q: When you went into the house, when you answered the call, did you have any occasion to go out on the porch?

A: No, I didn't.

Q: When the call had come in, what had you been told about the nature of the complaint that the people at 187 had?

THE COURT: Well, I know there is no objection by the Commonwealth, but I want to keep this within proper confines.

DEFENDANT PECK: All right.

Had the complainant told you that she had viewed us from her porch?

THE COURT: Well, we're going to go down a road we shouldn't. That is not admissible in evidence.

DEFENDANT PECK: All right.

I am going to show you the photograph —— To the best of your ability to recall, is that a fair representation of the house at 187 and the house in between 187 and 197?

A: Taken from where?

Q: This is from the porch. Is this a fair representation of the Gentiles' house as you might have viewed it from the yard or from — does this look like the Gentiles' house?

A: That looks like the Gentiles' house, yes.

Q: So this second window would be the bathroom window?

A: That is correct.

Q: Now, is there a chimney in front of it that's on the house in between?

A: I don't recall it.

Q: Can you see it in the photograph?

A: I can see it, but ——

Q: Is there also a tree that is in between the windows at 187 and closer to 187 than our house, in the photograph?

A: Yes.

Q: All right.

DEFENDANT PECK: I offer this as an exhibit, as our Exhibit No. 1.

MR. MILLS: Objected to as to relevancy, your Honor.

THE COURT: Hand it to the Clerk.

Exhibit No. 3

(Photograph handed to the Clerk, who handed it to the Court)

THE COURT: Would you tell me again what this is supposed to represent?

DEFENDANT PECK: This is 187, or the dark house is 187, and there's ——

THE COURT: This is looking out from your house?

DEFENDANT PECK: From our house, from our porch.

THE COURT: It may be marked as an exhibit, and you may show it to the jury if you wish.

(Photograph received in evidence and marked EXHIBIT 3)

(Exhibit 3 handed to the Foreman)

THE COURT: You may go ahead.

Q: I'd like to show you another photograph. Does that look like a fair representation of 187 viewed from Malcolm Road?

A: Viewed from the street, yes.

Q: Viewed from the street. And would this be 197 in back of it?

A: Yes, it would. Porch right there.

Q: And that's the porch that we were viewed on?

A: Yes.

Q: And this is the porch at 187 that you didn't go out on but could have?

A: That's correct.

(Photograph shown to Mr. Mills)

MR. MILLS: Same objection, your Honor.

THE COURT: You are looking at the back porch, are you, at 187 in this photograph?

DEFENDANT PECK: Yes.

THE COURT: It may be marked as an exhibit and shown to the jury.

(Photograph received in evidence and marked EXHIBIT 4)

(Exhibit 4 handed to the Foreman)

Q: Now, on Friday I had also asked you if you had any prior information about the occupants of 197 Lakeview, before you came to the scene on March 9, and I will ask you that question again.

A: No, I didn't.

Q: Now, I will show you a statement made by you in district court concerning this matter:

"Q: *Had he or had anyone told you about the nature of the case prior to your arrival in the home of the Gentiles?"*

YOUR ANSWER: *"Yes."*

"Could you tell the Court what he told you?"

"A report came in to our office about a week before from Detective Ellis."

Did you ever make this statement?

A: Yes, I did.

Q: And were you under oath at the time?

A: Yes.

(Document shown to Mr. Mills)

DEFENDANT PECK: I am going to ——

(Defendant Peck whispers to Mr. Mills)

MR. MILLS: If Miss Peck represents that this is a piece of the transcript from the district-court proceedings, on her representation, there is no objection from the Commonwealth.

THE COURT: Objection to what?

MR. MILLS: To whatever she wishes to do with it.

THE COURT: Will you pass it up?

(Paper given to the Court)

THE COURT: It may be marked as an exhibit.

(Document received in evidence and marked EXHIBIT 5)

Q: I am going to show you a photograph and ask you if that is a fair representation of nude males and nude females?

A: Yes.

(Photograph shown to Mr. Mills)

(Photograph shown to the Court)

THE COURT: I see the photograph, and ask you why is it before me, or before the Court? Do you offer this in evidence?

DEFENDANT PECK: Yes, that's correct.

THE COURT: It's excluded.

DEFENDANT PECK: May I make an offer of proof at this point, for this evidence, and also when you excluded my question about whether he ——

THE COURT: Your offers of proof must be made without the hearing of the jury or else you have it before the jury. Mr. Reporter, will you come to the side of the bench?

First of all, I will make it easy for you. I will ask the reporter to mark that document, the exhibit you want in evidence, which I excluded, as an exhibit for identification only, which, if you wish, can constitute the offer of proof as to that.

THE COURT: These are technical matters, Mr. Foreman, ladies and gentlemen, which do not concern you, but certain procedural steps are necessary to protect the record, and we will take care of that.

Excuse me, Miss Peck. Did you finish your examination?

DEFENDANT PECK: Yes, I have.

THE COURT: All right. Doctor, you may proceed.

CROSS-EXAMINATION BY THE DEFENDANT MANY

Q: Detective McNulty, in your testimony originally you mentioned that you work for the Cambridge Police Department as a member of the Crime Detection Squad, is that correct?

A: Crime Prevention Bureau.

Q: Crime Prevention. Is that commonly known as the Vice Squad?

A: That's encompassed in it, yes.

Q: It's part of the Vice Squad?

A: No, the Vice Squad is part of the Crime Prevention Bureau.

Q: In your experience as a detective, how long have you worked for the Crime Prevention Bureau?

A: Six years.

Q: Six years. Now, in your experience, you must have come up against many similar cases in which this law was applied?

MR. MILLS: I pray your Honor's judgment.

THE COURT: He may answer this yes or no.

A: No.

Q: No. Could you tell me briefly, describe what the central difference is in this particular case?

THE COURT: As compared to what, Doctor?

Q: As compared to the many previous cases that you have come up against, utilizing this law?

MR. MILLS: I pray your Honor's judgment.

THE COURT: Sustained.

DEFENDANT MANY: I take exception.

On the photographs that the Commonwealth presented, could you tell me whether, from these photographs, whether the day was bright and sunny or cloudy and gray? Is there any way you can tell from those photographs?

A: I would say it was bright and sunny.

Q: Bright and sunny. Now, can you tell me whether the roof here — and this is the roof of the house between 187 and 197 — intrudes at waist level for well over a half of the portion of the porch?

MR. MILLS: I pray your Honor's judgment.

DEFENDANT MANY: May I clarify what I'm asking?

THE COURT: Please do. Not to me, but to the witness.

Q: I am suggesting this house right in between 187 and 197 actually juts out to such an extent that well over half of the porch is excluded from the view of the persons at 187.

A: I would say close to half.

Q: I present your own pictures in evidence of the statement I have just made and ask you again whether or not that is the case, that the roof actually excludes at least half of the porch at least from the waist up?

MR. MILLS: I pray your Honor's judgment. May the defendant be cautioned from testifying?

THE COURT: Well, it's a question. The witness may answer.

A: I would say it's close to half.

Q: You testified earlier that these were probably taken with a telephoto lens. Is it your opinion that this represents a photograph that has been blown up considerably?

A: I couldn't say.

Q: You testified that you went to a private home, 187, the home of a fellow officer, and from that home you made certain observations. Now, would you point in this photograph which window it was from which you made the observation?

A: I would say it would be this one. *(Pointing)*

Q: And this is the bedroom window?

A: Yes.

Q: Not the window from which the pictures were taken — or is it? I don't know; I'm asking you.

A: I think they were taken from both this window and that window.

Q: The day that you made the observation, were the blinds drawn on that window or were they up?

A: I don't recall.

Q: You don't recall whether you were looking through the blinds or through an open window?

A: No, I don't.

Q: You have previously testified before this Court that your presence was — to the best of your knowledge, that no notice was taken of your presence by the defendants, is that correct?

A: Correct.

MR. MILLS: I pray your Honor's judgment.

THE COURT: Well, he may answer the question. Go ahead.

Q: Now, I would like to call your attention and the attention of the Court to the indictment and ask you to read the last two sentences of the indictment against the defendants.

A: Starting where? Last two lines?

THE COURT: If you will read them to yourself, Mr. Witness, please.

Q: Now, for the purposes of examination, these lines read, "The defendants —— "

MR. MILLS: I pray your Honor's judgment.

DEFENDANT MANY: I would like to explain the question that I'm going to ask, and I can explain that best by reading from the indictment.

THE COURT: Well, the jurors are going to have that, anyway. No reason why you can't do this, without elaboration. Just read the words.

DEFENDANT MANY: "The defendant" — and this indictment is towards myself, the other one is toward Carolyn — "The defendant was guilty of open and gross lewdness and lascivious behavior in the presence of Edward D. McNulty."

Q: And you have just testified, Mr. McNulty, you have just testified that to the best of your knowledge I had no knowledge of your presence. Yet you have claimed on the indictment that I was in your presence.

I wonder if you could explain the nature of that indictment and the conflict between the indictment and your testimony?

MR. MILLS: I pray your Honor's judgment. Matter of law.

THE COURT: The objection is sustained. You don't ask the question that way. You may inquire as to what he saw or anything else about the facts, but the law is reserved to the Court to tell the jury later.

DEFENDANT MANY: I take exception.

THE COURT: Doctor, as I say, you may ask him about any of the facts in the indictment. You may ask him any of the facts having to do with the indictment or the facts that gave rise to it. He is not precluded from such questions as to the facts.

Q: Was this crime in your presence — this alleged crime?

A: Yes.

Q: It was. Did you make any effort to notify or let the defendants know that you were present?

A: No, I didn't.

Q: Did you observe any behavior that aroused lustful thoughts?

MR. MILLS: Objection, if that's the end of the question.

(Laughter)

THE COURT: Just a minute. We are in Superior Court. The spectators are welcome to be here, as long as they comport themselves properly. If they wish to laugh from amusement or merriment, they can carry those activities on outside the Court House building.

I don't want to have to say that again.

Are you directing your question, Doctor, to the witness's own feelings or own reactions?

DEFENDANT MANY: I am addressing my question to the objective fact of the behavior.

Q: And my question again is, did he observe any behavior calculated to arouse lustful thoughts?

MR. MILLS: The Commonwealth's objection, your Honor.

THE COURT: The objection is sustained.
DEFENDANT MANY: I take an exception.
THE COURT: Yes, Doctor.
You may ask him what he observed.
Q: Did you observe behavior calculated to corrupt or debauch you or any other persons?
MR. MILLS: Same objection, your Honor.
THE COURT: Sustained.
Let me explain to the jurors, and, hopefully, to the defendants ——
DEFENDANT MANY: I take exception.
THE COURT: And, hopefully, to the defendants: Neither of these defendants are lawyers, and they have at their own wish — this is their privilege; they have a right to try this case themselves. So naturally it's a little bit more difficult than a case tried by lawyers, but the problem is this: whether or not a certain act, as has been alleged — and we will use the word "alleged" — in this indictment, is lewd or lascivious or otherwise — that is the province of the jurors, to find on the facts of the case, and on the law as I give it to you at the end of the case.

It's not for the witness or for the district attorney or the defendants to discuss the law or the ultimate conclusion which the jury may or may not find, as the case may be.
Q: Were there any objective manifestations of sexual conduct, Mr. McNulty?

A: That I observed?

Q: Yes.

A: No.

Q: Were there any objective manifestations that you observed of lustful conduct?

MR. MILLS: I pray your Honor's judgment.

THE COURT: Now, we're getting back again into the jury's province, Doctor.

The objection is sustained.

DEFENDANT MANY: I take exception.

Q: Did you observe any attempts to commercially exploit ourselves or, in like manner, engage the interests of other persons?

MR. MILLS: Objection, your Honor.

THE COURT: Sustained.

DEFENDANT MANY: Exception.

THE COURT: Let me say something further to the jury, to make it a little more understandable: You are new at jury service. Forget this case for the moment. I don't want to say anything that impinges on this case.

If you had an automobile-accident case, you would have lawyers who would ask the various witnesses what they observed — how fast they were going, were they stopped or moving, and the like; but no witness in an accident case can be asked the question, "Were you negligent or was the other man negligent?"* That is a function for the jury to determine, and under the law given to them by the Court.

So in this case we are trying to stick to the facts in the case, as far as the witnesses are concerned. What the ultimate conclusion is will be for the jurors.

Q: Did you observe any behavior calculated to invite or to include others?

MR. MILLS: Same objection, your Honor.

THE COURT: Sustained.

Q: Did you observe any invitational behavior, any inclusion of other persons in what was going on in the porch?

MR. MILLS: Same objection, your Honor.

THE COURT: Sustained.

The trouble we're having, Doctor, is in the form of the questions.

DEFENDANT MANY: If you want me to argue the reasons why I'm presenting this ——

THE COURT: No, no. I won't hear arguments on the question, but you

*A witness may testify as to the effect — who and what was hit and what harm was done. The Court blocked analogous questions here.

may ask him, as I said before — well, I guess I'll withdraw the comment.

Q: Did the defendants make any actions to invite others in?

A: No.

Q: You have testified that you knew about a week prior to your arrival at 187 about the defendants in that house. Will you tell me what your prior knowledge was?

A: I testified that I didn't know of the defendants in the house. Now, I can clarify the remark that was made. I did receive a report from Detective Ellis that he had been to 197 Lakeview Avenue approximately a week before and was unable to gain entrance. At the time, he had no idea who the occupants of the dwelling were, and I had no idea who the occupants were until the time I got to 187 Lakeview Avenue, on the 9th.

Q: Did he have a warrant to get into the house, to the best of your knowledge?

MR. MILLS: I pray your Honor's judgment.

THE COURT: Sustained.

DEFENDANT MANY: Exception.

You testified earlier, Mr. McNulty, that the photographer attempted to get pictures from the outside as well as from the inside of 187, is that correct?

A: I believe my testimony was that the photographer was outside. I was not present with him when he took pictures outside.

Q: Did he get pictures from the outside?

A: I have no idea.

Q: Had you discussed the case with anybody prior to arriving at 187?

A: On the occasion that I had the conversation with Detective Ellis, approximately a week before that morning, I had a telephone call, a radio call, to make a telephone call to the police station to talk to my superior officer, and he told me to go to 187 Lakeview Avenue and check into a situation.

DEFENDANT MANY: I rest on the questions.

THE COURT: Well, do you mean you have finished your questions with this witness?

DEFENDANT MANY: Yes.

THE COURT: Further questions from the government?

MR. MILLS: Just a few, if your Honor please.

REDIRECT-EXAMINATION BY MR. MILLS

Q: Detective, on cross-examination it was brought out that there was a prior court proceeding in this case, and there has been some suggestion that there was prior inconsistent testimony by you. Now, I ask you, on March 9, 1970, when you went to No. 187 Lakeview, did you know the names of the persons who dwelt in there?

A: I did not.

Q: Had you prior knowledge that some activity had been taking place in there and that you had gone to 187 for the purposes of investigating that activity?

A: I did, sir.

Q: Did you go to persecute any particular person?

A: I don't understand.

Q: Did you know the names of the people? Did they mean anything to you, or did you go to investigate activity?

A: I went to investigate activity.

MR. MILLS: Thank you. Nothing further. Thank you, your Honor.

THE COURT: You may step down, Officer.

(*Witness excused*)

MR. MILLS: Mr. Amoroso, please.

JOSEPH A. AMOROSO

(*Sworn*)

DIRECT EXAMINATION BY MR. MILLS

Q: Mr. Amoroso, would you be kind enough to state your name, your occupation and your station of duty?

A: Joseph A. Amoroso, police officer of the City of Cambridge, in charge of the BCI, Cambridge Police Department.

Q: Are you an officer, detective, sergeant?

A: Detective.

Q: And did you have occasion to be present in No. 187 Lakeview Avenue with Detective McNulty on March 9, 1970?

A: Yes, I did.

Q: And, Detective, from somewhere in No. 187 Lakeview, did you have occasion to observe No. 197 Lakeview Avenue?

A: Yes, sir, I did.

Q: At No. 197 did you observe the defendant, Miss Peck, and the defendant, Dr. Many?

A: Yes, I did.

Q: And when you observed them, were the defendants completely clothed?

A: No, they were not.

Q: Were they totally nude?

A: Yes, they were.

Q: Would you be kind enough to describe to the Court and the jury the activity, if any, which you saw the defendants take place in — anything you saw them do, anything you heard them say, if you heard anything, please?

A: On that specific morning of March 9, as a result of a radio call, we were dispatched to go to 187 Lakeview Avenue, and on arriving, we were met by Mrs. Gentile, who stated of the activities that were going on next door. She brought us up into the ——

Q: Detective, we can go through that but I don't think it's necessary.

When you were in No. 187 and you were viewing portions of No. 197, you testified you saw the defendants?

A: Yes.

Q: What did you see them do, if you saw them do anything? What did you hear them say, if you heard them say anything?

A: I observed Miss Peck on the porch and Dr. Many on the porch. They were both in the nude, and at times they appeared to be looking at some pictures or something. He had a hammer and he, Mr. Many, would step up on a chair and appeared to be nailing something on the sill up there. And they were in one particular corner there for quite a while, looking at something there — I couldn't make it out.

And they would go into their apartment and come out, and their porch was enclosed with a clear plastic vinyl, and it was a bright, sunny day this particular day. And they would enter their apartment different times, come out.

One particular time, Miss Peck was alone on the porch. She was looking towards the Gentile house. I was standing at the windowsill, the shade was up, and I observed Miss Peck, what appeared to me to be plucking hair from her pubic area. And then she would go into the apartment and then she would come out.

WE SEEN 'EM! ALL of 'EM!

And they were there for about an hour, the whole length of time, so I called Sergeant Galligan over, and he viewed some of this, and we decided to call the Crime Prevention Bureau — this is their line of work — and see what was to be done.

Q: Sir, with reference to the defendant, Miss Peck, if you recall, is there any portion of her body which you did not view exposed?

Was there any part of her body which you could not see nude?

THE COURT: We would be direct about this: did you see any of her private parts at the time you looked at the female defendant?

THE WITNESS: Yes, I did.

THE COURT: What about the male defendant — did you see his private parts for a certain time?

THE WITNESS: Yes, I did.

Q: My last question, sir: During this time, were members Killion, Galligan and McNulty of your Police Department with you?

A: Well ——

Q: Better question: Who was with you?

A: Well, they were all there — Sergeant Galligan, Killion — but Killion, we called the Crime Prevention, Killion and McNulty arrived probably 15, 20 minutes after we were there.

MR. MILLS: Thank you, sir.

No further questions.

CROSS-EXAMINATION BY THE DEFENDANT PECK

Q: For the whole time you were there, you were in either the bedroom or the bathroom — the bedroom in 187?

A: I was in the bedroom. I was in the kitchen — I had a cup of coffee there which Mrs. Gentile made.

Q: Why didn't you go into the back yard?

THE COURT: I didn't hear the last part of your question, Miss Peck?

Q: Why didn't you go into the back yard of 187?
MR. MILLS: I pray your Honor's judgment.
THE COURT: Well, I will permit the question.
THE WITNESS: When McNulty and Killion arrived, they continued to conduct this investigation. We just dropped out of it. We didn't follow McNulty or Killion or — I believe our photographer, Eddie Colleran, was there.
Q: Would it be fair to say that you didn't go into the back yard because you didn't want to be seen by us?
A: No, we left. While they were still there, we had left.
Q: Could you have taken a view of our house from the back yard?
A: I don't know. I was never in the back yard.
Q: How did you know it existed?
A: Pardon?
Q: How did you know the back yard existed?
A: Well, there was a back yard next to the Gentile house. There's sort of — there's a back yard there — a little white house and then your house.
Q: And there's a yard also with the Gentiles' house?
A: I have never seen it.
Q: Oh, I thought you had testified to that?
A: I never did.
Q: You also testified that I was nude — was I nude at all times when I was on the porch when you were viewing me?
A: When we first arrived, you — when I first viewed you, you had come out onto the porch, you had panties on.
Q: What color were my panties?
A: White.
Q: And how long was I out there when I had something on, when I had my panties on?
A: Probably five minutes.
Q: All right. And what was the total time that you saw me out there when I was totally undressed?
A: Say about an hour.
Q: About an hour?
A: Yes.
Q: And when I was looking towards — you testified that I was looking towards the Gentiles' house at some time when I was alone?
A: Yes. Right.
Q: On the porch, is that correct?
A: Yes.
Q: At that time did I make any gestures to you, did I call out to you?

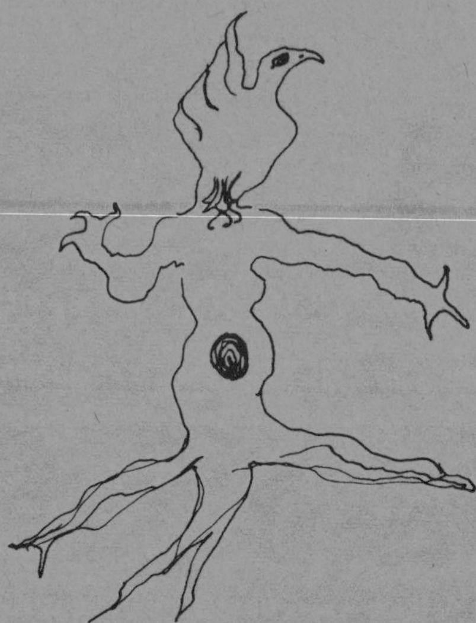

A: No.

Q: Did I make any gestures with my body like beckoning?

MR. MILLS: The same objection; and I think exceptions have been saved to the questions, your Honor.

THE COURT: Well, she may ask it again with the same result. This is a new witness. The objection sustained.

DEFENDANT PECK: I thought you allowed it.

DEFENDANT MANY: Exception.

Q: Well, did I make any sexual overtures to you?

MR. MILLS: Same objection.

THE COURT: Wait a minute. Wait a minute. Quite right. The objection was overruled last time. Of course, the witness may testify as to what he observed these defendants doing, and I withdraw my ruling on that. You may ask those questions.

Q: All right. I will ask again: Did I make any gesture to you of a beckoning sort? Did I in any way ask you to come over?

A: No.

Q: Did I make anything that you consider a sexual overture to you, directly at you?

MR. MILLS: Objection.

THE COURT: Sustained. We are in a subjective area. He may still testify and testify about what he observed, but not ——

DEFENDANT MANY: That was allowed earlier, your Honor.

THE COURT: You can ask him what he observed.

Q: Did you observe me recognize you in any way?

MR. MILLS: I pray your Honor's judgment.

THE COURT: She may ask this. These are close questions, but the defendants are entitled to bring out in full detail precisely what conduct they are alleged to have been engaged in at that time, and the witness may answer what he saw.

A: Repeat that question, please.

Q: Did I recognize you in any way?

A: I don't know.

Q: Not that you know of.

Did we exchange smiles?

A: No.

Q: Did I smile at you?

A: (*The witness shakes his head*)

Q: Do you know if I ever looked at you directly in the eyes, like I'm looking now?

MR. MILLS: I pray your Honor's judgment.

THE COURT: Objection overruled.

Q: Did you see my eyes looking at you?

THE COURT: Just a minute, Miss Peck. I am overruling the Commonwealth's objection. You may have that first question.

Q: Did I look directly at you, look into your eyes as I'm looking now?

A: You appeared to be looking my way.

Q: But can you tell whether I was seeing you?

A: Well, you were approximately, I would say, approximately 60 feet distance between us. I don't know whether you saw me or not.

Q: What day of the week is March 9, to the best of your memory?

A: I couldn't tell you. It was a weekday, I know.

Q: It was a weekday?

A: Yes.

Q: Before you went to the window, you had some knowledge about what you might see when you looked out the window?

A: Yes, I did.

Q: Would you say that you willingly subjected yourself, then, to the vision that you were going to see?

MR. MILLS: I pray your Honor's judgment.

Q: Whether it was in the course of your business or not, you willingly went to that house to look out?

A: I was sent to ——

THE COURT: Just a minute, please. She may have the question.

MR. MILLS: May it be dissected into parts, your Honor — the question, I mean?

THE COURT: That's a simple enough question. If the witness is having any trouble with it — you can answer that question, can't you?

THE WITNESS: Yes.

THE COURT: Will you answer it, please?

Q: Did you willingly go to the window and look out, knowing that you were going to see nude human beings?

A: I received a complaint on it and ——

Q: Just answer the question. Did you willingly go there of your own free will to look out the window, knowing that you were going to see nude persons?

A: It's my job.

Q: All right.

THE COURT: Is your answer yes?

THE WITNESS: Yes.

THE COURT: All right.

DEFENDANT PECK: Thank you.

I would like to again offer — make an offer of proof for Exhibit A that we have gone through again and do that for each witness as he comes.

THE COURT: Well, if it's necessary, if you want the record extended, I can say that if those are offered again, I will exclude them for the same reason. You can't make it any stronger by doing it twice, but go ahead. Are you finished with this witness?

DEFENDANT PECK: Yes, I am.

CROSS-EXAMINATION BY THE DEFENDANT MANY

Q: Mr. Amoroso, would you tell us, did you observe the defendants' behavior in the house?

A: In the house?

Q: Yes.

A: No, I did not.

Q: I would like to call your attention to your testimony at our first trial. On cross-examination I asked you: "Would you say I was in my house?"

Your answer: "Yes."

DEFENDANT MANY: I offer this certified statement of the district-court trial or record of the testimony of Mr. Amoroso in offering of proof to the conflict in his testimony today.

MR. MILLS: Objected to precisely on those grounds, because it shows no conflict, your Honor.

THE COURT: First of all, why don't you ask the witness whether he made the statement, and we'll deal with it ——

Q: Did you make that statement in district court?

THE COURT: Do you want to say what the statement was, for the record, please, Doctor?

DEFENDANT MANY: Yes. I will read this line of questioning, because it points out the context in which the statement occurred.

Q: *"You testified that it was a clear, bright, sunny day?"* — *my question.*

ANSWER: *"Right."*

MY QUESTION: *"What did you see the defendant doing?"*

ANSWER: *"I saw you in the nude."*

QUESTION: *"What was I doing in the nude?"*

ANSWER: *"I saw you in the nude."*

QUESTION: *"Would you say I was in my house?"*

ANSWER: *"Yes."*

Did you make such statements?

A: I may have.

Q: You may have? Yes or no: Did you make such a statement? I don't want to ——

A: If it's there, I made it, then.

Q: Thank you.

DEFENDANT MANY: I have no further questions.

REDIRECT-EXAMINATION BY MR. MILLS

Q: Detective, as a matter of fact, when you went to the window at 187, did you go as a police officer?

A: Yes, I did.

Q: Were you there in the course of duty?

A: Yes, I was.

Q: Were you assigned to be there?

A: Yes, I was.

Q: If you had had a choice — and this is a hypothetical question — between having a day off and being at 187 Lakeview, which would you have chosen?

A: I would take my day off.

THE COURT: Excluded. Excluded, gentlemen. The jury will disregard the question and the answer, which is absolutely immaterial to this case.

Q: As to your testimony in a previous proceeding in this case——

DEFENDANT MANY: Did you want that? Here.

Q: —— to your recollection, did you ever testify that you saw the defendants other than the portion of the building at 197 which we have been involved with during the course of this trial?

A: No, I did not.

MR. MILLS: Thank you. No further questions.

THE COURT: You may step down, Officer.

(*The witness steps down*)

THE COURT: Any further witnesses for the Commonwealth?

MR. MILLS: Yes, your Honor.

Miss Ridley, please.

SANDRA RIDLEY
(*Sworn*)

DIRECT EXAMINATION BY MR. MILLS

Q: Is it Miss or Mrs. Ridley?

A: I usually use Mrs. I am divorced and have a daughter, so I choose to use "Mrs."

Q: Mrs. Ridley, could you give us your full name and your occupation, please?

A: Sandra Ridley, 183 Lakeview Avenue in Cambridge. I work at the Cambridge Hospital.

Q: Yes. And do you live somewhere in this area?

THE COURT: Madam, what is the nature of your occupation? Are you a nurse?

THE WITNESS: No, I work in the billing office.

Q: We've been talking about March 9 in this courtroom, and you've been in the courtroom. I ask you if on some date subsequent to March 9, did you have any occasion to observe the roof-top of No. 197 Lakeview Avenue?

DEFENDANT PECK: Objection. Objection, your Honor.

THE COURT: Just a minute. Just yes or no on this question. Just yes or no.

THE WITNESS: Yes. I had seen it before, but hadn't observed ——

THE COURT: Are you talking now about after, after the date of the alleged crime?

MR. MILLS: Yes, your Honor.

DEFENDANT MANY: Object.

THE COURT: Before we delve into that in any great detail, can you tell me any basis on which ——

THE WITNESS: I can't help seeing the roof-top when I go down my back stairs.

THE COURT: Just a minute. Stand down there. Move the witness down there.

MR. MILLS: I will stand wherever you want me to.

THE COURT: Go ahead.

Don't tell me what she is going to testify to. I want to know how it's material.

MR. MILLS: Her observations subsequent to March 9, and other witnesses' observations prior to March 9 —

THE COURT: Talking about after the date ——

MR. MILLS: After the day. —— will be offered to show the intention of the defendant as of March 9, 1970.

THE COURT: Retroactive intention?

MR. MILLS: No, your Honor. As a matter of ——

THE COURT: Do you have a case that sets that out?

MR. MILLS: Yes, several.

THE COURT: I learn something every day.

First of all, do the defendants object to this line of testimony?

DEFENDANT MANY: Completely.

MR. MILLS: I believe that Commonwealth vs. Leventhal, 236 Mass. 5 ——

THE COURT: Excuse me. Do you have the cite?

MR. MILLS: 236 Mass., your Honor.

THE COURT: The page, please?

MR. MILLS: 516.

THE COURT: I think what I will do, I will excuse the jury for a few minutes. I will excuse the jury.

You may stand down, Madam, please. Excuse the jury. We will be back in a few minutes.

(*The witness stepped down*)

(*The jury leaves the courtroom at 11:12 a.m.*)

THE COURT: Any particular page, Mr. Mills?

MR. MILLS: 254 Mass. at 69.

THE COURT: This involves the sale of intoxicating liquor. Do you have a page on this?

MR. MILLS: No, your Honor.

THE COURT: Are you saying that states that subsequent acts may be received in evidence?

MR. MILLS: I have nothing that says explicitly subsequent acts, but the cases say evidence of similar activity, with no distinction between subsequent and precedent.

THE COURT: Apart from conduct amounting to an admission, I am not aware of any cases that say that subsequent activity can be allowed in on the question of intent — certainly on the civil side of the court. It's obviously inadmissible.

I am going to exclude that evidence, but if you wish to give me a precise case later on, that says that it's admissible, I will reverse my ruling.

MR. MILLS: The Commonwealth would like to proceed to a precedent activity.

THE COURT: That's a different story.

DEFENDANT PECK: We object to that.

THE COURT: Might as well take that up right now, then. I take it you're going to offer in some questions of intent, openness, intentional exposure?

MR. MILLS: Well, from the definition which I have been able to glean from the law of the Commonwealth as to just what this open and gross behavior is to include, the intention of the defendant seems to be at the apex of the activity as well as the activity itself; and in order to show intention, the evidence of a similar activity precedent to the activity in question, even if that activity is potentially criminal in itself, may be offered — of course, in the Court's discretion — to show exactly the defendants knew what they were doing and that it was not an accident or some other happenstance, but a part of a scheme or plan or a general behavior, a recurring event.

But I think that the testimony that will be offered by the Commonwealth will be far from remote, and it will meet the criteria of the law of evidence as to similar activity.

THE COURT: Why don't we discuss it now rather than when the jury is here? Can you summarize what the evidence will be?

MR. MILLS: Yes, your Honor. There will be several witnesses — as many until I get very tired, and then we can stop ——

THE COURT: I don't think I'll let you get to that point.

MR. MILLS: Thank you. There will be several Commonwealth witnesses who will testify as to their observations of the defendants on dates other than March 9, which will be about the date of the lunar eclipse, which — I don't know exactly whether it was in the first week of March ——

THE COURT: Let me ask you this: Are you alleging, then, that this evidence would tend to show that their conduct was brought home to them in some way, or simply they were observed?

MR. MILLS: They were observed engaged in similar activity as the activity which is alleged to be criminal in this case. And also there will be one witness who will testify of his attempt to call upon the defendants and discuss their activity with them. And this testimony relates to a date prior to March 9.

DEFENDANT PECK: Your Honor, I suggest that seven peeping Toms don't prove intent any more than one would, or that we have any knowledge. It would be ——

THE COURT: I'll come to you in a minute. I'm just trying to find out what the evidence is, and then we will hear from you in due course.

You're raising a second point. You say there was an alleged discussion with the defendants about their conduct?

MR. MILLS: Not both defendants. I believe one defendant, your Honor.

THE COURT: An actual discussion? You used the word "attempted." I wonder if you meant the word "attempted."

MR. MILLS: I haven't been over the case with the witness who will testify. The substance of it is — I have spoken and said hello — the said substance of his attempt, as I understand it, will be that he spoke with, I believe, Miss Peck and not Dr. Many.

THE COURT: Now, the Leventhal case, which has to do — it's an arson case. They brought in similar acts having to do with burning buildings for the insurance, to show a pattern of conduct.

MR. MILLS: Yes, your Honor.

THE COURT: Leading to an attempt to commit arson in the case being tried. I am not following you too well in your first point. You say evidence of similar acts in the community on the porch of the house could be received in evidence as to their intentional exposure on the day in question?

MR. MILLS: No, other similar acts of nudity, not necessarily confined to the porch of the house.

DEFENDANT MANY: Acts of lewdity?

MR. MILLS: No, nudity. Acts of nudity.

Our starting place is the — I think the most substantial case is the Commonwealth vs. Wardell, in 128 Mass. 52, defining the nature of this crime. And that case seems to put great emphasis on the proof of intention and the fact of intention — not the intention of being open, gross or lewd, but the intention of doing the activity, as opposed to an accidental activity, an activity which happens if the shade goes up all of a sudden, but intentional exposure.

THE COURT: I know, but that case doesn't deal with previous activity, does it?

MR. MILLS: No, it has to do with the elements that the Commonwealth must prove in this case.

THE COURT: Can you cite me a case that deals with previous activity, other than ——

MR. MILLS: In this type of criminal action, your Honor?

THE COURT: Yes.

MR. MILLS: In open-and-gross cases?

THE COURT: Exactly.

MR. MILLS: I have no case ——

THE COURT: Well, I'm going to rule that evidence out, too. Do you care to be heard on this?

DEFENDANT PECK: Yes. The way in which he is using intent reduces it to nothing, as it means any time anyone does an act while they're conscious, that's intent.

That's not the kind of intent that the criminal law requires for any specific statute. Thus, if I walked around clothed and the next day I was seen walking around clothed, that has nothing to do with my intent on that day and what meaning I put on being clothed.

And this act is supposed to look at what we intended to do. We intended to be open. That means that we must have known or been able to reasonably foresee that other people would see us, that we intended to be lewd and gross and lascivious, that it had certain sexual or — the legal meanings of those words, that we intended those meanings.

The fact of acts that are neutral, that may or may not fit those standards, have nothing to do with it. It would be like looking at our habits that have nothing to do with that specific act.

THE COURT: I am going to rule that evidence of criminal acts prior to March 9 out, but I am willing to reopen the matter if you produce a case for me. Doctor, do you wish to say anything on this point? I am going to rule in your favor, so it really isn't necessary.

DEFENDANT MANY: I'd better keep my mouth shut.

MR. MILLS: May I ask you, Judge, would you require a case as specifically the 272, Section 16, case, other than open and gross cohabitation, or whatever it's called?

THE COURT: Well, it seems to me that this crime which is called open and gross lewdness and lascivious in this Commonwealth has its counterpart in all the states, and I should think that there must be at least one case somewhere in the country that deals with the question posed. Wouldn't you think so?

MR. MILLS: I think probably.

THE COURT: All right. The third thing we are dealing with now is apparently alleged conversation held between the police officers and the defendants with respect to their conduct prior to March 9?

MR. MILLS: Yes, your Honor. A police officer.

THE COURT: Do you represent that — what do you want that for — to bring home the fact that the conduct was observed?

MR. MILLS: Yes, your Honor.

Can we have the morning ——

THE COURT: Well, I will deal with that when it comes up, but I will — at the moment we'll take the morning recess.

(*Court recessed at 11:25 a.m.*)

(*Court reconvened at 11:53 a.m.*)

DEFENDANT MANY: Your Honor, I have several comments on intent that I would like to make at this time.

THE COURT: Well, this is not the time, Doctor. I will take it up with you prior to my charge to the jury.

MR. MILLS: Your Honor, I think that I would like to approach the bench.

THE COURT: Pardon?

MR. MILLS: I would like to approach the bench.

THE COURT: How long will it take?

MR. MILLS: Very shortly. It has to do with an offer of proof as to a witness's testimony, and I want you to be aware of it.

THE COURT: I will send the jury out again, this time literally. Five minutes.

(*The jury leaves at 11:55 a.m.*)

DEFENDANT MANY: Your Honor, may I just — it won't take just a second.

THE COURT: Now that the jury is gone, you may. We'll take your point. Go ahead, Doctor.

DEFENDANT MANY: I really feel that the question of intent is important, and I am in a paradoxical situation because I want the district attorney to bring forth all the evidence he has as to intent about the criminal nature of our acts — that is, to the extent that the acts were lewd or lascivious or prior behavior will bear on these points. I would appreciate it if he would bring that into evidence.

Now, I think the question of intent deals with the criminal nature of the act, and if he has some such evidence, I am certainly open to that, and I would want to hear it. Now, as far as ——

THE COURT: I don't follow you, Doctor.

DEFENDANT MANY: In other words ——

THE COURT: Do you want him to bring in evidence as to your prior conduct?

DEFENDANT MANY: Prior conduct as to the criminal nature of the act, not prior conduct as it reproduces an activity already well-described, namely, nakedness, because I think, as Carolyn argued, that constitutes nothing but the reproduction of the crime itself — that is, the alleged crime.

In other words, if he has evidence as to my lewdness, then I think that that should be admitted, and if he has evidence as to my gross or my lascivious behavior, even though that may have taken place at a prior time, I think that should be admitted.

And I can't say that my counsel is of a similar mind, but ——

THE COURT: Is that true, Miss Peck?

DEFENDANT PECK: I'm really confused by the whole thing.

THE COURT: Go ahead. Then I will make a ruling on it. What do you say about all this?

MR. MILLS: Well, first, all of the evidence which the Commonwealth introduces is introduced for one purpose only, and that is to show the violation of a legitimate statute enacted by the Great & General Court.

Number two, as far as similar activity, not remote, precedent to March 9, it is our contention that it is admissible under the rules of evidence — and one of the assistants has agreed to go to the library, and he is there. I do not know of the existence of any one particular case dealing with open and gross lewdness or whatever the crime is called, in any jurisdiction, and as far as the introduction of evidence in this particular type of case, that ruling will be yours.

As far as what I wanted to bring up, it has nothing to do with ——

THE COURT: On the first point, let's defer that, Doctor, until 2 o'clock, at which time we will have some law on it, and I will make my ruling then. Now, let's take up the new point.

MR. MILLS: The new point is that the testimony of a Cambridge police officer, your Honor, on March 1, a Cambridge police officer called at the address, 197, rang the bell, and identified himself as an officer and stated he wished to discuss a complaint with the occupants of the dwelling. He never said "a complaint for open and gross lewdness" or a complaint that someone was nude, or anything else. And Miss Peck said some things to him, and he said some things to Miss Peck.

I want to introduce this to show some prior knowledge of the fact that this was not an all-of-a-sudden, an unfair police — but the fact that the police, the police wished to show the intention of the defendant, of the continuing nature of their acts.

I think if the police officer had said, "I am here to discuss a complaint with you from neighbors that there are nude people on the porch," I think that there would probably be little argument as to the admissibility of that. I don't want a mistrial and I don't want to be unfair.

THE COURT: I understand what you allege to be the evidence from the officer as to conversation — are you alleging that the evidence will be that he brought home to the defendants that they could be seen on the back porch by neighbors, in a naked state, or not?

MR. MILLS: Yes.

THE COURT: And what about it? What is it alleged that they said in reply? Not in detail, just the substance.

MR. MILLS: I think there was a slam of the door, your Honor. And Miss Peck, five minutes later, reappeared and told the police officer that this matter would be discussed only after all of the members of the dwelling had been consulted.

DEFENDANT PECK: I will make several stipulations at that point about that evidence. I don't know if he wants to go farther.

I went to the door. The officer refused to tell me the nature of the complaint or who made the complaint. I refused to let him in until that information was given to us, and I also said, as he said, that if it involved all of us we all would want to talk about it together, and that we would make an appointment with him, and he wouldn't make it.

THE COURT: Is it agreed that he told you people, or whoever answered the door, that there was — that he wanted to discuss the matter of being naked in the back porch?

DEFENDANT PECK: No, I don't stipulate to that. That's not ——

THE COURT: I will go ahead with this and take it up step by step. I will rule on it as we go along. Will the jury come back in, please?

(*The jury enters the courtroom at 12:01 p.m.*)

MR. MILLS: May Miss Ridley return to the stand, your Honor?

SANDRA RIDLEY (*Resumed*)

MR. MILLS: Your Honor, where do you prefer counsel to stand?

THE COURT: I don't mind where you stand, except I don't like to have you stand right alongside the bench. Anywhere in the entire room.

DIRECT EXAMINATION BY MR. MILLS, CONTINUED

Q: Miss Ridley, on March 9, 1970, were you in the neighborhood of 197 Lakeview?
A: Yes, I live at 183.
Q: And at any time during the day on March 9, 1970, did you have occasion to see either or both of the defendants unclothed?
A: I just saw Dr. Many.
Q: And where was he at the time?
A: On the porch on the side of their house.
Q: Was he partially clothed?
A: He was naked.
Q: Totally naked?
A: Yes.

MR. MILLS: Thank you. No further questions, your Honor. Your witness.

CROSS-EXAMINATION BY DEFENDANT PECK

Q: Miss Ridley, is this your porch here?
A: Yes, it is.
Q: And from this angle (*showing witness a photograph*), how much of our

sun-porch could you see?
A: Almost the entire sun-porch. Probably my right-hand side of it.
Q: Was the sun shining out there?
A: Yes, it was.

CROSS-EXAMINATION BY DEFENDANT MANY

Q: What activity was I engaged in?
A: I don't know what you were doing. You were bending over.
Q: Bending over?
A: Yes.
Q: And that was all you saw? That's the only activity?
A: Yes. I went in the house.
Q: Yes. Now, could you describe the parts of me which you found objectionable?
MR. MILLS: I pray your Honor's judgment.
THE COURT: Well, in that form. You may ask what she saw. But the word "objectionable" goes out.
Q: What did you see?
A: Saw your naked body from, I would say, right above the knees, up.
Q: Had you had ——
THE COURT: Excuse me. Excuse me.
Mrs. Witness, where were you at that time?
THE WITNESS: On my back porch.
THE COURT: Which is what level?
THE WITNESS: What level? Second floor.
THE COURT: And where?
THE WITNESS: 183.
THE COURT: Which would be one house farther removed from 187?
THE WITNESS: Yes.
DEFENDANT MANY: I think I can clarify the position in another picture.
THE COURT: All right.
Q: Is this the porch from which you made your observation?
A: Yes.

Exhibit No. 6

DEFENDANT MANY: I will present this. This is the porch here.
(*Showing to Mr. Mills*)
THE COURT: I am going to ask you to stand down while the Court looks at this. It may be marked as an exhibit and shown to the jury, if you wish.
(*Photograph received in evidence and marked EXHIBIT 6*)

DEFENDANT MANY: May I indicate to the jury, your Honor ——

THE COURT: Yes, you may.

DEFENDANT MANY: This is the house in question, 183, with the back porch. This is 183 here. This roof is the roof of our house, and our sun-porch is actually down here, below the ——

MR. MILLS: I pray your Honor's judgment.

THE COURT: Well ——

DEFENDANT MANY: I am showing the picture ——

THE COURT: You may go ahead and do it. Try to prevent yourself from testifying, that's what we try to do.

DEFENDANT MANY: Okay. Were there any questions about what ——

THE COURT: We can't have you interrogate the jury, Doctor.

THE WITNESS: Dr. Many, I live on a hill, also.

Q: That picture was taken from the street, so it doesn't — I don't think it accurately represents the angle, because we couldn't go up to her house and take the picture.

THE COURT: Doctor, you can't testify as counsel. The jury will disregard that statement. Go ahead with the interrogation.

Q: Had you gone out on the porch that day with the knowledge that you would see me?

A: Yes. My five-year-old daughter had come in and told me about you.

Q: Had you talked about the nature of the behavior taking place on that sun-porch with other persons?

A: Yes. The parents of the children that — the parents of the other children who used to stand in my driveway and watch them.

Q: And what were the nature of your discussions?

A: Well, naturally we didn't like our children watching that.

Q: But you didn't mind, yourself?

A: I went out, looked for a second, and went back into the house, and I did mind.

Q: You did mind. Did you feel that it was harmful to you?

A: I don't want to see your naked body.

THE COURT: Just a minute. Even in the absence of an objection, I am going to rule that line of questioning out in this case. We are not interested in the subjective opinion of a viewer in this case.

Q: Did you observe behavior that upset you?

A: Yes.

Q: What was that behavior?

A: That my daughter has to look at it.

Q: The behavior you observed was that your daughter has to look ——

A: I don't want my daughter to have to look at your naked body.

THE COURT: I am going to ask the jury to disregard your statement. That is not the issue.

I will tell the jury later the precise crime being alleged here, and you must be guided by that, but not subjective feelings of any witness, police officer or anybody else — their reactions to these matters.

Q: Could you describe the behavior which upset you, the behavior on the part of the defendant?

MR. MILLS: I pray your Honor's judgment.

THE COURT: Well, the word "upset" cannot be used. You can find out what she saw.

DEFENDANT MANY: I'm trying to.

THE COURT: Ask her.

THE WITNESS: The fact that you were naked.

Q: The fact that I was naked?

A: And visible from my house and the street, yes.

Q: Was there any behavior that was designed to engage you in what I was doing?

A: No. You were working ——

MR. MILLS: Object.

THE COURT: I didn't hear your question, Doctor. Was there any behavior ——

Q: Was there any invitational behavior on my part towards you?
A: No.
Q: Was there any behavior that suggested I took note of your presence?
A: I'm sure you didn't.
DEFENDANT MANY: I have no questions.
THE COURT: Miss Peck, do you have any questions?
DEFENDANT PECK: No.
THE COURT: Anything further?
MR. MILLS: Nothing further.
THE COURT: You may stand down, Madam.
MR. MILLS: Mr. Ellis, please.

RONALD ELLIS
(*Sworn*)

DIRECT EXAMINATION BY MR. MILLS

Q: Please state your name and occupation.
A: Ronald Ellis, police officer, City of Cambridge.
Q: Officer Ellis, is the clothing that you are wearing today, out of your uniform?
A: Yes, sir.
Q: Did you, sir, on or about March 1, 1970, have occasion to call at No. 197 Lakeview Avenue?
A: Yes, sir.
Q: At that time how were you dressed?
A: In a sport jacket, tie.
Q: And what time of day did you call at the house?
A: 12:10 p.m.
Q: Did you knock at the door?
A: Yes, I did.
Q: When the door was answered, did you identify yourself as a police officer?
A: Yes, I did.
Q: In what manner?
A: With the credentials and a badge.
Q: And did you — first of all, who answered the door, if you know?
A: At the time, I didn't, but now I know it was Miss Peck.
Q: The same Miss Peck who is a defendant in this courtroom today?
A: Yes, sir.
Q: And did you say anything to Miss Peck?

A: Yes. I identified myself. I told her that I had received a complaint from the neighbors, and I would like to speak to the owner and/or the occupants. At that time she told me she would see, and she closed the door. She returned five minutes later and told me that I could not speak with any of the occupants until they all got together and decided if they would speak with me.

I asked to speak to the people present.

She said no.

I asked her her name.

She refused to give it.

I asked her who owned the house.

She told me, "It's a matter of public record; find out."

At this time she slammed the door.

Q: Did you ever enter this building known and numbered as No. 197 Lakeview?

A: No, sir, I did not.

THE COURT: Mr. Witness, what is the first thing you said to this lady when you met her?

THE WITNESS: I identified myself as a police officer, detective assigned to the Bureau of Criminal Investigation, and that there had been a complaint in the neighborhood and I would like to speak to the owner and/or the occupants of the house.

THE COURT: Did you describe the nature of the complaint?

THE WITNESS: No, I did not.

THE COURT: Go ahead.

Q: Were you present at 197 Lakeview that day in the course of duty as a police officer with the City of Cambridge?

A: Yes, sir, I was.

MR. MILLS: No further questions. Thank you. Your witness.

CROSS-EXAMINATION BY THE DEFENDANT PECK

Q: Do you recall what day of the week March 1 was?

A: Sunday.

Q: Do you ordinarily investigate complaints on a Sunday?

A: Yes.

MR. MILLS: I pray your Honor's judgment.

THE COURT: Objection overruled. You may answer.

THE WITNESS: Yes, we investigate complaints 24 hours a day, seven days a week.

Q: Do you recall whether I asked you who had made the complaint against us, when we talked at the door?

A: I told you the neighbors made a complaint.

Q: Did I ask you specifically which neighbor — that we would be willing to speak to the neighbor?

A: No, you did not.

Q: I did not ask you that?

A: No, you did not.

Q: Did I ask you what the nature of the complaint was, do you recall?

A: No, you did not.

Q: Do you recall whether I asked — told you that we would be willing to make an appointment with you to discuss the matter?

A: No, you did not.

DEFENDANT PECK: I have no further questions.

THE COURT: Dr. Many, do you have any questions?

CROSS-EXAMINATION BY THE DEFENDANT MANY

Q: What was the nature of the complaint against us?

A: I spoke with Mrs. Carole Gentile at 11:45 a.m. on March 1, and she represented to me, and her child, nine years old, that a man and a woman had appeared on the rear porch at several occasions, naked, the latest being February 26, 1970, at 3 P.M., and lasting for one hour. Her attention was called to this by her child and another child that was playing in the rear yard and came up to the house to report it.

Q: And that was the only communication you had about that complaint, is that correct?

A: At that time, yes, sir.

Q: Did you feel the law was being broken?

A: I ——

MR. MILLS: I pray your Honor's judgment.

THE COURT: Just a moment. Sustained.

THE WITNESS: I was conducting an investigation ——

THE COURT: Just a minute. Mr. Witness, you cannot testify to that.

THE WITNESS: I'm sorry.

Q: Did you make further investigations?

A: No, sir, I did not.

Q: Did you contact others who would continue that investigation in the police force?

A: Yes, I did.

Q: Did they make an attempt to contact us?

MR. MILLS: I pray your Honor's judgment. If he knows.

THE COURT: Well, if he knows.

A: I have no knowledge, your Honor.

Q: Did you actually cite the words of the complaint?

MR. MILLS: I pray your Honor's judgment.

THE COURT: Objection overruled. He may answer.

Q: Did you cite the words in the complaint to Carolyn — did you cite the words of the complaint when you met her at the door?

A: No, I did not.

MR. MILLS: I object.

THE COURT: He may answer.

THE WITNESS: No, I did not.

Q: Is that routine? Is that part of, you know — are you part of the Crime Prevention Bureau?

A: I am not part of the Crime Prevention Bureau.

Q: Is that ordinary procedure, not to cite the nature of the complaint?

A: I asked to speak to the occupants of the dwelling, and I was refused permission to do so. I didn't know if she was a visitor, occupant — she didn't identify herself — so, unless I was sure, I was not going to cite the nature of the complaint. She may have been a maid.

DEFENDANT MANY: A maid.

Thank you. That's all.

REDIRECT-EXAMINATION BY MR. MILLS

Q: Just one further question. Mr. Ellis, you said you did not read the complaint. As a matter of fact, had there been any complaint, to your knowledge, issued as of March 1, 1970?

A: There was no complaint.

Q: Did you have a complaint in your possession?

A: No, I did not.

Q: Did you have a complaint to read?

A: No, I did not.

MR. MILLS: Nothing further. Thank you, your Honor.

RECROSS-EXAMINATION BY THE DEFENDANT PECK

Q: What did you have in your possession?

A: What did I have in my possession?

Q: Was a complaint in the technical sense — you had a complaint from the neighbors; you used that word before?

A: Yes.

Q: How did you mean that word?

A: At 11:45 ——

Q: No. What does that word mean, when you use "complaint" as you have used it in your first testimony? Does ——

THE COURT: To shorten this up: You didn't have a formal piece of paper from the court?

THE WITNESS: No.

THE COURT: But one of the neighbors had said something which indicated displeasure with something that was going on, is that it?

THE WITNESS: Yes.

Q: You call that a complaint, what you meant by "complaint"?

A: Yes.

RECROSS-EXAMINATION BY THE DEFENDANT MANY

Q: Did you inquire of that neighbor why she didn't make any attempt to carry out her objection on her own part?

MR. MILLS: I pray your Honor's judgment.

THE COURT: Sustained. You may step down.

THE COURT: I wish now to instruct the jury as to this testimony, that it's in for a very limited purpose. These defendants are not on trial for any conduct, if there was any conduct, at any time other than on March 9 of this year. Any evidence you have heard from this witness as to what might have transpired as to their conduct on a previous date is not received in evidence as to other crimes; it's in evidence only for one purpose, and that is to the extent if the jury cares to believe it and cares to give it credence, to the intent which may have existed in the mind of the defendant Peck as to any conduct she may have been engaged in on March 9 or subsequent date. I will say more about this when we come to the charge. Go ahead.

MR. MILLS: Call the next witness, your Honor?

Ruth Murphy, please.

THE COURT: Is this the last witness of the Commonwealth?

MR. MILLS: No, your Honor. The testimony will be brief, your Honor.

THE COURT: All right.

RUTH MURPHY

(*Sworn*)

DIRECT EXAMINATION BY MR. MILLS

Q: State your name and occupation, if you have one, and tell us where you live.

A: Ruth Murphy, 3 Malcolm Road, and I am a housewife.

Q: Mrs. Murphy, referring to the chalk that we have here, is this Malcolm Road?

A: Yes, it is.

Q: Would you step up and just mark your house there with a piece of chalk?

(*Witness goes to the board*)

Q: Mrs. Murphy, while you are at the chalk board here, are there any dwelling houses, trees, fences, between your house and No. 197 Lakeview?

A: Nothing to block a view at all.

Q: Would you please take the stand?

(*The witness resumes the stand*)

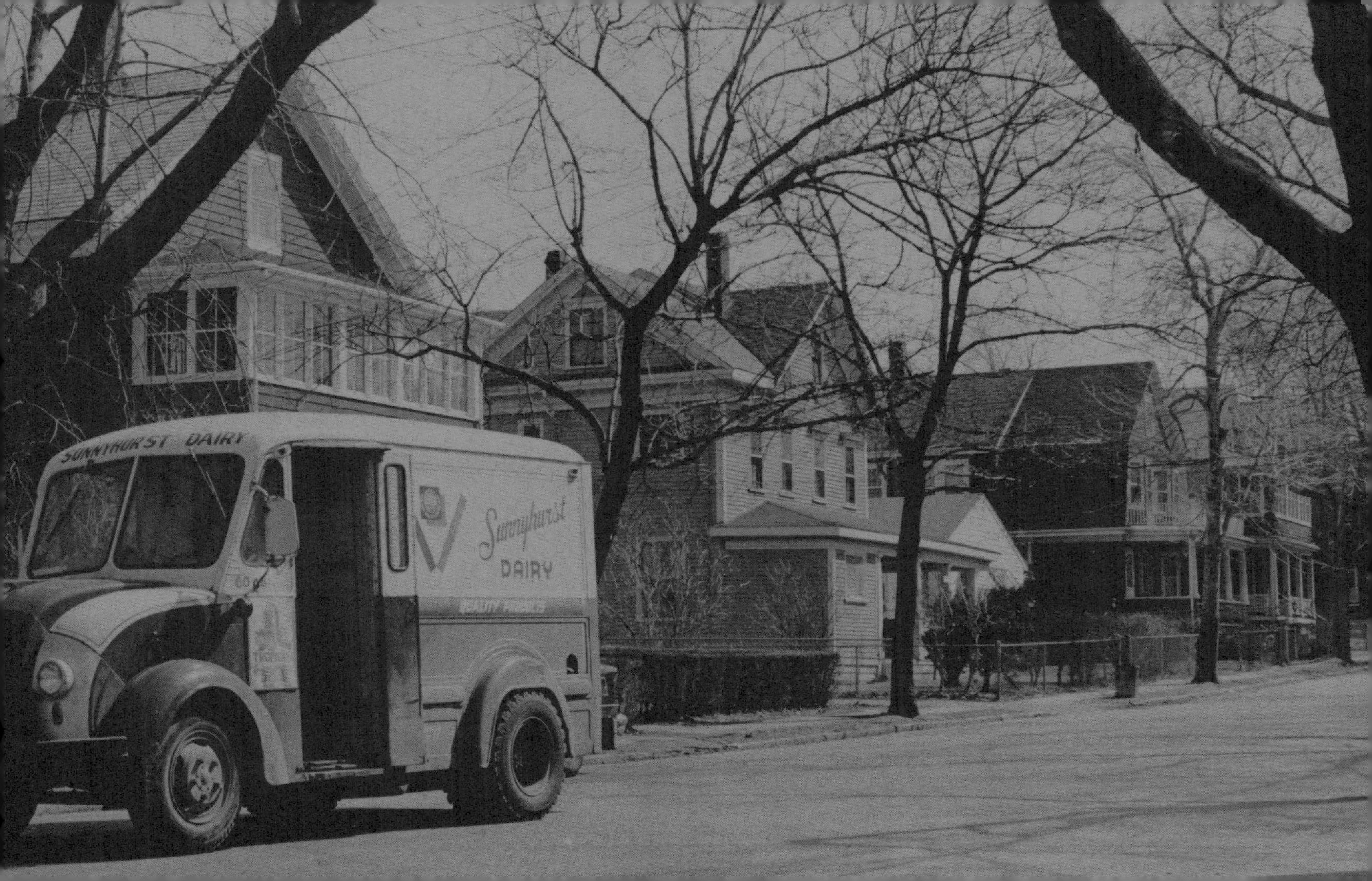
SUNNYHURST DAIRY
Sunnyhurst
DAIRY
QUALITY PRODUCTS

Q: I am going to ask you only about March 9, 1970, and you will please restrict your remarks only to that date.
Were you home on March 9?
A: Yes, I was.
Q: Did you have occasion to look in the vicinity of 197 Lakeview?
A: Yes, I did. I happened to be shaking a rug out the window and I glanced just in that direction and I could see very clearly the whole porch there.
Q: Did you see at 197 Lakeview either or both of the defendants who are in the courtroom?
A: Yes, I did. I saw them both.
Q: You saw them both. And were they clothed at the time, partially or totally?
A: I believe when I first looked out, the girl had on a slight pant, but later on I looked out again, just curiosity, I guess, and she did not, and he had nothing but a band on his hair.
Q: What do you mean by "a band"?
A: Like one of those bands they wear around their hair.
Q: Who is "they"?
A: The man. (*Pointing*) Dr. Many.
Q: Do you know or could you tell from where you were what the defendants were doing?
A: Well, they seemed to be putting up like a clear covering on a window, and at one time, sweeping.
Q: Mrs. Murphy, I show you Exhibit 1 and Exhibit 2 in this case, and ask you if they are the same porch which you have just described in your testimony?
A: It looks it. Yes, it does. I see it from an entirely different angle.
MR. MILLS: Thank you very much. Nothing further, your Honor.

CROSS-EXAMINATION BY DEFENDANT PECK

Q: How long have you lived at 3 Malcolm Road?
A: Eleven years.
Q: How old are you?
MR. MILLS: I pray your Honor's judgment.
THE COURT: She may have that answer.
Approximately?
THE WITNESS: Approximately 38.
Q: Thirty-eight.
What is your religion?
A: I'm a Catholic.
Q: Now, the first time you looked out, how long did you look?

A: I really don't know.
Q: But you had a chance to see both of us?
A: Oh, definitely.
Q: That's when you were shaking the rug?
A: Originally, yes.
Q: Did you stop shaking the rug to watch?
A: I sure did. Curiosity.
Q: Yes. And when you came back out the second time, when you went back in ——
A: I was in the house the whole time. It was out a window.
THE COURT: I'm going to ask these men to step down from that jury box. I don't want any reaction to testimony. Those three men on that ——

People are welcome to attend the trial. They are not part of the trial in this case.

(*Two assistant district attorneys leave*)

THE COURT: The reporter may stay. This is not an entertainment section of the court. They will govern themselves accordingly.
Q: You were standing on the porch, shaking the rug?
A: No.
Q: Where were you shaking the rug?
A: In my room.
Q: Oh, from your room?
A: Yes.
Q: That's on the first floor?
A: Yes.
Q: In the rear of the house?
A: Yes, it is.
Q: And were you shaking the rug out the window?
A: Yes, I was.
Q: Now, at the time that you were doing that, do you know whether I saw you?
A: I don't believe you did.
Q: Did I make any gestures towards you, or did we exchange anything?
A: I don't even believe you knew I was there.
Q: Oh, all right. And as to Seth?
A: I don't believe he knew I was there.
THE COURT: Pardon?
THE WITNESS: I don't believe they knew I was there. I don't believe they knew I was there at all.
Q: You just said ——
A: I don't know if you could see me or not. I was out a window. I don't know.

Q: So it would be harder for us to see you?
A: I don't know. I've never been in your house.
Q: When you looked the second time, how long did you look?
A: Just glanced, looked. I really don't know, to be honest. It was a long time ago, and I never thought it would come to this.
Q: Neither did we!
MR. MILLS: May that remark be stricken, your Honor?
THE COURT: Yes, that may be stricken. Continue your questions.
DEFENDANT PECK: I take exception.
THE WITNESS: I really, because of the children, I do feel it's something the

children — this is how it was brought to my attention originally — seeing the children stand in the street, pointing, and I have four and——

Q: Were the children there that day?

A: Not that day, there was not, no.

Q: Was that a school day?

A: It was a school day.

Q: Did you ever make any effort to talk to us about your concern?

MR. MILLS: I pray your Honor's judgment.

THE COURT: Sustained.

DEFENDANT PECK: Exception.

Thank you.

CROSS-EXAMINATION BY DEFENDANT MANY

Q: Mrs. Murphy, I'm really not clear on your testimony. You felt that something was going to harm your children?

A: Well, I feel that children should have respect for some things, and——

THE COURT: I am going to, without any objection from the Commonwealth, to expedite this, I am going to strike out the question and answer. We're not concerned with this witness's reaction.

DEFENDANT MANY: I take exception.

THE COURT: As to what she saw, you may inquire.

Q: What observations did you make that you felt would be harmful?

MR. MILLS: I pray your Honor's judgment.

THE COURT: Sustained.

Q: What observation — you said that you saw us putting up something of a plastic and sweeping. Did you feel that — oh.

Was that the conduct that led you to make your complaint?

A: Conduct was the attire or lack of attire, I guess you would call it. It isn't what you were doing. That had no bearing on it. It was the way

you were dressed — undressed, I mean.

Q: Do you have other objectionable modes of dress?

MR. MILLS: I pray your Honor's judgment.

THE COURT: Sustained.

DEFENDANT MANY: Exception.

Q: Did you discuss with the other neighbors prior to your observations ——

MR. MILLS: I pray your Honor's judgment.

THE COURT: Well, he may have this.
You may answer.

A: Discuss you people?

Q: Yes.

A: Well, I had been told — that was my first observation, but I had been told that the children had seen you, and we really felt we didn't want the children to see you. That was the discussion with the neighbors. And we were going to try to avoid this.

Q: Could you tell me which neighbors you discussed it with?

MR. MILLS: Objection, your Honor.

THE COURT: Well, he may have it.
Go ahead.

A: Well, one was Mrs. Ruth Johnson, was one we had discussed it with, because her children had seen it.

Q: Who else?

A: I don't remember. I think she was the only one, but one child ran down the street like Paul Revere and said, "They're out! They're out!"

THE COURT: I'm going to exclude this. This has nothing to do with the case. We are not going into that matter. Go ahead.

Q: You discussed this with Mrs. Johnson. Now, on that day had you gathered, with any other persons to observe ——

A: Yes, I called her and told her what her son had seen was going on now, and if she wanted to come to my house she could see it then.

Q: You made an effort to include your other neighbors in the scene, but not those ——

MR. MILLS: I pray your Honor's judgment.

Q: —— who were engaged in the objectionable behavior?

THE COURT: Did you finish the question, Doctor?

DEFENDANT MANY: Yes.

THE COURT: The objection is sustained.

DEFENDANT MANY: Exception.

Q: Who did gather there that day?

A: Mrs. Johnson and Mrs. Crowley, because Mrs. Crowley was at Mrs. Johnson's house, I believe.

Q: Did they both look out the window?

A: Yes, they did.

Q: Did they look out the window voluntarily?

A: I believe they wanted to see what their children had seen, and I believe both their children had seen this.

Q: Are there shades on your window?

A: Yes.

DEFENDANT MANY: That's all.

THE COURT: Is that it?

MR. MILLS: Nothing further.

THE COURT: You may step down.

(*Witness excused*)

THE COURT: Is that the Commonwealth's case?

MR. MILLS: Five additional Commonwealth witnesses, your Honor, but I don't think that the testimony of any witness will be more than a minute or two.

THE COURT: Direct testimony?

MR. MILLS: Direct testimony.

THE COURT: Do you feel you need all five? I'm trying to expedite this case.
MR. MILLS: Yes, that's why I'm pausing.
I will be as brief as possible, your Honor.
THE COURT: Cumulative evidence?
MR. MILLS: I think of necessity in some instances it will be — part of the testimony of each witness may be cumulative, your Honor.
THE COURT: Well, I think we ought to take one of those five. We have to bring this case to an end some time.
MR. MILLS: Mrs. Pentz, please.

PRISCILLA PENTZ

(*Sworn*)

DIRECT EXAMINATION BY MR. MILLS

Q: Will you give the Court and jury your full name and address?
A: Priscilla Pentz, 183 Lakeview Avenue. That's the one on the corner.
Q: That's this house?
A: Yes.
Q: Is that a two-family house?
A: It's a two-family.
Q: And what floor do you live on?
A: Second floor.
Q: And do you have an occupation?
A: No, I'm a housewife.
Q: On March 9 — and I'm going to ask you only about March 9, 1970, and you will please restrict your answers to March 9 and no other date?
A: Yes.
Q: On or about March 9, did you have occasion to view No. 197 Lakeview?
A: I did.
Q: Did you see the defendant, Miss Peck, or the defendant, Dr. Many, one or both?
A: I saw both Dr. Many and Miss Peck.
Q: Were they clothed at the time?
A: They were unclothed, sir.
Q: Where were they?
Do you know what they were doing, or — excuse me. Will you tell the Court and jury what you saw by way of activity, if any?
A: Well, actually, I don't know what they were doing. Dr. Many was putting up something, standing on something, pounding, or reaching up above his head and pounding something. And Miss Peck was, at one

point, trying to straighten it out. I was hanging clothes, so I was in and out of the porch.

Q: What time of day was this?
A: Oh, gee, I'm not sure.
Q: Was it morning or afternoon?
A: It was in the morning.
Q: It was in the morning?
A: Yes.
Q: But you don't know exactly what time?
A: No, I do not.
Q: But are you sure that the two persons who are defendants in the courtroom were the same two persons that you saw on the porch?
A: Positive.
MR. MILLS: Thank you.

Nothing further, your Honor.

CROSS-EXAMINATION BY DEFENDANT PECK

Q: How long have you lived there?

A: I was born on Lakeview.

Q: Do you have a relationship with any of the other people who testified in this matter?

MR. MILLS: I pray your Honor's judgment. "Relationship."

DEFENDANT PECK: Related to.

THE COURT: Just a minute. Just a minute.

You may answer. Are you related to any of the ——

THE WITNESS: I am.

Q: To whom are you related?

A: Mrs. Ridley.

Q: What is your relationship?

A: I'm her mother.

Q: And what is your religion?

A: I'm ——

MR. MILLS: Objection.

THE COURT: Well, cross-examination. She may have it.

THE WITNESS: I'm a Protestant — Congregationalist.

Q: And had you discussed what — did you, when you went out on this porch, did you know what you were going to see?

A: I was hanging clothes.

Q: Had anyone told you that they were out again?

A: All you have to do is see the children, or hear them.

Q: Were the children there that day?

A: The children had been there.

Q: It was a Monday, wasn't it?

A: No. I don't know just what day it was.

Q: This is March 9 you're talking about?

A: Yes.

Q: That is the only day we're going to talk about now.

A: Yes, but I'm not positive just what day it was, whether Monday, Tuesday or Wednesday.

Q: Was it a school day?

A: Yes, it was a school day.

Q: Are the children usually in school on a school day?

A: Some of them are, some of them aren't.

Q: Had any of your neighbors telephoned you and told you to go out and take a look?

MR. MILLS: I pray your Honor's judgment.

A: No, I was hanging my clothes.

THE COURT: She may have the question. Objection overruled.

A: I was hanging out clothes.
Q: After you saw us on the porch, did you go inside and call any of your neighbors and tell them to take a look?
A: No. I went back in ——
MR. MILLS: I pray your Honor's judgment.
THE COURT: Objection overruled. May have it. You may answer, Madam.
THE WITNESS: I went back in and phoned the police.
Q: Did you thereafter talk to Sandra or to any of the other neighbors?
A: After that, yes.
Q: Within the same day?
A: Well, after I had made two calls to the police, yes.
Q: And then you spoke to some of the neighbors and told them what was going on?
A: Well, it was after that, yes.
Q: And who did you speak to about it?
A: Well, I spoke to practically all of them. I've known most of these people since they were children.
Q: Most of the people who testified here?
A: Yes.
Q: That would be Mrs. Johnson?
A: That's right.

Q: And Mrs. Murphy?
A: Mrs. Murphy is a neighbor, two doors down, and I've known her family.
Q: All right. And had you heard those neighbors talking about us before, about what was going on?
A: No.
Q: When you saw us out there, you went out on two separate occasions?
A: Yes. I was still hanging clothes out. I don't hang them out all at a time.
Q: And would you just glance over?
A: To see if you were still there, yes.
Q: Right. When you glanced, at any time did either Seth or I speak to you or gesture to you?
A: Not at that time, no.
Q: At any time on March 9?
A: No.
Q: And would you say what we were doing when we were out on the porch?
A: I said that he was putting something up. I don't know what it was. You were trying to straighten it out at one point. Another time you were over in the corner, which would be in the far end of the porch, which would be down at the back of it. I don't know what you were doing — kneeling down to something.
Q: Was there any other activity that we were engaged in?
A: I don't know. Not that I know of.
Q: Is being nude an activity?
MR. MILLS: I pray your Honor's judgment.
THE COURT: Objection sustained.
DEFENDANT MANY: Exception.
DEFENDANT PECK: Exception.
I have no other questions.

CROSS-EXAMINATION BY DEFENDANT MANY

Q: Mrs. Pentz, this is a picture taken from our porch ——
THE COURT: Dr. Many, do you want to identify that for the record by exhibit number?
Q: Exhibit No. 3. Can you identify your porch on this picture?
A: Not from your angle. We're above this. This part is the clothes-line, right there, part of the clothes-line from my porch. You see? I'm above this. You're on a lower angle than I am.
Q: Can you see any part of your house in this photograph?
A: This part here.
Q: Right here? (*Pointing*)

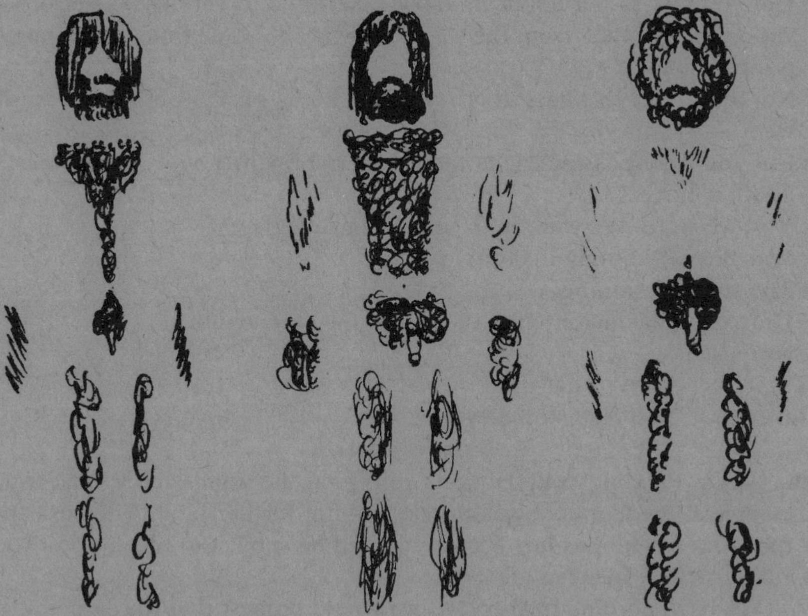

A: Yes.

DEFENDANT MANY: I would like to present this to the jury.

THE COURT: You may indicate where she pointed, Doctor.

DEFENDANT MANY: This is part of Mrs. Pentz's house, right here, this — just this corner right here. That piece of the roof. And here is a little black mark that she identifies as clothes-line. I hand that to you.

Q: Is this the house here in question that we're talking about?

A: That's right.

Q: And, again, is this the porch?

A: This is my porch; right. The first three lines.

Q: This is the porch.

(*Photograph shown to the Foreman and the jury, then given to the Foreman*)

THE WITNESS: You were on the lower level when those pictures were taken. You were on the street instead of ——

Q: This last picture is taken from the street?

A: Yes.

Q: Did you contact your daughter in order to have her come see what you were looking at?

A: I didn't contact her personally. I immediately went for the telephone and called the police.

Q: Did you talk to her about it, about making observations — her observations were made from the same place at the same time, according to prior testimony.

A: Not at the very same second, because I was on the phone before she went ——

Q: But you were passing each other back and forth. You were together, is not that correct?

A: Yes, we were. We were in the same apartment.

Q: Was the sun shining that day?

A: The sun was shining.

Q: Did you make any attempt to contact the defendants?

A: No.

DEFENDANT MANY: That's all.

THE COURT: You may step down.

(*Witness excused*)

MR. MILLS: Pending your Honor's ruling on the admissibility of certain evidence, the Commonwealth has nothing further now. I just ask that the witness who has just been dismissed be subject to recall upon your ruling as to evidence.

We have nothing further, but we would request that the case now be stopped pending preparation of the law requested by this Court.

THE COURT: I have to make a ruling on other questions in your absence, so we must suspend the case at this moment, and I am going to take it up at 2 o'clock with counsel in your absence. So I want you to know in advance about this interruption.

So when the officer announces that we are in recess until 2 o'clock, that will apply to the lawyers and to me. The jury will not be expected to return until 2:15.

(*Court recessed at 12:45 p.m.*)

AFTERNOON SESSION

(*The court reconvened at 2:05 p.m. The jury is not present*)

THE COURT: Yes, Mr. Mills.

MR. MILLS: Yes, your Honor. May we at this time consider the question of law that you proposed prior to the noon recess?

THE COURT: Yes.

MR. MILLS: And it is the Commonwealth's intention, depending on your ruling of law, to introduce testimony tending to show that the defendants, one or both of them, on days both subsequent to and precedent to March 9, 1970, were engaged in activities similar to that activity which is the ground for the complaint as to March 9.

THE COURT: Right.

MR. MILLS: Did your Honor make a definitive ruling as to subsequent activity?

THE COURT: Yes. That's out.

MR. MILLS: It's out. As to precedent activity, then, I think we can start with the case most on point, although it's not from this jurisdiction — State vs. Stice, an 1893 case from the Supreme Court of Iowa, which relies in its opinion upon the case of Commonwealth vs. Sawtelle, in 141 Mass.

THE COURT: Let me tell you why I'm semi-expert on this question: I got overruled on this point by the Supreme Court in Commonwealth vs. Welcome. I followed your reasoning in a similar action, and the case was overruled, and the case was retried, too.

Go ahead.

MR. MILLS: Well, the young attorney always respects the prudence of any court.

THE COURT: Go ahead, Mr. Mills.

MR. MILLS: In brief, your Honor, it's incumbent upon the Commonwealth to show that this act was intentional and not a mere accident, and, as the Iowa Supreme Court said in the Stice case, we know of no better way to establish the fact that the offense was designedly committed than to show the commission both before and, in that case, after the particular date in question, that similar activity had been engaged in by the defendants.

And in the Stice case, there was a careful instruction to the jurors that that evidence was admitted for the limited purpose only as to go into intent or purposefulness of the act — and, of course, that's all that the Commonwealth wishes from this evidence.

THE COURT: I am trying to find the Commonwealth against Welcome case. I don't have the proper book here, so I'm not able to do it.

MR. MILLS: Refer to the last volume of the Digest, your Honor, the table of cases.

THE COURT: I will show counsel. Dr. Many and Miss Peck may look at this, if they wish.

That was my case. Indecent-assault case, where the Supreme Court said it was prejudicial error and reversed the case for the reason that ——

MR. MILLS: Well, as to that rule, your Honor, of course, we recognize that there are all kinds of exceptions: The activity must be geographically proximate, or proximate in time, similar, substantially; and I know the name, Commonwealth vs. Welcome; I don't know what the case is about and I don't recall.

But I know there are several different reasons why the Court could have overruled it as far as not conforming to the norms required for preserving the defendant's rights when other similar activity is involved.

I think we have them all here: We're talking about a period of ten days; we're talking about precisely the same place, precisely the same defendants, and, in substance, the same acts.

THE COURT: Well, Miss Peck, do you care to be heard?

DEFENDANT PECK: Yes. I think the proof that he's offering is this proof of dissimilar acts. It isn't proof of the specific act to be open, the specific intent to be lewd, the specific intent to be grossly lewd or engaged in lascivious behavior. All it does is perhaps show intent to be nude, and I don't think that it's a clear question that to be nude is to be lewd.

So I think the evidence that he is going to offer is irrelevant on that ground, rather than on the question of what you are considering.

THE COURT: Doctor, do you have anything to say?

DEFENDANT MANY: I would like to add that if he believes that the intent to be nude can be demonstrated by showing that we were nude or naked persons, then he might rightfully look to all the examples of our nakedness, which would include conditions that have to do with taking showers, taking baths, being born, being examined medically, relating to other persons in our own affairs.

So I will have to agree with my sister and ascertain and assert that he is not really concerned with intent to break the law, but intent to be nude.

THE COURT: I am going to exclude the evidence. Bring in the jury, please. I recognize the authorities are split, but I don't think. . . . Does the Commonwealth have any further witnesses?

MR. MILLS: I don't think it would be necessary, your Honor. Could we request permission of the Court to excuse all the Commonwealth witnesses at this time; that is, if there will be no ——

THE COURT: Will the defendants require the presence of any of the witnesses for the Commonwealth? Do you need the witnesses for the Commonwealth here? If not, we will excuse them, if you do not.

MR. MILLS: May the Clerk announce that the Commonwealth's witnesses are excused, so there is no reason to stay?

THE COURT: The Commonwealth rests?

MR. MILLS: Yes, Commonwealth rests.

DEFENDANT PECK: I would like to make a motion.

THE COURT: Just a minute.

(*Jury now present*)

THE COURT: The defendants have advised me that they have a motion to make which must be heard in the absence of the jury. If you're not receiving much evidence, you're receiving a lot of exercise.

So we will excuse you now for a few moments until we finish with that.

(*The jury leaves the courtroom at 2:29 p.m.*)

DEFENDANT PECK: We move for directed verdict on the grounds that — shall we continue without the Clerk?

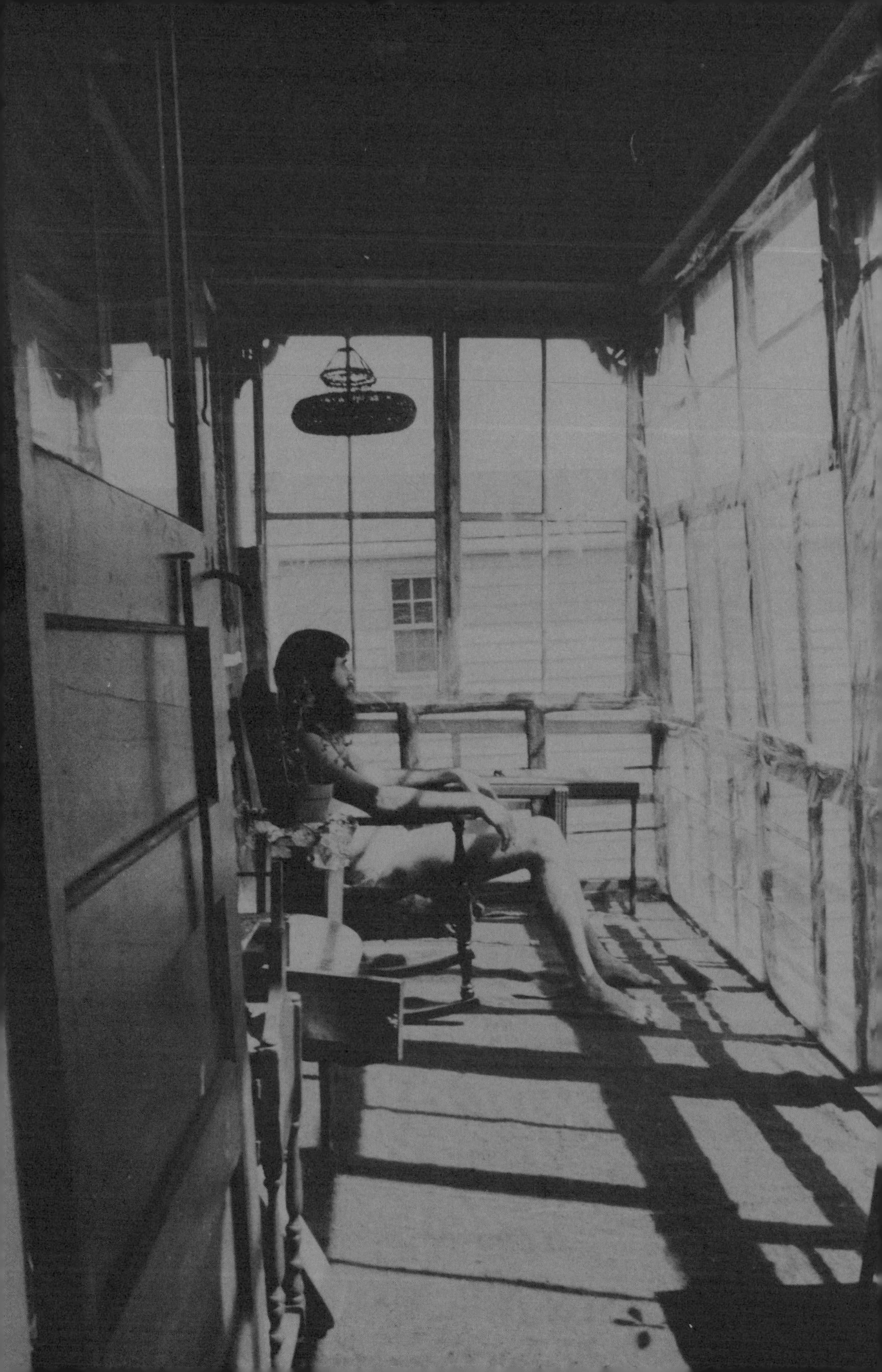

THE COURT: We have a reporter. I will hear you on the motion for directed verdict.

DEFENDANT PECK: I don't think that the government has proved beyond a reasonable doubt the case against us. I don't think they have introduced any material evidence about our intention to be open — that is, to be in a place where it is so public that we should have known people should see us, or that we knew that people of the general public would be watching.

I don't think there's any showing that our acts were lewd, or that we intended to be lewd. There is just evidence that we were nude on the porch. There is no evidence that there was any interaction — in fact, most of the witnesses admitted that they didn't think we could have even seen them — that we were looking for a crowd to have them view us in any way.

There is no evidence of anything sexual.

Most of the cases, if you can find a common strain in the cases, I think it is that there is some kind of sexual overture made between the defendant and another person who is unwilling — that is, the exposure of a private part is an incongruity in the context; that is, that this is a male, fully clad, except that he pulls out his penis and shocks somebody who comes alongside.

That isn't the case here. There is nothing that makes this stand out as stark and bold and offensive. It's something that happened in the context of our private home, porch — at least maybe it's open, but it's attached to our house. It's like porches that the other witnesses had.

There was testimony from the witnesses that they actually engaged in a certain amount of activity to get each other out there to look, that they called each other up — one witness even looked twice. They felt that they were willingly looking at it.

I don't think that this is the kind of case where somebody couldn't have avoided contact with something that was clearly offensive. I don't think the acts are things that are clearly offensive by community standards. That is a question of law, if you look around you; and regardless of whether you think it is an issue for the jury to determine, the community standards or yours, it is clear that there are lots of instances of nudity that are more sexual, more provocative, more titillating, more pandering and prurient in the sense that the Supreme Court of the United States has used when it has looked at obscenity cases.

This case lacks anything like that. It is an act that arose out of our lives, arose naturally and in the normal course of affairs. This actually was none of their business how we were living, how we chose to relate to each other in our home, or to the world around us.

THE COURT: Dr. Many, do you care to be heard?

DEFENDANT MANY: I would like to add to Carolyn's statement by noting that in the Roth case, which involved a lewd and obscenity statute pertaining to the United States mails, the trial judge was quoted as saying that the test of obscenity was not whether it would arouse sexual desires or sexually impure thoughts in those comprising a particular segment of the community — the young, the immature, or the highly prudish: The test in each case is the effect upon all those whom it is likely to reach.

Now, we have had no testimony regarding the effect upon those whom it is likely to reach. The prosecution has made no attempt to get at the nature of the effect on those whom, supposedly, the alleged criminal behavior did reach; and in view of this lack in the prosecution's attempt to get at and to prove and to demonstrate the burden of guilt, and in view of this lack to make this a crime by argument, and their lack of evidence in this case, I think that it's very clear that there is no evidence against us as far as lewdness, lasciviousness and grossness is concerned.

I would also mention that from the testimony it has become clear that there is no legitimate state interest operating here. There has been no testimony as to harm; there has been testimony that people acting as private citizens in concert with other private citizens utilized the arm of the law to enforce their own particular religious and moral standards.

I would maintain that as a part of the nature of this statute, which is vague and subject to interpretation at every point, that the state has not maintained its burden.

THE COURT: Mr. Mills?

MR. MILLS: Very briefly, your Honor, it is the Commonwealth's contention that our case has been sufficient, on the evidence; and we rely upon the case of Commonwealth vs. Cummings, in 273 Mass. at Page 229.

With respect to the defendant's claim that the activity took place on the porch and was therefore not open, I think that the defendants, as the defendant in the Cummings case, took their chances — although the Cummings case involved a public washroom, it was nonetheless closed, and the defendant was there alone with another consenting adult. The Court, however, held that they took their chances, and the chance of being discovered or viewed at any time. And then there was a sufficient proof of the intentional nature of their act, and the non-private or the openness burden was sustained by the Commonwealth.

THE COURT: What do you say about their point that there should be some sexual misconduct attendant to these exposure cases?

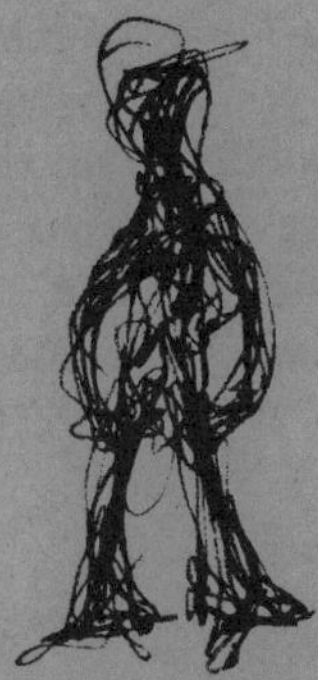

MR. MILLS: We rely upon the definitions of the offense as they are set forth in the decisions of the Supreme Judicial Court.

THE COURT: We all do that. However ——

MR. MILLS: Sorry I ducked, your Honor, but ——

THE COURT: It's not an easy question. Anything further to be said?

MR. MILLS: Yes. We have been precluded from directly showing activity on any other day, and under the case of Commonwealth vs. Parker, in 86 Mass. at Page 313, the Court is clear in saying that one act is certainly sufficient, a series of acts is not necessary, although it may be advisable to be proven under some circumstances.

And then, as to the intentional nature of the act, the Commonwealth relies upon the case of Commonwealth vs. Wardell, 128 Mass. at Page 52; and from there may we quote that —

> "The word 'open' qualifies the intention of the perpetrator of the act. It does not fairly imply that it must be public in the sense of being in a public place or in the presence of many people. It is enough if it is an intentional act of lewd exposure, offensive to one or more persons present. The fact of the act in a given case is most commonly proved, it is true, by evidence that it occurred in a public place or in the presence of many people, but it does not follow that the intentionally open and immodest character of the act may not be equally well proved by other evidence."

Thank you, your Honor.

THE COURT: The motion for directed verdict is denied. The exceptions of both defendants are noted to my action. Take a short recess, and we will be back with the jury.

(*Court recessed at 2:40 p.m.*)

(*Court reconvened at 2:43 p.m. Jury present.*)

THE COURT: You will find as you go through your monthly service that this happens frequently, especially on the criminal side of the court. There are many pieces of evidence to discuss, and obviously if the discussion were held in your presence, and then if finally it was held to be inadmissible, you already would have heard it.

Now, the Commonwealth has rested?

MR. MILLS: Yes, your Honor.

WITNESSES FOR THE DEFENSE

THE COURT: It is now in order for the defendants to go ahead. Does either of the defendants care to make an opening to the jury? — Miss Peck, you first, or Dr. Many.

DEFENDANT MANY: May I, first?

THE COURT: All right. You may proceed, Doctor.

DEFENDANT MANY: Our case will be an attempt to demonstrate and prove that we were not guilty of the crime as charged, the crime being open and gross lewdness and lascivious behavior. On each one of these counts we hope to demonstrate to your satisfaction that the crime as charged did not take place.

First, we suggest that as far as the open character of our behavior, the circumstances have been explained to a certain degree: It was the side sunporch of our home, and no intention was demonstrated to engage other persons in our behavior or to butt into their clothed way of life.

The openness of our acts is not open in the sense in which the statute describes behavior, and we hope to demonstrate that further in our own defense, that the acts were not gross that we engaged in.

There was no great, serious, flagrant, shameful, repulsive, sickening behavior that took place. The acts were not lewd; they were not such acts as are commonly referred to as frequenting a whorehouse, nor were they such acts that could be interpreted as a flagrant display of sexuality. The acts in no sense were lascivious, not was there any lascivious behavior that was described. If lust indeed was aroused from our behavior, that was not demonstrated.

In the second case, we hope to show that, although the prosecution has sought to impress upon us a different way of life, that our way of life and our faith and our commitments have to do with an open and honest relationship to the world around us, and that we have no shameful desire to conceal or to be dishonest in those relationships, and this includes our relationship to nature around us, to the water, to the earth, to the air and to the sun, and we hope to show that it's a very important condition of our life and our urban way of life, that we have the right

to expose ourselves to the sun and to use our window, even though our neighbors in this case might prefer that we erected a wall around our home.

We hope to show that there was no legitimate state interest, no legitimate Commonwealth interest in our particular behavior, but at most the question of diverse neighborhood values in contention, values which stem from the different religions and the different kinds of upbringing which, in turn have been subjected on each of the persons, both in the prosecution and in our defense, to in a different way interpret the central values in their lives.

We hope to show that, as the district attorney stated in this court on Wednesday, that this is a matter of taste and degree.

We hope to demonstrate that the right to be let alone was infringed by a small, vocal group, operating with the police force as one of their extensions, in making us accede to their way of life and in coercively prohibiting our way of life.

We hope to show that there is no readily identifiable community standard in this matter, but, rather, a hodge-podge of many standards.

Fourth, we hope to demonstrate that no substantial harm was or could be done to any witnesses of our behavior, and that the acts described resulted in, at most, mental upset, disquiet and displeasure, and that the cause of such displeasure and upset rested in the different ways in which each person has been taught to believe and to act, not from any substantial harm in the acts themselves.

We also hope to demonstrate that the acts described were not in substance different from those acts that are constitutionally protected and such as appear in art exhibitions, in theaters, in magazines and in

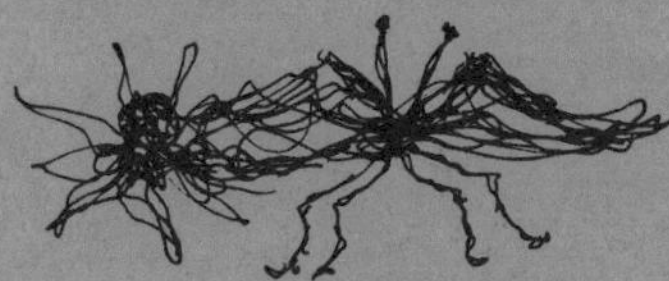

festivals, in movies and on beaches, and as are reported every day in the media, on TV and the radio and in the press.

We hope to show that the primary difference between us and these protected expressions lies mainly in the fact that for us there was no aspect of commercial exploitation — we were not attempting to sell anything. We are what we are, and our values flow out of our lives in relationship to each other, to each other person with whom we live.

Furthermore, we hope to show that there is no evidence that this society would crumble were you to find us not guilty.

Finally, we hope to demonstrate that, in the main, the prosecution has not sustained its burden of proof, but has sought to enforce a strict religious code, a strict religious ethic, upon our lives.

THE COURT: Miss Peck?

DEFENDANT PECK: The only comment I want to make is that this is a criminal statute of a serious nature. It's 200 years old, and it has serious implications for our lives.

I think all the Commonwealth has proved is that we were naked beings on a porch in our house. What nakedness means, we hope to demonstrate by our proof, to us; what it has meant to others who have viewed us is partly a product, as Seth has said, of how they were brought up, or their particular sensibilities, as in a negligence case, when somebody might have a particular vulnerability to damage, if you just touched them lightly and you break a bone, you're not held guilty of that. So, with us, if our neighbors have particular sensibilities, we should not be held guilty because things that we do offend them; that in this country there should be a wide range of tolerance for differences, for people who have different ways of looking at things, for people with different backgrounds and different beliefs, and that this is the nature of the conflict here — it's because we basically have very different ways of viewing the world, and that the ways in which we are different aren't ways in which the criminal law of the state should be concerned. They have to do with values, differences, basic beliefs, but they don't have to do with harm, damaging other people with acts of violence or infringement on other people's rights.

THE CLERK: May the witnesses be sworn?
THE COURT: Yes.
THE CLERK: First witness?
DEFENDANT MANY: I would like to call as our first witness, Ann Brown.

ANN A. BROWN
(*Sworn*)

DIRECT EXAMINATION BY THE DEFENDANT MANY

Q: Ann, would you state your age and your address and your full name?
A: I am 40. I live at 207 Lakeview Avenue. And what is the last ——
Q: Your name.
A: Ann Aubrey Brown.
Q: Would you fill in on the board just where you live? This is Lakeview Avenue, heading towards Fresh Pond Parkway.
Q: O.K. This is where you live? (*Pointing*)
A: Yes.

(*Witness draws*)

Q: 207 Lakeview Avenue.

(*Witness resumes the stand*)

Q: How long have you lived there?
A: Eight years.
Q: Eight years. Do you have any children?
A: Three.
Q: Three children. What are their ages?
A: Fifteen, thirteen and eight.
Q: Fifteen, thirteen and eight. Do you recall how you first became acquainted with us?
A: You invited everyone on the block to a party.
Q: Could you tell me, have your children or you ever been to our house?
A: Yes, all of us have.
Q: And have you observed us in our house?
A: Yes.
Q: Have you observed that any of us are naked?
A: Yes.
THE COURT: Now, wait a minute. Mr. District Attorney, do you have objection to that line of questioning?
MR. MILLS: To all of the questioning, your Honor.
THE COURT: Objection is sustained. What happened on another time or place or conduct except on March 9, 1970, we are not concerned with.
DEFENDANT MANY: I take exception, your Honor. In my opening state-

ment, I said that I would hope to show ——

THE COURT: Look, I also told you that Rule 71 does not call for argument on objections unless asked for. I rarely ask for argument. Exception is noted to my ruling.

Q: Does your son Colin come over regularly?

A: Yes.

MR. MILLS: Same objection.

THE COURT: Objection overruled.

I don't know where this will lead us, but we are not interested in any conduct other than on the day in question. If you were a lawyer, I would have to put this in a stronger way, but since you're not, I have to deal with it in this way.

Q: Has your son seen our sunporch, to the best of your knowledge?

A: I don't know. He has seen it from the outside.

Q: Do you know whether he has ever seen us sun-bathing in the nude?

MR. MILLS: I pray your Honor's judgment.

THE COURT: Sustained. Dr. Many, I order you to desist from this line of inquiry. I have given my ruling, and you are not entitled to pursue a line of questioning that I have ruled inadmissible.

DEFENDANT MANY: If you could clarify —— I feel like you've ruled out all my line of questioning ——

THE COURT: That may be.

DEFENDANT MANY: —— which we rest on the question of diversity of community standards.

If you do not permit me to make such a demonstration of diverse community standards, then what we are clearly faced with is the essential issue in this particular case, and that is the issue of whether one can express themselves openly and honestly, especially in a court of law.

THE COURT: Let me get, if I can, to your reasoning here. You seek to introduce evidence to show that other people other than those neighbors who complained had different views as to whether they approve or disapprove of nakedness in your house — is that about it?

DEFENDANT MANY: That's approximately correct.

THE COURT: Yes.

DEFENDANT MANY: That is one of the lines.

THE COURT: So that line of questioning I rule is out of order, and you may not introduce evidence in this regard. And I note your exception to my ruling, and that of your co-defendant.

Q: Are you familiar with the character and reputation of the defendants?

A: Yes.

Q: Would you allow your children to associate freely with those defendants?

MR. MILLS: I pray your Honor's judgment.

THE COURT: Sustained.

Q: What is the character and reputation of the defendants?

MR. MILLS: I pray your Honor's judgment.

THE COURT: I will hear the district attorney on this.

MR. MILLS: Is she speaking as of this year?

THE COURT: I think that ought to be shown.

MR. MILLS: Character of both of these defendants?

THE COURT: I think that to be so.

MR. MILLS: I don't think there is sufficient background shown for the basis of this witness's testimony.

DEFENDANT MANY: What does that mean?

THE COURT: He wants you to develop more information as to the witness's acquaintance with you and Miss Peck.

DEFENDANT MANY: That's what I've been trying to do, and he has objected to what — to that kind of a question.

Q: Have you come to visit us at ——

A: Yes.

Q: Has your son come to visit us?

A: Yes, he has baby-sat at your house.

Q: How frequently does he come?

A: Usually once a week.

Q: Once a week. For how long has it been going on?

A: Since school started in September.

Q: Since school started. And before that, in the summer, did he?

A: Not as a baby-sitter; as a visitor.

Q: As a visitor. And did he ever go to the beach with us?

A: Yes.

Q: Do you recall whether, in your conversations with us, you were aware of the fact that we were at times naked on the beach?

A: Yes.

Q: Did you consider that harmful?

MR. MILLS: I pray your Honor's judgment.

THE COURT: Objection sustained. If you want to ask her what your reputation was in the community, you may ask it.

DEFENDANT MANY: All right.

Q: Did you consider that fact, the fact of our nakedness, a sign of bad character?

MR. MILLS: I pray your Honor's judgment.

THE COURT: That is sustained. You may ask her, if you care to, about your general reputation in the community, but you may not ask this

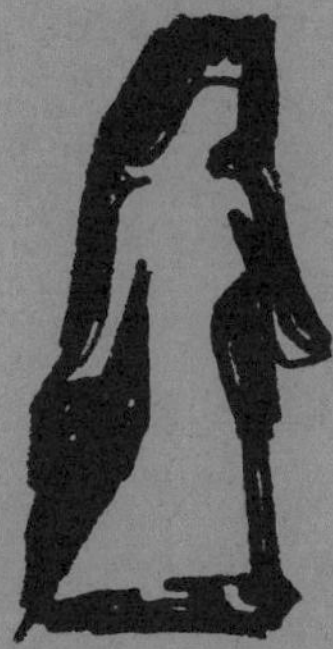

witness her subjective reactions to nakedness, Doctor. That is neither material or relevant to this case.

Q: In the community, do you know whether other people knew that we went around naked?

A: Yes.

MR. MILLS: I pray your Honor's judgment.

THE COURT: Sustained.

MISS PECK: May I be heard on that briefly?

THE COURT: No. No, you may not, Miss Peck.

Exceptions are noted.

This problem arises — I don't want you to hold them responsible — they are not lawyers. Beyond that, the subject of these particular statutes is a complex one, even for the Supreme Court of the United States, and lawyers. So the fact that they are not lawyers should not be held against them; and this case has to be run differently, you understand, than if lawyers were presenting the defense, because they are not familiar with our procedures.

Go ahead, Dr. Many.

Q: Is there such a thing in that community as a general reputation?

MR. MILLS: Objection, your Honor.

THE COURT: I'm going to sustain the objection.

Q: Can you describe anything about the nature of our general reputation?

A: It's diverse. Different people think different things about it.

DEFENDANT MANY: I rest, as far as questions.

THE COURT: Miss Peck, any questions?

DEFENDANT PECK: No questions.

THE COURT: Mr. Mills?

MR. MILLS: Nothing. Thank you.

THE COURT: You may step down.

DEFENDANT PECK: I would like to call Madeleine Drucker.

THE COURT: Are we going to have an order of presenting witnesses? Are you going to change back and forth?

DEFENDANT PECK: We will change back and forth.

THE COURT: Perfectly all right.

MADELEINE G. DRUCKER
(*Sworn*)

DIRECT EXAMINATION BY THE DEFENDANT PECK

Q: Would you tell us your name?

A: Madeleine Gilbert Drucker.

Q: Where do you live?

A: 173 Lakeview Avenue.

Q: Would you go to the board and try to indicate approximately where your house is?

A: Yes. (*Witness goes to the board and writes*)

(*The witness resumes the stand*)

Q: How long have you lived at 173?

A: Two and a half years.

Q: Do you have any children?

A: Yes, I have two.

Q: Could you give their names and ages?

A: Yes. Two boys — Benjamin, almost two; Elliott, almost three — almost four, excuse me.

Q: Could you tell us the occasion when you first heard about us?

A: Yes.

MR. MILLS: Objection, your Honor.

THE COURT: Just identify it by date, please, only.

THE WITNESS: I can approximate it. It was some time in the summer.

Q: Have you and your children ever been to our house?

MR. MILLS: I pray your Honor's judgment.

THE COURT: Well, this can be answered yes or no. She may answer.

A: Yes.

Q: And have you seen us in our normal attire?

A: Yes.

Q: Did you have any qualms about bringing the children to the house?

MR. MILLS: Objection.

THE COURT: Sustained.

DEFENDANT MANY: Exception.

Q: And are you familiar with or do we have a general reputation in the neighborhood?

A: You do, but it differs according to whom you speak to.

Q: And do you know what the reason for the difference is?

MR. MILLS: I pray your Honor's judgment.

THE COURT: Sustained.

Q: Does there seem to be one basic thing that makes a difference as to whether people believe we have good character or bad character?

MR. MILLS: I pray your Honor's judgment.

THE COURT: Sustained.

DEFENDANT PECK: Yes, I will take exception.

I don't have any further questions.

THE COURT: Any more questions?

DEFENDANT MANY: No.

THE COURT: Wait a minute. Just a moment.

Do you have any questions?

MR. MILLS: No, nothing. Thank you.

THE COURT: You may stand down.

DEFENDANT PECK: I'd like to call Jonathan Peck to the stand.

JONATHAN C. PECK
(*Sworn*)

DIRECT EXAMINATION BY THE DEFENDANT PECK

Q: Could you state your name?
A: Jonathan Charles Peck.
Q: And your address?
A: 1842 Commonwealth Avenue, Brighton, Mass.
Q: And your age?
A: Twenty-two.
Q: Do you have a relationship, blood relationship, to any of the defendants?
A: Yes. I'm your brother.
Q: And how long have you known Seth?
A: I would say about eight or nine years.
Q: And could you state what your religion is?
A: Well, not in terms that would affiliate me with any religion, specifically, any body of religion. I think that it would be related to ——
Q: Did you go to the Rock Festival at Powder Ridge?
A: Yes.
MR. MILLS: I pray your Honor's judgment.

THE COURT: Sustained.

DEFENDANT PECK: I take exception to that.

Q: I would like to show you a photograph. Is that a fair representation of two figures, nude figures?

A: Sure.

DEFENDANT PECK: I make this as an offer of proof.

THE COURT: Do you represent them to be photographs of the defendant or somebody else?

Q: Do you recognize the figures in that photograph?

A: Yes, I do. They're you and Seth.

MR. MILLS: Objected to.

THE COURT: Is this taken on the premises at 197 Lakeview Street, Cambridge?

DEFENDANT PECK: No, sir, it wasn't.

Q: Could you identify the journal that it appears in?

A: *Newsweek Magazine.*

Q: O.K. Do you know where that photograph was taken?

A: Yes.

Q: Where was it taken?

A: Powder Ridge.

Q: And was that in any way exceptional behavior at Powder Ridge?

MR. MILLS: Objection.

THE COURT: Sustained.

DEFENDANT PECK: I take exception to that.

THE COURT: Do you offer that?

DEFENDANT PECK: Yes, I offer this.

THE COURT: Is there an objection?

MR. MILLS: It's objected to, your Honor.

THE COURT: The objection is sustained. The evidence is excluded. It may be marked as an exhibit for identification as far as your offer of proof — identification only.

(*Page 20 of NEWSWEEK dated August 10, 1970, marked B for Identification*)

Q: Jonathan, have you visited at 197 Lakeview Avenue?

A: Yes.

Q: And have you visited there frequently?

A: Yes.

Q: Since the time we moved there, on January 1?

A: Well, I visited there infrequently from January 1 to August of this year, and frequently since.

Q: Do you recall efforts on our part to talk with our neighbors ——

MR. MILLS: Objection, your Honor.

THE COURT: Sustained.

Q: Did you attend an open house that we held for the neighborhood?

MR. MILLS: Objection, your Honor.

THE COURT: I will allow this. I don't know where it will lead us, at the moment. You may answer that yes or no.

A: Yes, I did.

Q: And did a lot of neighbors come?

MR. MILLS: Objection, your Honor.

THE COURT: Overruled. You may answer.

A: Yes.

Q: And did we discuss at that time with them some of the differences that we felt we had?

MR. MILLS: I pray your Honor's judgment.

THE COURT: Sustained.

DEFENDANT PECK: I take exception to that.

Do you recall whether ——

May I withdraw that?

In the community in which you're a member, do we have a reputation?

MR. MILLS: Objection, your Honor.

THE COURT: Let her finish her question. Have you finished your question, Miss Peck?

DEFENDANT PECK: Well, I don't know whether you heard the finish of it.

THE COURT: I heard it, but I don't know whether you were finished with it.

DEFENDANT PECK: Do you know whether ——

Oh, yes, I've finished with it.

THE COURT: Objection sustained.

Q: In the community in which you are a part, do you know whether the reputation we have is good?

MR. MILLS: Objection, your Honor.

THE COURT: Sustained.

DEFENDANT PECK: Could you tell me what the ground for this is, and maybe I can rephrase the question?

THE COURT: I'm sorry, but I do not do that. That's why I urged you defendants to have a lawyer.

DEFENDANT PECK: O.K. I don't have any further questions.

EXAMINATION BY DEFENDANT MANY

Q: Can you describe the conditions at 197 Lakeview?

A: Yes.

Q: Would you?

MR. MILLS: I pray your Honor's judgment. "Conditions."

THE COURT: Well, make your question more precise, will you, please?

DEFENDANT MANY: I would like him to describe the setting of the sunporch and the room and place it in the context of the house and the neighborhood.

A: The sunporch would be on the side, the rear side on the second floor, on top of the house. It slopes so that you may get out on it.

Q: And the roof?

A: Well, the roof is above, and it faces towards the back of the house, and it's blocked partially by a slanted piece going down, blocking to the side.

Q: And you have observed us on the roof or sunporch naked, is that correct?

A: Yes.

Q: Did that behavior — could you describe any behavior that showed us communicating with the neighbors in any other way in that respect?

THE COURT: Just a moment. Are you talking now about the incident of March 9, 1970?

DEFENDANT MANY: I'm not talking about that particular incident, your Honor.

MR. MILLS: Object on that ground.

THE COURT: Objection sustained.

Q: Have you ever seen any forms of sexual impurity while you were at our house?

MR. MILLS: I pray your Honor's judgment.

THE COURT: Sustained. Whether he has or has not is absolutely immaterial to this case.

DEFENDANT MANY: I take exception. I guess that's all.

THE COURT: Any questions from the Commonwealth?

MR. MILLS: Nothing, your Honor. Thank you.

THE COURT: Miss Peck, any questions?

DEFENDANT PECK: Do I — I already asked him.

THE COURT: All right. You may step down.

DEFENDANT PECK: Like to call Lou Benhan to the stand.

LEWIS G. BENHAN
(*Sworn*)

DIRECT EXAMINATION BY DEFENDANT PECK

Q: Would you state your name and address?

A: Lewis Glenn Benhan, 1713 Mass. Avenue.

Q: State your occupation.

A: I'm a student and I have a part-time job as a model.
Q: And what kind of modeling do you do?
A: I do modeling for classes in portrait-drawing and figure-drawing.
THE COURT: What school do you attend as a student?
THE WITNESS: I attend Harvard Law School.
THE COURT: What year are you in?
THE WITNESS: First year.
Q: And while you're modeling, are you nude?
A: I am ——
MR. MILLS: I pray your Honor's judgment.
THE COURT: Do you represent this is on March 9, 1970?
DEFENDANT PECK: No, sir.
THE COURT: That is excluded.
DEFENDANT PECK: I take exception.
Q: Have you ever visited our home?
A: Yes, I have.
Q: Were you comfortable there?
A: Yes.
MR. MILLS: Pray your Honor's judgment.
THE COURT: Sustained.
DEFENDANT PECK: I take exception.
No further questions.

EXAMINATION BY THE DEFENDANT MANY

Q: Do you have knowledge as to our general reputation in the Cambridge community?
A: Yes, I have some knowledge.
Q: Would you relate that knowledge?
THE COURT: Is that objected to, Mr. District Attorney?
MR. MILLS: If he has knowledge of their reputation in the community, not objected to, your Honor.
THE COURT: Go ahead.
A: The community, by your appearances within it, are biased against you, and are quite impressed that you are a doctor, and so for that reason you are respected.
THE COURT: Repeat your answer.
THE WITNESS: Because of the dress, the appearance — your appearance, your reputation is probably low in the esteem of most of the people in the community, and they are quite amazed to know that you are a doctor and can still be free.
Q: Could you explain what you mean by "still be free"?

COMMENCE
DISROBING ....
Check guns
shoes + boots
pipes + cigs
HERE...

A: I mean that you don't subscribe to the general standards of the community.

Q: Which community is that?

A: The community that people usually associate with doctors.

MR. MILLS: Your Honor, the Commonwealth asks that that entire answer be stricken, as I thought that the witness was going to testify as to the defendant's reputation in the community.

DEFENDANT MANY: Which community are you talking about?

THE COURT: Just a moment, please. The objection is overruled at this time. The Commonwealth had a chance to object earlier and did not, so the answer stands. You may go ahead, Doctor.

Q: Could you define more specifically the community in which I am held in respect?

MR. MILLS: Pray your Honor's judgment.

THE COURT: Overruled. He may answer.

A: In the community in which you are held in respect are people who have somewhat liberal ideas about the freedom of people to do as they feel so long as it doesn't interfere with other people in the state, people who have been exposed to different ideas; whereas the people who would be opposed to you are somewhat limited in their experience and the ideas that they have been exposed to.

Q: Could you comment on Carolyn's general reputation in the community?

A: Carolyn is a respected person in the community. She has a respected job and is well thought of. I am acquainted with the people she works with. She is thought of very well at her place of employment and is a respected lawyer.

Q: And what is that place of employment?

A: She works at the Center for Law & Education.

Q: Whose center?

A: It's — as I understand, it's under the guidance or under the — it's part of Harvard, and funded by the federal government.

DEFENDANT MANY: That's all. Thank you.

THE COURT: Any further questions of this witness?

MR. MILLS: Nothing.

THE COURT: You may stand down.

DEFENDANT MANY: Ralph Fanelli, please.

RALPH FANELLI
(*Sworn*)

DIRECT EXAMINATION BY DEFENDANT MANY

Q: What is your religion now?

MR. MILLS: I pray your Honor's judgment.

THE COURT: I missed the question.

DEFENDANT MANY: I asked what his religion was, your Honor. The question has been allowed.

THE COURT: Why don't we find out who he is?

THE WITNESS: My name is Ralph Fanelli.

Q: And what is your religion?

MR. MILLS: Objection.

THE COURT: Let's find out where he lives.

THE WITNESS: 5 Upland Road, Cambridge.

THE COURT: Now put the question.

Q: What is your religion?

MR. MILLS: Objection.

THE COURT: Sustained.

DEFENDANT MANY: Exception.

Q: How old are you, Ralph?
A: I'm 38.
Q: Do you have a present occupation or an occupation or an avocation?
A: I've been a teacher for 11 years, and right now I'm a playwright.
Q: Could you tell us what kind of plays you write?
MR. MILLS: Objection, your Honor.
THE COURT: At this stage I will allow the question. You may answer.
A: I write plays that protest the war in Viet Nam. I write plays that protest minority rights, and write ——
THE COURT: You protest in favor of the minority, I assume?
THE WITNESS: Yes. And I write plays that deal with openness, plays that deal with people getting together; and I attempt in my plays to raise people's consciousness to the consciousness of Level III, as expressed in *The Greening of America*. And I deal with people on that level.
Q: Who is *The Greening of America* by? Do you know the author?
MR. MILLS: I pray your Honor's judgment.
THE COURT: Sustained.
DEFENDANT MANY: Exception.
Did you recently write and produce a play?
A: I did.
MR. MILLS: Objection, your Honor.
THE COURT: Well, sustained.
DEFENDANT MANY: Exception.
THE COURT: Suppose we come back to this particular case that we're trying.
DEFENDANT MANY: With due respect, I believe we have been on this particular case.
Q: Have you come at all to our residence and home?
A: Yes, I have.
Q: Could you tell us what you observed there?
MR. MILLS: Objection, your Honor.
THE COURT: Well, are you referring to a particular part of the premises, Doctor?
DEFENDANT MANY: I'm referring to ——
THE COURT: Will you please specify exactly where?
DEFENDANT MANY: I can't do that. It has to do with what he is. I cannot specify what I want him to talk about. That's not part of the ——
THE COURT: That is your function, as your own lawyer. Well, ask the question and we'll see how it turns out.
Q: Have you visited our residence?
A: Yes.
Q: What did you observe there?

MR. MILLS: Objection. Same objection.

THE COURT: Observe with respect to what? That's the problem.

Q: Observe with respect to us, our persons, our character, our behavior, our hopes, our ideals, our thoughts or feelings.

MR. MILLS: Same objection, your Honor.

THE COURT: Objection sustained.

DEFENDANT MANY: Exception.

Q: Do you have any knowledge as to . . .

(*Defendants Many and Peck confer*)

Q: Are you familiar with our character in the community and reputation?

MR. MILLS: Pray your Honor's judgment.

THE COURT: Well, are you referring only to reputation, Doctor?

DEFENDANT MANY: Character and reputation.

THE COURT: Do you object to this?

MR. MILLS: I think that he should set a foundation first, your Honor.

THE COURT: Well, the answer to this is either going to be yes or no, and then he can set a foundation. Yes or no, please?

A: Yes.

Q: All right. Could you first describe the community that you will be talking about — you know, like who are — what is our community?

MR. MILLS: Pray your Honor's judgment.

THE COURT: If he is going to define the community in which he says he knows the reputation, he may do that.

MR. MILLS: May I be heard, your Honor?

THE COURT: No. You will have a chance to object later, however. Go ahead, Mr. Witness.

THE WITNESS: I know the people that the defendants know. I know of good things that these people have said about them.

THE COURT: Now, you're talking about a community. Business community? What community?

THE WITNESS: They are people that live in Cambridge, and their community is a community that is larger than a specific street number or specific location. They are united in a spiritual way and in an open way, and they are not tied to a street number.

THE COURT: Are you or are you not talking about a geographical community?

THE WITNESS: Not in that specific sense.

THE COURT: Put your next question, Doctor, please.

Q: Confine yourself for the moment to the geographical community of Cambridge. Now, can you attest to my general reputation in that geographical community?

MR. MILLS: I pray your Honor's judgment. No foundation.

THE COURT: Do you want to go further — the opportunity to learn of reputation, whatever it might be?

Q: Have you attended the concerts on Sunday in the Cambridge Common?

A: Yes, I have.

Q: And would you say that a large number of persons gather there to enjoy and partake of those concerts?

A: Yes.

MR. MILLS: Pray your Honor's judgment.

THE COURT: Let me phrase the question for you.

Would you tell me the manner in which you became aware of the reputation of the defendant that you are about to testify to?

THE WITNESS: Through some of my friends and through direct observation and by listening to them.

THE COURT: Where would this be?

THE WITNESS: On the Cambridge Common, and in their home.

THE COURT: Go ahead.

Q: Can you tell me what were the observations you made as to my character and reputation in that community?

MR. MILLS: Objection, your Honor. Observations are heard and not made, and furthermore, I think he has restricted himself out of the realm of testimony to which he is competent by failing to show a foundation for his opinion.

THE COURT: The community to which you have referred — Cambridge Common — during the concerts, is that what you're talking about?

DEFENDANT MANY: No. I suggested that that is where we first met. This is where we gathered and learned from each other.

THE COURT: I think I will save a lot of time if I let him answer your question. Go ahead.

DEFENDANT MANY: Thank you.

THE COURT: Put your question.

Q: Could you testify as to the observations you made about my character and the nature of my reputation from our meetings on the Cambridge Common?

A: Dr. Many was explaining his views about life to a large group of people

that were standing there, listening very attentively. It was my — I observed people listening who seemed to be in ageement with many of the things that hc was saying. I supported many of the things that he said about the war, about oppression in our society. I felt that there was a camaraderie between us and among the other members of the commune.

MR. MILLS: The Commonwealth asks that the answer be stricken as not ——

THE COURT: It may be stricken, and the jury will disregard it, as having absolutely nothing to do with this case — absolutely nothing to do with it.

DEFENDANT MANY: Exception.

THE COURT: Certainly. Certainly. This witness, if you want him to, can testify, if he knows, about your reputation.

DEFENDANT MANY: That is what he's doing, your Honor.

THE COURT: Well, then proceed to something else.

Q: Within the smallest geographical community specified by the boundaries of 197 Lakeview, can you testify as to the reputation and character with which I am held in that community, also known as the Cambridge Commune?

MR. MILLS: Objection, your Honor.

Q: A community of some seven persons?

MR. MILLS: Same objection.

THE COURT: Sustained.

DEFENDANT MANY: Exception.

That's all I have.

THE COURT: Any questions, Miss Peck?

DEFENDANT PECK: No.

THE COURT: Mr. Mills?

MR. MILLS: Nothing, thank you, your Honor.

THE COURT: You may stand down.

DEFENDANT MANY: I'd like to call Michael Finn.

MICHAEL E. FINN
(*Sworn*)

DIRECT EXAMINATION BY DEFENDANT MANY

Q: Please state your full name.

A: Michael Edward Finn.

Q: And your age?

A: Twenty-six.

Q: And would you state your religion?
MR. MILLS: Objection, your Honor.
THE COURT: Sustained.
DEFENDANT PECK: Exception.
DEFENDANT MANY: Exception.
Q: Would you state your ground of being?
MR. MILLS: I think I object.
DEFENDANT MANY: I'll be glad to explain what that means.
THE COURT: Thank you, no. Sustained. Would you give your address?
THE WITNESS: 197 Lakeview Avenue.
Q: Are you related in any way to any of the defendants?
A: Yes.
Q: In what way?
A: We're all people.
Q: Now, how long have you lived in this area?
A: All my life.
Q: All your life. Where were you born?
A: Cambridge.
Q: And where did you go to school?
MR. MILLS: Objection, your Honor.
THE COURT: I don't know where it's going to lead, but I will let him continue on, to save time. You may answer.
A: Well, it started off in, I guess, informal education at home, and then formal education in Newton, where I went through high school, and then college at Tufts. And then I started learning for myself.
Q: Are you familiar with the fact that Cambridge was historically a part of Newton?
MR. MILLS: I pray your Honor's judgment.
THE COURT: Sustained.
Q: Michael, in the last two years, what has been your preoccupation and your vocation?
MR. MILLS: Pray your Honor's judgment.
THE COURT: He may have it as a preliminary question. What is your occupation?
DEFENDANT MANY: I asked his preoccupation, first. That comes before occupation.
THE COURT: It may come before occupation in your question, but not in mine. Let's have your occupation first, please.
DEFENDANT MANY: Exception.
THE WITNESS: He asked during the last two years. Should I give all of them?
THE COURT: I didn't hear what you said.

THE WITNESS: He asked for the last two years. Should I give all of them in the last two years?

THE COURT: That's up to Dr. Many.

THE WITNESS: He asked for them.

Q: Yes.

A: So I'll give them. Well, let's see. I guess two years ago I was an electro-optical engineer, and then I became a retail jeweler. Then I became a — let's see — yes, a chef. You know, a chef. And I guess now I'm preoccupied with living with Carolyn and Seth and the other people in the commune, and in learning how to get along peacefully.

MR. MILLS: May the last portion of the answer be stricken, your Honor, as non-responsive?

THE COURT: Well, it's not, but I'll let it stand. Go ahead, Dr. Many, please.

Q: Are you familiar with the set-up, with the sunporch and the houses surrounding?

A: Yes.

Q: I'm going to ask you to take a look at several of the pictures. Now, this picture, which is Exhibit 2 — both from your experience as an electro-optical engineer — and do I understand that you also at one time engaged in photography for remuneration?

A: Yes. It wasn't ——

Q: Now, from your experience, from this picture, can you describe any of the characteristics that make it unusual and take it out of the context of an ordinary picture?

MR. MILLS: Objection. No foundation has been shown.

THE COURT: First of all, what is the exhibit number to which you are referring, Doctor?

DEFENDANT MANY: Exhibit 2.

THE COURT: All right. Are you trying to get him to testify in his capacity as an expert in photography methods?

DEFENDANT MANY: More like a person very familiar with the nature of photography, and one who has taught photography and one who has been involved in optical problems. I think there's something very specific about this picture that I'm ——

THE COURT: Do you object to his expertise in this field?

MR. MILLS: Yes. There has been no expertise shown or ruled upon.

THE COURT: All right. We have to find out whether or not he is an expert in the field, before he can testify. Will you inquire in that direction, Doctor?

DEFENDANT MANY: O.K.

Q: Who did you work for as an optical engineer?

A: I worked for Itek Corporation.

Q: Is it the case, then, that you had security clearance?
A: Yes.
THE COURT: Let me shorten this up. Do you have any experience as a photographer in taking pictures?
THE WITNESS: Yes.
THE COURT: Over how long a period of time?
THE WITNESS: Well ——
THE COURT: Just roughly.
THE WITNESS: Well, different types of taking pictures.
THE COURT: Just generally.
THE WITNESS: Well, I would say five years.
THE COURT: All right. Have you become familiar with different types of cameras?
THE WITNESS: Yes.
THE COURT: Exposure of film, development of film?
THE WITNESS: Yes.
Q: Is it true you maintain a dark-room in our house in order to carry ——
A: Yes, I do.
THE COURT: Put your question, Dr. Many.
Q: Does this picture represent an enlargement or telephoto lens?
A: Well, there's two grounds on which I can describe what separates this from a realistic representation. One is the quality of the picture clearly indicates that if this was truly a sunny day ——
THE COURT: Just a moment. We have competition with an automobile outside. (*Pause*)
THE WITNESS: Well, because of the low contrast throughout the picture, it's clearly either — it's clearly a blow-up, an enlargement, of a smaller, you know, real-life representation.

And the other thing is — well, I guess this has to do with just common sense: just knowing that somebody 60 feet away, as was testified by one of the private photographers ——
THE COURT: We can't have you give testimony on that. You say that's a blow-up?
THE WITNESS: Yes. You mean I can't know that fact?
THE COURT: Dr. Many, I will have to ask you to stand, like the others.
DEFENDANT MANY: Excuse me.

Here are two exhibits, Exhibit 1 and Exhibit 3, both of which purport to have been taken from the same distance, one from 197, looking to 187, and one from 187, looking to 197, and they have both been admitted into evidence, one over objections — that is, Exhibit No. 1 was admitted over objection, which was not sustained, and Exhibit No. 3 was admitted into evidence as an adequate and fair representation.

Now, can you explain what the difference between these two pictures is?

THE COURT: From what point of view?

DEFENDANT MANY: From the point of view of a photographer who is familiar with the relative exposure, expansiveness of the picture, quality of the lens, perhaps telephoto lens was used.

THE COURT: He may do that.

A: Well, if Exhibit No. 3 is a fair representation, then Exhibit No. 1 would have to be a blow-up of around four times Exhibit No. 3, because the scale is about four or five times different. So, clearly, this would be a blow-up — this being Exhibit 1, would be a blow-up of Exhibit 3.

Q: Thank you. Now, you lived in that house at 197 at the time of the alleged crime, is that not correct?

A: (*Witness nods*). Right. Yes.

Q: At that time of the alleged crime, were you at home?

MR. MILLS: I pray your Honor's judgment.

THE COURT: He may answer that, if he was home — on the morning of March 9, 1970, are you talking about?

DEFENDANT MANY: Yes.

A: No, I was not.

Q: Where were you at that time?

MR. MILLS: Pray your Honor's judgment.

THE COURT: He may have his question. Objection overruled.

A: I think I was working in my capacity as a jeweler.

Q: As a jeweler. And what time did you leave that morning?
A: Roughly 8 in the morning.
MR. MILLS: Objection, your Honor.
THE COURT: Objection overruled. He may answer.
Q: Was that a sunny day, to the best of your knowledge?
A: Yes.
Q: Now, you are familiar with the porch on 197 Lakeview, is that correct?
A: Yes.
Q: Now, could you testify to the best of your knowledge that this picture, No. 3, represents the picture taken from the corner of our porch? — and I call your attention to the fact that there is a chimney sticking up in the middle of the porch of that house adjacent to us, which obscures most of the bathroom window. And I call attention to the fact that the bedroom at 187 is also partially obscured by that roof.
A: Well ——
MR. MILLS: I pray your Honor's judgment.
THE COURT: I'm not sure what the question is.

What is your precise question, Doctor? I know you called his attention to something, but what is your question?
DEFENDANT MANY: My question is whether this represents an adequate representation, an adequate and fair representation of the view from our porch to the Gentiles' house at 187.
THE COURT: May answer that.
A: Yes, very close. In fact, this was taken with — well, a 55-millimeter lens gives an accurate real-life representation, and this is very close to it.
Q: Now, you are familiar with our porch. Again, this is a picture, Exhibit 1, which is entered into evidence by the prosecution.

Can you describe what you see coming through the middle of the picture from the left-hand side, and obscuring well over one-half of our porch and part of the rest of the porch from the waist up?
MR. MILLS: Objection, your Honor.
THE COURT: Overruled.
Q: Are you familiar with that? What is that obstruction?
THE COURT: Do you want him to describe your porch? Is that a portion of your porch?
THE WITNESS: Picture.
DEFENDANT MANY: He is familiar with the view of our house.
THE COURT: I understand that. Do you want him to describe that portion of your porch which is depicted in that photograph?
DEFENDANT MANY: Yes.
THE COURT: He may do that.

THE WITNESS: All right. In this photograph — I guess Exhibit 1 — a good 75 percent of the porch, from roughly — well, the porch would cut me off around here, and it cuts off roughly 75 percent of the porch, from this angle. (*Indicating*)

By the way, I could — there is another thing here which suggests this was taken by a telephoto lens, which is the effect of the — this house is essentially foreground, and with the telephoto lens, the background and foreground tend to come together, and this shows this kind of an effect where this house and this porch look as though they're pretty close together. The depth is, you know — sense of perspective has been changed by the telephoto lens.

Q: Could you again tell us what exhibit that is you just referred to?

A: Exhibit 1.

DEFENDANT MANY: I would like to show these two pictures to the jury.

THE COURT: You may do so.

DEFENDANT MANY: In order for them to compare the different representations of the distances involved.

THE COURT: Dr. Many, I suggest you hand them to the Foreman and let him pass them around the jury.

DEFENDANT MANY: That finishes my questions, your Honor.

EXAMINATION BY DEFENDANT PECK

Q: How long have you known Seth and me?

A: I think about three years.

Q: And during those three years, have you observed us in normal activities and human interactions?

A: Yes.

Q: Could you describe some of those interactions that might have given you a basis for a judgment on our character?

MR. MILLS: Objection, your Honor.

THE COURT: Sustained.

Q: Are you familiar with the reputation and character that we may have in the community?

A: Yes.

Q: And how did you become familiar with that reputation and character — that reputation of our character?

A: By living with you and knowing you for three years — that's how I became familiar.

Q: And is our reputation a good one or a bad one?

MR. MILLS: I pray your Honor's judgment.

THE COURT: Let me find out first, what community are you talking about?

THE WITNESS: Well, I lived with and experienced things with them in a wide variety of communities, so I feel competent and capable of describing them in a wide variety of communities. Do you want to know what they are?

THE COURT: I want to know what the geographical or other community is that you're talking about, when you say "reputation in the community." It's not your assessment of character and reputation, but what the general reputation in the community may be. What is the basis for your forming an opinion as to that?

THE WITNESS: What is the basis for it?

Q: During the two years you have known us, have we lived in Cambridge or known you in Cambridge, primarily?

THE WITNESS: Well, I think I have two questions ——

THE COURT: To save time, let me shorten it: Is the community you're talking about the City of Cambridge?

THE WITNESS: Well, it includes the City of Cambridge. That's certainly one of the communities I've experienced them in.

THE COURT: One might be sufficient.

Go ahead, Miss Peck.

THE WITNESS: I don't think so.

THE COURT: Go ahead. We have enough problems with this case without your interposing your feelings about the case.

THE WITNESS: You're right.

THE COURT: I accept your apology, and we will proceed, Miss Peck.

Q: What is this reputation of our character in this community?

A: Can I think about it for a minute?

MR. MILLS: I suppose we're speaking about Cambridge, Massachusetts. I assume we're talking about Cambridge, Massachusetts.

THE COURT: You may.

THE WITNESS: I knew the question was going to come, and looked up the words in the dictionary, and I'm not sure that the definition is going to allow me to — if I follow the definition, I might ——

THE COURT: Just give your answer to the question.

THE WITNESS: I'm trying to say that I have some difficulty in answering.

THE COURT: Why don't you do the best you can?

THE WITNESS: Okay.

Well, the reputation in the general community, by a process of reckoning — that is the only process I have, right? Okay.

So — well, most — of course, all of my observations are only from their acts, that's all. I'm going to describe their acts.

THE COURT: Why don't you come directly to the reputation?

THE WITNESS: Yes. The acts ——

THE COURT: Not the acts. The reputation.

THE WITNESS: Well, the thing is that — well, I think we're talking about the same thing, because these ——

DEFENDANT PECK: He's concerned with what is in other people's minds.

THE COURT: I'm not the slightest little bit concerned. I just want an answer to your question, one way or the other.

THE WITNESS: All right. I have, by process of reckoning, I have ascertained that Seth and Carolyn, in regards to the Cambridge community, have acted with sensitivity ——

MR. MILLS: Pray your Honor's judgment.

THE COURT: Let him finish.

Have you finished your answer?

THE WITNESS: No.

THE COURT: Finish your answer.

THE WITNESS: Okay.

— a great sensitivity for and awareness of the needs of other people, but not necessarily taking on their needs as their own needs, but living their lives independently and yet as a part of the community in which they are living in. So they try not to superimpose their values on other people, and they try not to have, you know, without some meaning in their lives, to accept the values blindly which other people want them to have.

So, essentially, I have experienced and watched some of the integrity and honesty with regards to other people's views and their own.

THE COURT: What you say adds up to the reputation is one of honesty and integrity?

THE WITNESS: No, there's more to it.

THE COURT: Go ahead. Go ahead.

THE WITNESS: Okay. Well, there's another thing, which is, it's sort of empathy — you know, I mean, the caring for others, thoughts for other people. Taking the time and the energy to be with everybody that they're with and, you know, and have respect for what they are and treat them as people, you know, as best they can, you know.

Oh, and another characteristic is real commitment to non-violent living. Now, that's been demonstrated ——

THE COURT: I think we'll stop right there.

Go ahead ——

MR. MILLS: Before you stop, may we request that the entire answer be stricken as not responsive and not an answer?

THE WITNESS: I haven't finished it, though.

THE COURT: As far as you've gone, it's stricken, and the jury will disregard it.

DEFENDANT MANY: Exception.

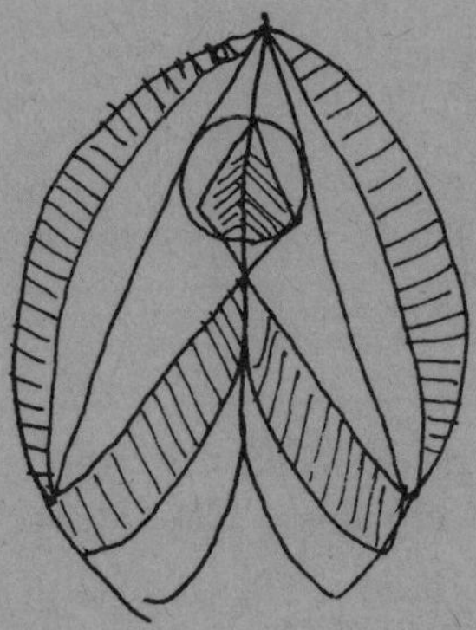

DEFENDANT PECK: Exception.
DEFENDANT MANY: Exceptional exception.
THE WITNESS: Should I continue, or ——
THE COURT: Just wait for the next question.
THE WITNESS: I haven't finished the first question.
THE COURT: You have, sir.
THE WITNESS: I have?
THE COURT: Miss Peck, would you ask another question, please?

What we are dealing with, Mr. Foreman, ladies and gentlemen, are questions of law as to evidence. Certain things are admitted into evidence and certain things are not, and you have to accept my rulings in this case as to what they are.

Q: Harkening back to March 9 of last year, I would like you to describe the condition of the porch, what kinds of coverings there were, if any, to your knowledge, at that time, the time of the alleged offense.

A: Well, the coverings — does that include the characteristics of the coverings?

Q: Yes, if you would.

A: The coverings consisted of complete enclosure, with glass panes, not — in other words, it wasn't just sheer glass; there were smaller panes with dividers all throughout, and over that was put a layer of transparent plastic, and this plastic had the characteristic of reflecting light in a very strange way — well, it sort of ripples, like this, you know. It wasn't just a straight piece of plastic.

And visioned from the — well, this is a characteristic that I have observed — visioned from the outside, from the street or from any other place in which, you know — well, actually, where it's situated, the sun reflects right off it, in other words, increasing its characteristic of reflections.

THE COURT: What time of day?
THE WITNESS: All times of day, because the sun passes right across it.
Q: Have you observed the sun on it at any time from about 10 to noon?
A: Yes.
Q: Is the characteristic more marked then, or less marked, than maybe 4 o'clock in the afternoon?
A: Well, it's hard to make that kind of comparison, but there's definitely more light around it, and the possibility of that happening is fair enough.

And also, from those hours of 10 to 12, the sun is more, like, behind 187 and shining directly on that porch. So it's more likely that someone viewing it from those directions would be more subject to the glare and reflections.
Q: Also, again calling your attention to the condition of the porch, is there a railing at about waist level on the porch that you remember?
A: Well, different height for different people. I think it's a little below my waist.
Q: And are there slats in the railing?
A: Yes.
Q: Do you know about how many inches apart the wood slats are from your waist level down?
A: About — the spacing between them is about an inch and a half to two inches.
Q: So that they are like slats on a bannister going up the staircase — would you liken it to that?
A: Yes. Could I see a picture to remind me, if there is one?
Q: Okay.
A: Just, you know ——

(*Photograph shown to the witness*)

THE WITNESS: Kind of spaced apart here. Can't tell. The light is obscuring what's behind — I can't see it.
THE COURT: We are going to stop at this time, and I am going to remain for a moment to talk to the defendants and counsel. I will excuse the jury now.

You may stand down, Mr. Witness.

THE COURT: The same admonition that I will give you in every case, I will give you in this case: Don't discuss the case with anybody, including the members of your family, and do not permit anybody else to discuss the case with you.

You are not to make up your minds about the case or any part of it until we have officially and formally given it to you for a verdict. You are excused now. See you back again tomorrow morning at 10 o'clock.

I shall remain. The jury may leave.

(*The jury leaves*)

THE COURT: I will take a recess in order for the jury to have a chance to get their coats.

(*Court recessed at 4:00 p.m.*)

(*Court reconvened at 4:05 p.m. Jury not present*)

THE COURT: My purpose in having you here is, for the record, to state that as part of the defense in this case, there is no necessity for the defendants or either of them to take the stand in their own defense unless they care to do so. If either one does not take the stand in his or her own defense, no comments may and no inference may be drawn against the person who does not take the stand.

You may know it anyway, but I want the record to show that you have been instructed.

And the second thing I want to say is, how many more witnesses does the defense have?

DEFENDANT MANY: Five to seven.

THE COURT: Stand in recess until tomorrow morning at 10 o'clock.

(*Court recessed at 4:07 p.m.*)

Tuesday, January 12, 1971

(The court convened at 10:59 a.m.)

THE COURT: Sorry we're late. I had a land-damage case which I carried over from my sitting in Plymouth in November or December, with some motions, and I have a capital case, a murder case, beginning on the 18th, which is the primary reason I am here in this county, and I had some preliminary motions to take up with counsel. We are now ready to resume the case on trial.

DEFENDANT PECK: Mr. Finn was on the stand. I would like to resume questioning.

MICHAEL FINN
(Resumed)

EXAMINATION BY THE DEFENDANT PECK, CONTINUED

Q: To get back to where we were, I believe you testified that you lived in Newton all your life, and that you have known us for the past three years?

A: *(Witness nods)*

Q: Is that correct?

A: Yes.

Q: Newton or Cambridge, for all your life?

A: Yes.

Q: And that you're familiar with our reputation in the community?

A: Yes.

Q: How did you become familiar with this reputation of ours in this community?

A: By living with you and knowing you and watching you do things in the community with the community.

Q: Could you tell us some of those things?

A: Yes. I recall an event that occurred not too long ago between some of the, I think teen-age kids in the neighborhood, which resulted in a knock on the door one night, and one of the kids ——

THE COURT: I think we can have this information, Miss Peck, in a general way. We don't have to relive the daily lives of these people.

THE WITNESS: I was trying to relate the act.

THE COURT: In a general way, if you will.

THE WITNESS: Okay. What had happened was a fight had occurred, someone was knocked out, and required Seth. Well, Seth had to go down to see what had happened — I mean, in his capacity as a doctor, actually;

and he went there and tried to relate to the people involved, showing concern for them and trying to turn their concern towards themselves and towards the condition and state of the boy who had been knocked out. He tried to make them aware of the medical as well as common-sense realities connected with this child's state.

Q: Had there been other occasions ——

MR. MILLS: Pray your Honor's judgment.

THE COURT: Well, I'll let that stand. Why don't we come to the central question, Miss Peck? Are you going to ask him as to the reputation that you and the other defendant have?

DEFENDANT PECK: Yes.

THE COURT: Do that.

Q: State what reputation Seth and I have in that community.

A: Well, the word "respect" would be applicable — respect for your concern and the fact that you have taken the time and the energy to care about people in their states, in their — you know, as they come around.

So, respect. And some other aspects of reputation would be — well, just state of alertness and living-ness. So many people are — well, just the fact that they're alive and caring is just well-known throughout the community by various people, particularly in the neighborhood who have had a chance to in some ways confront us and find out that, you know, we're not oblivious to what's going on, but care about it and want to be a part of it — you know, consider us, consider themselves a part of what's going on.

So it's this caring and being a part of the community which the community is aware of.

Q: Are you familiar with our reputation that we have for being truthful and honest people?

A: Well, yes. With regards to community — let me think a minute.

Q: That question is just asking you if you're familiar with our reputation. Can you describe the reputation we have with regard to truthfulness and veracity?

A: I have experienced it in — you know, by observing, have seen you in the process of being honest and truthful.

MR. MILLS: Pray your Honor's judgment and ask that the answer be stricken.

Q: Just in regard to our reputation ——

THE COURT: Just a moment. Not your own feelings, Mr. Witness. Just what the reputation is in the community.

THE WITNESS: Well, it wasn't a feeling. It was an observation. I observed truth and honesty ——

THE COURT: Is that what you're saying is the reputation in the community?

THE WITNESS: That's one of the characteristics, yes.
THE COURT: Is that what you say is their reputation in the community?
THE WITNESS: Well, it's one of the representative characteristics of their reputation.
THE COURT: Let the answer stand.
Q: Did you study art when you were in college?
A: Yes.
Q: Were you an art minor?
A: Yes.
Q: And did you do some traveling in Europe and look at museums and art in them?
A: Yes.
Q: I would like to show you a photograph. Do you recognize that photograph, what it is a representation of?
A: Yes.
Q: Is it a fair representation of a work by Botticelli entitled "The Birth of Venus"?
A: Yes.
Q: And would you describe what you see?
MR. MILLS: Pray your Honor's judgment.
THE COURT: Sustained.
DEFENDANT PECK: I take exception to this, and make an offer of this as proof. No further questions of the witness.
THE COURT: Dr. Many, do you have any questions?
DEFENDANT MANY: No questions.
THE COURT: Anything from the Commonwealth?
MR. MILLS: Yes.

CROSS-EXAMINATION BY MR. MILLS

Q: Mr. Finn, would you describe to the Court and jury what you mean by "the community." You have just answered questions propounded by Miss Peck dealing with the community. What do you mean by "the community"?
A: Well, what do I mean?
Q: What do you mean by "community" in your answers to Miss Peck's questions?
A: I sort of accepted what the Judge required me to accept — that the community in question was the Cambridge community.
Q: Cambridge community. Do you mean all the citizens, some of the citizens, one of the citizens?
A: Well, I think when the Judge said "Cambridge community," he meant ——

THE COURT: The question, sir, is what you meant.

THE WITNESS: Well, you see, he asked me what I mean by "community." I include not just the Cambridge community ——

Q: In your answers, sir, when you referred to "community," what did you mean in your answers when you referred to "community"?

A: Oh, all right. "Community" to me is just the people living together in an area, or ——

Q: What size area?

A: Not necessarily an area.

Q: Neighborhood, house, one room?

A: Well, there are different levels which you can look at. If you can look at the community of the self, the community of the home ——

Q: Which were you referring to in your answers, sir?

A: All of them.

Q: All of them?

A: (*Witness nods*)

Q: And you spoke about the defendant's reputation for certain things. How many people in Cambridge, Massachusetts, have indicated to you their opinion of the character of either Dr. Many, Miss Peck, or both of them?

A: How many people?

Q: Yes.

A: Have offered their opinion — verbal opinion, or do you include — you know, people can express how they feel by a non-verbal communication of a frown or a smile.

Q: What did you mean by "opinion" when you gave your answers to Miss Peck's questions before this jury in court?

A: When I said "opinion," I was referring to verbal as well as non-verbal indications.

Q: Have you ever spoken with Mrs. Murphy of the Lakeview Avenue neighborhood?

A: Not verbally. We've had non-verbal communication.

Q: Have you ever spoken with Mrs. Pentz?

A: Non-verbal communication.

Q: When you gave your opinion as to the character of Dr. Many and Miss Peck, did you include within your answer any of the non-verbal communication that you had had with Mrs. Murphy or Mrs. Pentz?

A: I included verbal as well as non-verbal communication with everybody that I have had verbal and non-verbal communication with in the Cambridge community.

Q: And did you also have non-verbal communication with Mrs. Ridley?

THE COURT: I don't think we want to travel down that road.

A: I don't remember.

Q: How many persons in Cambridge have you discussed the reputation of Dr. Many and Miss Peck with?

A: Discussed verbally and non-verbally?

Q: Let's start with verbally.

THE COURT: Let's completely divest ourselves from non-verbal communication.

DEFENDANT PECK: Take exception to that.

Q: How many persons have you discussed reputation concerning Dr. Many and Miss Peck with in the Cambridge community?

A: Could you tell me what you mean by "reputation," or do you want me ——

Q: You spoke of reputation ——

THE COURT: Mr. District Attorney, will this interrogation be lengthy?

MR. MILLS: No, your Honor.

THE COURT: Let's hope it is not. Ask a few simple questions.

MR. MILLS: I have no simple questions, your Honor, and no further questions.

THE COURT: You may stand down, Mr. Witness.

(*Witness excused*)

DEFENDANT MANY: I would like to now call Marsha Hanlon.

MARSHA HANLON

(*Sworn*)

DIRECT EXAMINATION BY DEFENDANT MANY

Q: Marsha, can you tell us your full name and your age and your address?

A: Marsha Hanlon. I am age 28. I live at 177 Lakeview Avenue.

Q: Could you fill in on the board where you live?

(*Witness goes to the board, writes, and returns to the stand*)

Q: So you live right on the corner of Malcolm Road, which is opposite

the home of Priscilla Pentz, is that correct?
A: Yes, that is.
Q: And opposite the residence and home of Sandra Ridley?
A: Correct.
Q: Marsha, how long have you lived in that area?
A: I lived in that house since 1966. Four years.
Q: Before that time, did you live in the Cambridge area?
A: I was born in Cambridge and I subsequently have lived elsewhere, returned to Cambridge, yes.
Q: Now, as a resident of the Lakeview area, have you had an opportunity to speak with residents, other residents of the Lakeview area, and to speak to them, more specifically, about the defendants, and more specifically about the character and reputation of the defendants?
A: Yes, I have.
Q: Could you tell us what your observations were with respect to other persons' understanding of that reputation and character?
MR. MILLS: Pray your Honor's judgment.
THE COURT: Well, it's inartistically expressed, but what you want to know, Doctor, is what she knows of your reputation in the area?
DEFENDANT MANY: Yes.
THE COURT: You may tell us that.
THE WITNESS: The people with whom I have spoken on Lakeview Avenue feel a great admiration for the defendants for living the kind of life that they believe in, and I would say that these are people who would not share the life-style but who admire the defendants for living it.
THE COURT: Excuse me. Are you going to introduce evidence as to the reputation as to truth and veracity and the like? We're not going into life-styles here. That's a different question entirely.
DEFENDANT PECK: Your Honor, I object. It has to do with the character and the reputation that dwells in their minds, and there is no way to develop that unless to develop some kind of context for those words.
THE COURT: Whatever that means, I'm not sure, but the objection is overruled.
DEFENDANT PECK: I take exception.
THE COURT: Yes. You may tell us the reputation for truth and veracity in the neighborhood. Tell us that.
Q: Is it widely held that we are truthful persons?
A: I don't think I have ever spoken to anybody about whether you are truthful persons, although — I would only have to guess.
MR. MILLS: I pray your Honor's judgment.
THE COURT: Well, she said, in effect, she doesn't know.
Q: Do you know that people believe that we live honestly and openly?

MR. MILLS: Pray your Honor's judgment.

THE COURT: Again, we are talking or should be talking about reputation known to this witness. Phrase your questions in that way, please.

Q: Do we have a reputation for living openly and honestly in commitment to our ideals?

A: Definitely, yes.

DEFENDANT MANY: Thank you.

That's all.

THE COURT: Do you have any questions, Miss Peck?

DEFENDANT PECK: No, I haven't.

MR. MILLS: Nothing, your Honor. Thank you.

THE COURT: You may stand down.

DEFENDANT MANY: I call Suzanne McMillen.

THE COURT: How many more witnesses do the defendants intend to call? *(To Suzanne McMillen)* Just a moment, Madam.

DEFENDANT PECK: Four, altogether.

THE CLERK: Do you solemnly swear that the testimony you shall give the Court and jury in the issues now depending between the Commonwealth and these defendants shall be the truth, the whole truth and nothing but the truth, so help you God?

SUZANNE MCMILLEN: Yes. However, I need no God to help me.

THE COURT: In other words — I'm not criticizing you, I'm just asking you — you do not care to take the oath?

SUZANNE MCMILLEN: I intend to tell the truth, but I need no God to help me.

THE COURT: I just want you to answer my question. Do I understand you to say that you do not feel conscientiously that you can take the standard oath that the witnesses take?

SUZANNE MCMILLEN: Yes, I can.

THE COURT: You can.

SUZANNE MCMILLEN: I said, "I do."

THE COURT: Do you want to take the oath as read to you, or do you not?

SUZANNE MCMILLEN: Yes, I will.

THE COURT: Give her the oath again.

(To Suzanne McMillen) If you want to take the oath, fine.

Give her the oath.

THE CLERK: You will raise your right hand.

Do you solemnly swear that the testimony you shall give the Court and jury in the issues now pending between the Commonwealth and these defendants shall be the truth, the whole truth, and nothing but the truth, so help you God?

SUZANNE MCMILLEN: I do.

SUZANNE C. McMILLEN
(*Sworn*)

DIRECT EXAMINATION BY DEFENDANT MANY

Q: Suzanne, how old are you?

A: Seventeen.

Q: What is your name?

A: Suzanne Christian McMillen.

THE COURT: And your address?

THE WITNESS: 197 Lakeview.

THE COURT: You may proceed, Doctor.

Q: Suzanne, could you tell me how you became familiar with the reputation of the defendants?

A: I baby-sit for the kids in the neighborhood.

Q: And could you tell me what is the nature of that reputation, based on the people that you know in the neighborhood?

A: Well, I know a lot of people in the neighborhood, and people that I baby-sit the kids for — well, just the fact that they allow their kids to be over — accept Seth as a very high person. Plus, I know people across the street — and this is hearsay — but they think, they call — they're called Communists because they live in a commune.

THE COURT: I can't hear you.

THE WITNESS: The people across the street, who are opposing us, think we are Communists because we live in a commune and we share ——

THE COURT: I will strike that answer. You must address yourself to the questions asked of you — okay? — reputation as to character, honesty, truth, and veracity. You will please limit yourself to that.

Dr. Many, do you want to put another question?

Q: Would you speak, Suzanne, as to the honesty, veracity, and the reputation, the reputation for honesty, veracity, truthfulness? What is that reputation among the persons that you know?

MR. MILLS: Objection, your Honor. No basis has been shown.

THE COURT: I will let her answer. She says she knows the neighborhood. Go ahead. Have you heard this reputation discussed among the neighbors?

THE WITNESS: Yes.

THE COURT: You may answer the question.

A: It's held in high esteem by the people that I baby-sit for — the reputation.

MR. MILLS: I ask that that question — that the "answer" be stricken, your Honor, as non-responsive.

THE COURT: Well, the motion is denied. I will let it stand.

(*Witness starts to leave stand*)

MR. MILLS: May the Commonwealth inquire, your Honor?

THE COURT: Take the stand again, please.

CROSS-EXAMINATION BY MR. MILLS

Q: Miss McMillen, will you please tell the jurors and the Court what persons you baby-sit for on Lakeview Avenue?

A: Ann Brown and Michael and Lucy Bates.

Q: Now, how many families do those people represent?

A: Two.

Q: Are their houses located or indicated on the board?

A: Yes, they are.

Q: How many houses would you say there are in the neighborhood? — and you are the one who mentioned "neighborhood."

A: How many houses are in the neighborhood?
Q: Yes.
A: Well, on our block, what I can see on the board is ——
Q: Not from what you see on the board, but from what you know.
A: I never counted the houses on the street.
THE COURT: I can't hear your answer.
THE WITNESS: I don't count houses on the streets.
Q: You have baby-sat for two families on the street?
A: Yes.
Q: Do you know how many families live on the street?
A: No.
Q: Have you ever spoken with Mrs. Murphy?
A: Non-verbally, yes.
Q: We are talking about verbal communication.
A: No. I have no need to talk to her.
Q: You testified as to the reputation that the defendants have in the community. Have you ever spoken with Mrs. Pentz?
A: No.
Q: Have you ever spoken with Mrs. Ridley?
A: No. I don't even remember ——
Q: Have you ever spoken with anybody besides the two families that you baby-sit for?

A: Yes.
Q: Who?
A: People across the street, but I don't know their names.
Q: You don't know their names?
A: No.
Q: Just that family across the street and the two families that you baby-sit for?
A: The two families across the street, I do not baby-sit for them.
MR. MILLS: No further questions.
DEFENDANT MANY: Redirect.

REDIRECT-EXAMINATION BY DEFENDANT MANY

Q: Suzanne, does one of the families that you sit for, Michael and Lucy Bate, is it not the case that they live here (*pointing*), right next to us, between us and the Gentile residence?
A: True.
Q: Do you know what that number is?
A: 195.
Q: 195 Lakeview. Is it not the case, Suzanne, that you also know and have close relationships and have talked with the people who live right behind us?
MR. MILLS: I pray your Honor's judgment.
Q: Right here? (*Indicating*)
THE COURT: Wait a minute.
A: Yes.
Q: Right here, right behind us, in full observation of the porch, the house, the kitchen, etc.?
A: Yes.
THE COURT: Just ——
DEFENDANT MANY: He brought these questions up, your Honor.
THE COURT: Just a minute. The objection is overruled. She may answer. She has answered. What is your next question?
DEFENDANT MANY: Could you clarify that answer? Would you read that answer, because I didn't hear it.
THE COURT: Do you want to repeat your answer? Say your answer again. We didn't hear you.
THE WITNESS: Yes, I have talked to those people.
Q: These people right here (*pointing*), behind our house?
A: Yes.
Q: Do you know who they are?
A: They are two nurses. One of their names is Carolyn, and I don't know who the other is.

Q: And can you tell what is their opinion about our reputation?

MR. MILLS: I pray your Honor's judgment.

Q: —— from your speaking with them?

A: They told ——

THE COURT: Just a moment.

Objection?

MR. MILLS: Yes, your Honor.

THE COURT: Sustained.

DEFENDANT PECK: Exception.

DEFENDANT MANY: Exception.

Q: Have you talked to the persons who — in fact, there is a road right here that goes right through here? (*Indicating*)

MR. MILLS: I pray your Honor's judgment.

Q: Now, there is a, there is a private road ——

THE COURT: Excuse me. Just a minute. Excuse me. I will permit him to develop the people she has talked to about the defendants, but I will not permit him to tell us or have the witness tell us what they said. You may go ahead.

Q: Now, there are two houses right here on this private road. One is here and one is here. (*Pointing*) Now, have you talked to members of both those houses, including ——

A: Yes.

Q: —— including a lot of children that belong to those houses?

A: Yes, I have.

Q: And what is the reputation of the defendants, from those persons?

MR. MILLS: I pray your Honor's judgment.

THE COURT: Sustained.

DEFENDANT MANY: Okay.

Now, taking into consideration all these persons whom you have talked to, who surround us, who represent our particular and circumscribed geographical community, can you form a general opinion as to the reputation of the defendants?

MR. MILLS: I pray your Honor's judgment.

THE COURT: Sustained.

DEFENDANT MANY: I take exception.

A: The ——

THE COURT: Just a minute. There is no question before you. Doctor, any further questions?

(*Defendant Many shakes head*)

MR. MILLS: Nothing from the Commonwealth.

THE COURT: You may stand down.

DEFENDANT PECK: I'd like to call Jonathan Brush to the stand.

JONATHAN BRUSH: I don't want to take any oath.

THE COURT: You have an alternative method.

Give him the affirmation, Mr. Ewell.

THE CLERK: Do you solemnly swear that you will truly affirm such questions as shall be put to you by counsel, and the answers thereto?

JONATHAN BRUSH: I'll tell the truth. I will not affirm or swear.

THE COURT: Will you tell us the reason for that belief?

JONATHAN BRUSH: I tell the truth to the best of my knowledge at all times. I will continue to do so in this court.

THE COURT: I will accept that as an affirmation. You may take the stand.

JONATHAN BRUSH
(*Affirmed*)

DIRECT EXAMINATION BY DEFENDANT PECK

Q: John, will you state your name?

A: Jonathan Brush.

Q: And where do you live?

A: 197 Lakeview Avenue, Cambridge.

Q: Could you give us some idea of your background?

A: I was born in Ames, Iowa. I moved around until I was five. I lived with my parents in New Jersey until I was 18, going to school. I went to college in Indiana, at Earlham College. I went to the graduate school at Michigan.

In 1968 I worked for the Department of Corrections in New York City. In 1969 I worked for a camp in Vermont, a farm building in which nudity was approved. The end of 1969 I moved to Cambridge and began living in a commune, Cambridge Commune. And in 1970 I began working for the City of Cambridge in the Cambridge City Hospital as a ——

Q: What do you do?

A: I am a therapist. I work in the psychiatric ward.

Q: Have you been on the sunporch that is the scene of the alleged crime in this case? And would you describe it, briefly?

A: It's a sunporch on the southeast corner of the residence at 197 Lakeview Avenue. I would say it's about 20 feet long by about eight feet or six feet wide.

At the time of March 9, it was enclosed by glass panes, and I think we are in the process of putting up plastic insulation — clear plastic.

Q: Okay. And have you been on that porch when it's been sunny in the winter?

A: I have.
Q: And what is the temperature there on a sunny ——
MR. MILLS: I pray your Honor's judgment.
THE COURT: Objection overruled. He may answer.
A: I can't give you an exact estimate of the temperature, but ——
THE COURT: You're talking about March of 1970?
THE WITNESS: March.
DEFENDANT PECK: Yes.
THE COURT: Go ahead.
Q: Could you say warm, cool, on winter days?
A: Quite hot. When the sun is hot, the sun shines right in there, and there's very little air circulation, and it becomes quite warm on the sunporch.
Q: And do you have any idea of the purpose of that porch?
MR. MILLS: I pray your Honor's judgment.
THE COURT: Well, in that form, the objection is sustained. You may ask what it's used for.
Q: Could you tell us what the porch was being used for?
A: It was being used for enjoyment of the sun by the occupants of 197 Lakeview Avenue.
MR. MILLS: May the answer be stricken, your Honor?
THE COURT: No, it may stand. The motion is denied.
Q: Do you recall whether there were any plants that we put out there?
A: We put some plants out there, yes.
Q: And you have been on that porch, or you were on it during March of 1970 or February some time?
A: Yes. The end of February is when we closed it in, and then I was out there from then through part of March.
Q: On those occasions when you were on the porch, did you ever observe people from the house at 187 or the house at the corner — I can't recall the numbers any more ——
MR. MILLS: I pray your Honor's judgment.
Q: Did you make any observations of other people's presence when you were on the porch?
MR. MILLS: Object to that, your Honor.
THE COURT: Just a moment. He may answer.
A: No.

Q: You never saw people looking from their windows?

A: No, I never saw anyone, to my knowledge, take any notice of any activities that were going on in that sunporch.

Q: Now, have you had occasion to observe — have you had occasion to become familiar with the reputation that Seth and I have in the Cambridge — in the community of Cambridge?

A: This is going to be the same problem that we had before.

I believe I am familiar with the reputation in the circles in which I move, which include people on the Cambridge Common in the summer, people who work in the Cambridge Hospital along with myself, and people whom I meet in the course of my daily life.

MR. MILLS: Your Honor ——

Q: Are some of those people who work in the hospital, are they also neighbors?

MR. MILLS: I pray your Honor's judgment on the basis of the witness's last response — that his testimony will be — I think it's irrelevant.

THE COURT: Miss Peck hasn't completed the interrogation as to foundation. Go ahead.

Q: Are some of the people that you come in contact with in your employment also people who reside in our neighborhood?

A: Yes, they are.

Q: And do you have contacts with people in the Cambridge community as you travel and as you work?

A: Yes.

Q: Based on those observations and those feelings, can you make a statement — do you have — did you form an opinion as to what that character and reputation that we have is, in that community?

MR. MILLS: I pray your Honor's judgment.

THE COURT: Do you want to rephrase that question? You're asking whether he knows your reputation for character and honesty and truthfulness in the Cambridge area, is that it?

DEFENDANT PECK: Yes.

THE COURT: Do you have such a knowledge?

THE WITNESS: Yes.

Q: Would you tell us what your knowledge is?

A: You have a reputation ——

MR. MILLS: Objection.

THE COURT: Objection overruled. You may answer.

A: You have a reputation for, if nothing else, truthfulness, honesty, integrity. Many people don't believe in the same values that we believe in, but they certainly believe that you and Seth are honest, truthful, and individuals of high integrity.

DEFENDANT PECK: Thank you.
THE COURT: Any questions, Dr. Many?
DEFENDANT MANY: I have no questions.
THE COURT: Mr. Mills?
MR. MILLS: Nothing, your Honor. Thank you.
THE COURT: You may stand down.

(*Witness excused*)

DEFENDANT MANY: I would like to call my star witness, Carolyn Peck.
THE COURT: Without going into it again, Miss Peck ——
DEFENDANT PECK: I'm sorry?
THE COURT: Without going into it again, you are aware of what I said to you after the jury left yesterday?
DEFENDANT PECK: Yes.
THE COURT: You still wish to take the stand?
DEFENDANT PECK: Yes, I do.
THE COURT: All right.

CAROLYN R. PECK
(*Sworn*)

DIRECT EXAMINATION BY DEFENDANT MANY

Q: Would you state your name?
A: Carolyn Ramsey Peck.
Q: And your age?
A: I am 28.

Q: And your place of residence?
A: I live at 197 Lakeview Avenue in Cambridge.
Q: Would you state your religion?
MR. MILLS: I pray your Honor's judgment.
THE COURT: Sustained.
THE WITNESS: Are we taking an exception?
DEFENDANT MANY: I take exception.
Q: Would you state the things that occupy you centrally in your life?
MR. MILLS: I pray your Honor's judgment.
THE COURT: Sustained.
Q: Could you tell me what your — what you spend most of your time doing?
MR. MILLS: I pray your Honor's judgment.
THE COURT: Sustained. Excuse me. If you are asking about her occupation, that's different.
DEFENDANT MANY: That is correct. I was trying to get at that through this line of questioning.
THE COURT: Go ahead.
Q: Can you tell me what you make money at?
A: I make money by being an attorney at the Center for Law & Education, which is a poverty-program agency.
MR. MILLS: I pray your Honor's judgment.
THE COURT: She may tell us what she does. She has a right to give us general information about herself. You may answer.
A: (*Continued*) Which is concerned with reforming the educational system to try to make it more humanistic, and, in particular, as it affects minority groups like black people and poor people and rural people — people who are often left out.
Q: Now, Carolyn, you have heard the testimony of Detective Ellis, that he came to your home approximately a week before the date of the alleged crime.

Now, I am going to — in that testimony he made several allegations. One of those allegations had to do with interaction that was between you and he.

Now, I want to ask you, what did he say when he came to the door?
A: He identified himself as a police officer, said he was Detective Ellis, and he showed me his credentials. He said that he had a complaint. And I asked him what the nature of the complaint was, and he wouldn't tell me. I asked him who had made the complaint, and he refused to tell me that, also.

He said he wanted to come inside the house, and I said that I wouldn't let him inside the house unless he told me what he wanted to

talk to us about. His manner was fairly aggressive and blunt.

He wouldn't give me any other information, and I didn't feel that he was a friendly person that I wanted to have in my house.

Q: Was he dressed in uniform?

A: He had a trench coat on and a sports jacket and a tie.

Q: And do you remember the day that he came to the house?

A: Yes. It was a Sunday. It was March 1.

Q: At any time did he indicate that the nature of his investigation had to do with possible future or past acts of nakedness?

A: No, he didn't. And I had no reason to think that — I knew we had moved in there on January 1; I knew that we looked different from most of our neighbors, having long hair; and I knew that a lot of neighbors viewed us with suspicion, mostly from their non-verbal communications — staring at us when we walked down the street, and not speaking and not saying "Good morning." So I had no reason to know what the specific nature of the complaint was.

MR. MILLS: Request that the answer be stricken, your Honor.

THE COURT: The motion is denied.

Q: Now, there has been some conflict in the testimony with respect to what this house includes.

Now, at 197 Lakeview Avenue, we have a home here. Do you know how many rooms it is?

A: It's a 14-room house. It's a very large house.

Q: Right. Now, would you say that the porch is a part of the house?

A: Yes, it is. It's directly over ——

MR. MILLS: I pray your Honor's judgment.

THE COURT: She may answer.

THE WITNESS: It's directly over where we eat our breakfast and meals, primarily, which is a part of the kitchen, and this is just an extension of that, so it doesn't jut out from the main body of the house. It's part of the main body of the house. Its door leads directly into my room.

Q: Now, at the time of the alleged crime, was there a window or a series of windows that surrounded that porch?

A: Yes. There were main — two windows here with panes, with wood strips between the panes, and then about four windows facing directly south, two windows east and four windows south.

Q: In other words, at the time of the alleged crime, the porch in question constituted a room that was totally enclosed by glass; in effect, a hot room?

A: Except that it was covered by ——

MR. MILLS: I pray your Honor's judgment.

THE COURT: No, the question is leading, but we will save time by having an answer. Is your answer yes or no, Miss Peck?

THE WITNESS: Yes. And the roof is solid, too.

Q: The roof is solid. Now, can you tell me what the intention of the defendants was in the construction of that room?

MR. MILLS: I pray your Honor's judgment.

THE COURT: Sustained.

Q: Can you tell me on the day in question what kind of activity we were engaged in in that room?

A: Yes. We had enclosed it in glass, and we had — we were enclosing it in plastic to make it warm so that the plants could grow there, and so we could go out there and get the winter sun. It was a very pleasant place to read.

We were at that point putting up plastic to block out the worst currents of air between the panes, so it was like putting on storm windows. And on that day, the temperature when we were working there gets up to about 90 degrees, because we brought a thermometer out to see how we were doing, and you could get the sun in the winter-time, which is a rarity.

Q: Are you familiar with the word "solarium"?

A: Yes.

Q: Would you consider that that room was, in fact, a solarium?

A: Yes.

MR. MILLS: I pray your Honor's judgment.

THE COURT: Well, the answer may stand.

Q: What was the specific act that you saw me engaged in while I was up there? Did you see any specific behavior that you could describe?

A: Yes. You had a staple gun and you were stapling the plastic to the

wood panels and wood strips, and at times I would assist you, help you hold the plastic.

Q: Did you notice any behavior on my part that had to do with persons outside of our home?

A: No.

Q: Was there any behavior that you engaged in that had to do with persons outside our home?

A: No. I had no awareness of being watched by persons or that persons were present. I didn't see anybody. I didn't hear any voices call out. I didn't even — I didn't look around. I didn't see any people watching in the back yards or in the other windows. I thought Seth and I were alone.

Q: Now, it has been suggested that this room had a special purpose — that is, to get the sun and to allow us to partake of the winter sun. Now, with respect to that special purpose, can you describe the extent of your clothing or lack of it on that day?

A: When I had first come out, I recall having on a turtleneck that had blue and white, red stripes, and a pair of panties. Because it was hot, and it became uncomfortable to work in that garb, I first took off my turtleneck, and later, several minutes — not long, since it was so hot — took off my panties, too, so that I would be comfortable working.

Q: Were there times when you came into that room, that solarium, naked, from the house itself?

A: Yes, yes.

Q: Could you explain how it is that you came into that room naked, rather than disrobing there in the solarium?

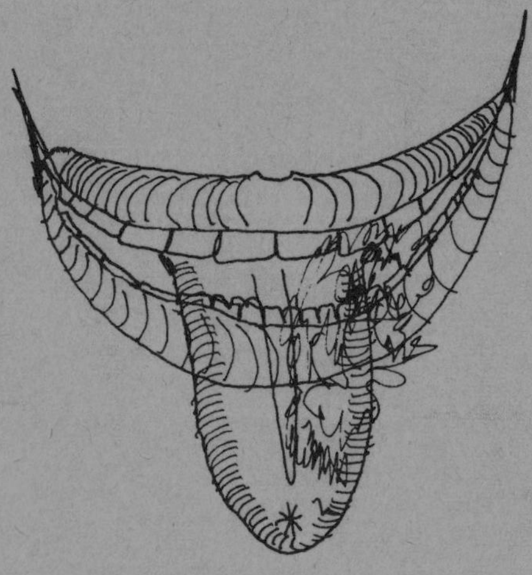

A: Well, my bedroom adjoins the sunporch, and so it was easy to just throw my clothes off in my room. I suppose I also felt that the act of disrobing is somehow more provocative, and I think it was just my feeling, not even knowing that I was watched, but that you don't disrobe in front of other persons, that you do it, really, in the most private way that you can. I suppose I had some sense that that might be sexual — to disrobe, whereas when I was actually naked, I, I — you know — felt natural. It wasn't going through stages to get there. It wasn't provocative, teasing; it just felt natural.

MR. MILLS: Request that the answer be stricken, your Honor.

THE COURT: The motion is denied.

Q: Did you feel at any time — did you at any time engage in behavior that was morbid?

A: No, I did not.

MR. MILLS: Objection, your Honor.

THE COURT: I will strike the question and the answer. If you want to preface that, Doctor.

Q: Were your acts sexual in nature, Carolyn?

MR. MILLS: I pray your Honor's judgment.

THE COURT: Well, Doctor, why don't you preface that, to be more specific?

DEFENDANT MANY: Did you engage in behavior that ——

I don't know ——

THE COURT: You can ask her what she did.

DEFENDANT MANY: Yes.

Q: What did you do?

A: I assisted you and I talked to you. I mean, those were the things that I did. What I was at that moment was naked, but it wasn't doing anything; it just was how I happened to be, just as I happen to be dressed now.

MR. MILLS: May the last half of the answer be stricken, your Honor?

THE COURT: Motion denied.

Q: Do you recall whether the shades on the house, the private home of Mr. Gentile, do you recall whether those shades were up or down?

A: I really don't recall. Frequently they are down all the way, and I have never seen anyone on their rear porch, and I have never seen anyone on the rear porch of the corner house or where Mrs. Johnson testified from; I had never seen anyone out there while we were on the sunporch. I had no reason to think that there would be.

Q: This is Exhibit 3, looking out of that solarium, or sunporch. Now, to the best of your knowledge, is it possible to see from that sunporch to the home from which Priscilla Pentz and Sandra Ridley testified that they saw you?

A: I don't think I can see in that home at all.

Q: Can you see in this picture any part of their sunporch, their porch?

A: Yes, I can see the top part of their porch.

MR. MILLS: I pray your Honor's judgment.

THE COURT: You may answer. Objection overruled.

THE WITNESS: I can see the top part of their porch that extends in the rear of their house.

Q: Can you point that out?

A: Yes. Right here. (*Pointing*)

Q: Now, wait. You're talking about Mrs. Gentile's house here?

A: Yes.

Q: I asked you a question about Sandra Pentz.

A: Oh.

Q: Sandra Ridley and Priscilla Pentz' home, beyond that house on the corner — can you see that porch?

A: No, I can't, from that photograph.

Q: But you can see the porch of the Gentiles?

A: Yes. And I can see their windows, but I can't see in them.

Q: How long were you out on the porch, approximately, that day?

A: Well, you know, it took place over about an hour, but I would just go out on the porch for about ten-minute periods, because it would be too hot. It was too uncomfortable. So then I would go outside again.

So I would say maybe, maybe I was there for 30 minutes — you know, ten-minute sequences, with some minutes in between, going in and getting lemonade or something.

DEFENDANT MANY: I have no further questions.

THE COURT: The witness is representing herself. She may ask herself questions if she wants to. If she wants to — I'm not urging her to. I am saying just that she has a right to. Anything you want to develop?

(Defendant Many and the witness confer)

THE WITNESS: I would like to ask myself if that day was an extraordinary day in any way.

And I would like to answer that it wasn't.

MR. MILLS: I would like to object, your Honor.

THE COURT: Well, let's go ahead.

THE WITNESS: That it wasn't unusual for me to be naked, that I often am that way in my own home. It's the way I prefer to be. It's the way I feel comfortable, it's the way I can interact directly with people, and maybe it even eases some kind of communication, because then people aren't always wondering about what's behind the mask, and the way clothes can be a mask, and when it's all out in front, with all your blemishes and all that you are, that doesn't become an issue any more, you can get to the things that really trouble human beings in getting together and being together. That's my only ——

THE COURT: Mr. Mills, go ahead.

CROSS-EXAMINATION BY MR. MILLS

Q: Miss Peck, could you tell the jury approximately how many times during the month of February you appeared unclothed upon this sunporch?

A: Well, we had just finished construction of the porch at the end of February, so it was too cold to go out there. I don't think I had ever appeared in February.

Q: Do you know approximately how many times during the month of March? Was it a daily event or —

A: I do recall one other time when I went out and sat in the chair and read for about half an hour.

Q: So are you telling the Court and the jury that there were two occasions during the month of March in 1970 when you appeared nude on that porch?

A: Yes.

Q: Two, and two only?

A: That's all I recall right now. I might have gone out there — as I say, it wasn't an extraordinary act for me.

Q: Did you ever appear on the roof of No. 197 nude? And I specifically direct your attention to the date, March 1, 1970?

A: No.

Q: Do you recall what date in 1970 an eclipse of the sun took place, in March of 1970?

A: Well, I know, because I called the Harvard Observatory, and it was a Friday, the 6th of March.

DEFENDANT MANY: The 7th.

THE WITNESS: 7th. I don't even remember it from ——

Q: On that day, did you appear nude on the roof of No. 197 Lakeview?

A: No, I did not.

MR. MILLS: Nothing further. Thank you, your Honor.

THE COURT: You may step down.

DEFENDANT MANY: Your Honor, I would like to ask that that line of questioning and the answers be stricken as being — applying to precedent facts and observations which were denied by your Honor earlier.

THE COURT: The motion is denied.

DEFENDANT MANY: Exception.

THE COURT: I think at this time we may take a short recess.

(*Court recessed at 11:54 a.m.*)

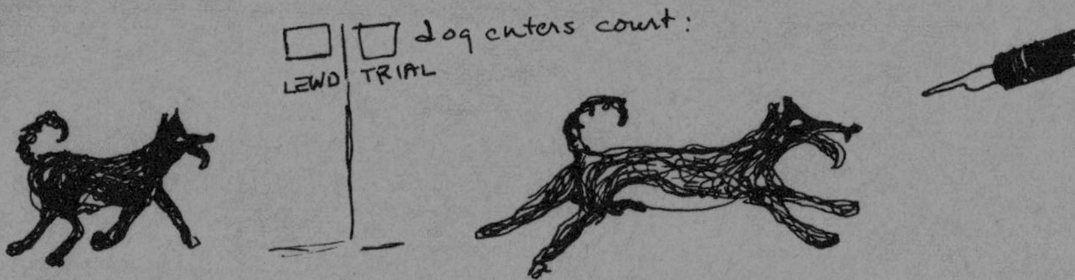

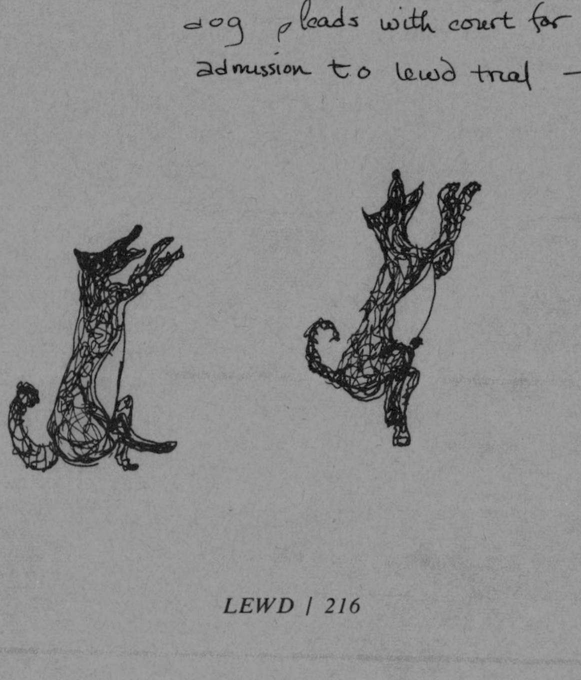

(*Court reconvened at 12:12 p.m.*)
(*Jury not present*)

THE COURT: I am advised you have a motion.

DEFENDANT PECK: Yes, for mistrial, on the grounds that you wrongfully allowed in evidence regarding prior acts of nudity on the premises — this was during the D.A.'s questions — and that that is inconsistent with your prior rulings — you disallowed evidence which would have allowed us to cross-examine those people, and the jury is left with a prejudicial inference from the questions and the fact that this evidence was wrongfully allowed in.

THE COURT: Dr. Many, is there anything you care to add?

DEFENDANT MANY: No.

THE COURT: Do you join in the motion?

DEFENDANT MANY: I join, yes.

THE COURT: Well, this situation comes as a direct result of you two defendants not following my strong urgings to get lawyers. I am not your lawyer.

What I would have done, had that evidence been objected to, is one thing, but you cannot bootstrap yourselves from your refusal to have lawyers, now, to get a mistrial because evidence came in that you think was improper.

The motions are denied. Bring in the jury, please. I would still urge you, even at this late stage, to get the advantage of an experienced trial lawyer in your case. What you do is your decision. I gather you would say no?

DEFENDANT MANY: No.

DEFENDANT PECK: No.

THE COURT: The exceptions of the defendants are noted. (*The jury enters the courtroom at 12:15 p.m.*)

THE COURT: However, I am going to take it upon myself to say to the jury that you will disregard any evidence you may have heard in this case about any nakedness of the defendants, as to either one of them, at any time prior to March 9, 1970.

DEFENDANT PECK: I call Dr. Many to the stand.

THE CLERK: Will you raise your right hand?

DEFENDANT MANY: I can't take the last part of it (the oath) — I don't believe in God — but I will affirm to the rest of it (the truth).

THE COURT: All right.

Will you give the witness, please, the affirmation?

THE CLERK: You solemnly swear that you will truly affirm such questions as shall be put to you by counsel, and the answers thereto?

DEFENDANT MANY: I do.

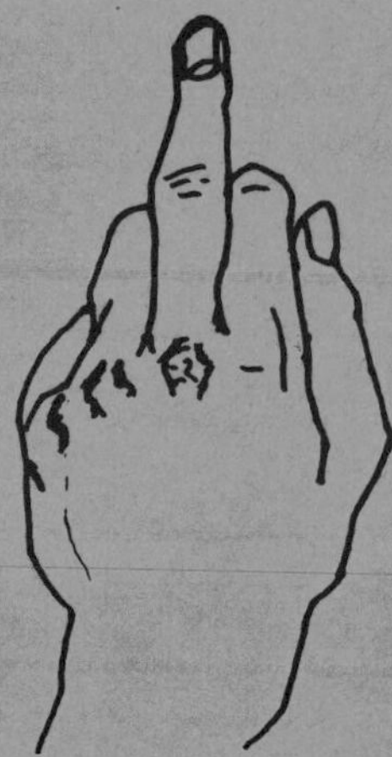

THE COURT: Mr. Foreman, ladies and gentlemen, we have a procedure, to satisfy the conscience requirements of all witnesses, and we provide for the oath to be taken, and if the witness for any reason of conscience feels he cannot take that, then we have another procedure which is called an affirmation; and you are not to draw any conclusions one way or another as far as this case is concerned. It has nothing to do with the merits of the case.

SETH E. MANY
(*Affirmed*)

DIRECT EXAMINATION BY DEFENDANT PECK

Q: Harkening back to March 9, 1970, could you tell the jury why you were on the porch of 197 Lakeview on March 9?

A: I was in a room that had been a porch but was at that time a solarium, totally enclosed by glass.

Q: Now, why were you in that solarium?

A: I was in the solarium on that particular morning in order to put the finishing touches on the plastic which we were setting up all around to help block out breezes and to maintain the heat level at a more constant level, appropriate both to the growth of humans and to the growth of plants.

We hoped to use that solarium and we would have used it both as a place to get the winter sun for ourselves and for the sake of the green plants that we love to have around us.

And so I was there that day with an instrument in my hand, a stapling gun, and I was stapling on some plastic in the corners, in order to block out those breezes. That was the main purpose.

The other purpose was that it was a beautiful day that day, a bright, sunny day, and it was one of those early winter times when one gets a chance to get out and partake of the sun, because in March the sun has then begun its passage through the sky to a level which allows the rays to play in upon that porch. And so, in order to take advantage of that, I was on the porch, dawdling around and doing some work with the plastic and hoping to block out those nasty little breezes that keep you from enjoying the total scene and the environment.

And it was a very beautiful day out, and I can remember seeing the blue sky and the sun and thinking what a really good place the city would be if people would just open themselves to the natural environment around them, if they wouldn't close it off, if they wouldn't try to keep it closed. And I was thinking that Cambridge was a really good place to live.

Q: Did you have any other purpose in your mind, any other purpose that might be called an evil purpose, that you recall?

MR. MILLS: I pray your Honor's judgment.

THE COURT: Well, inartistically expressed, but I will allow the question to be answered.

MR. MILLS: Can I have just a continuing objection to all the line of inquiry?

THE COURT: No. State of mind is an important factor in this case, perhaps one of the most important ones, and you may tell us.

A: I had no evil purpose. I did have a social purpose, which was to enjoy being out there with you, with my co-defendant, and to enjoy the sun together, because it's always a pleasure to discuss the small things and the important things and the problems that you're having, and the difficulties, and to discuss it in a pleasant and peaceful environment; and that's what we were doing.

Q: Did you have any conscious purpose in your mind to show yourself to the neighbors?

A: I had no conscious purpose to show myself to the neighbors or, indeed, to any persons, neighbors or policemen or non-neighbors or any other persons, other than to be with the person that I enjoyed being with, which was you at the time.

I was there in my own home, and I felt, indeed, it was a home in the sense that one is peaceful and can feel comfortable about a home. It was my castle, and I didn't realize it at that time, that a castle has to have a wall around it, and that wall has to block out the sun as well as the view of other persons; and, not realizing that, I was fully partaking of that sun and enjoying the temperature and the social company, which was excellent.

Q: Did you see any of the neighbors while you were there?

A: No, I didn't see any of the neighbors while I was there. In fact, during that day, I can't — I never saw any neighbors. It was very unusual, and it still is unusual, to see any neighbors in that neighborhood in the winter, because they all go indoors and they hide and they keep themselves from other persons, and they are not part of the neighborhood in any sense that I can discern. There is no openness to that neighborhood. It is a neighborhood which has, up to the present time, entailed a bunch of people living in geographical proximity, but without any close interpersonal relationships, and with a great deal of fear and concern — fear and concern lest new persons, new black persons, new niggers, new hippies, new anybody, should move in and disrupt their peaceful, their peaceful way of life.

And thus we have had contact with the neighbors and that contact had suggested that there was an element of disruption already — people were concerned about our long hair, about our mode of dress, about the fact that we lived together. They were concerned, but they never expressed those concerns to us directly; they were expressed in hurried whispers and glances aside, and the snickers, and you could see this.

THE COURT: I am not going to let this continue any longer. This is highly prejudicial testimony in any case, whether used against or for these defendants. It plays no part in these proceedings.

THE WITNESS: The testimony was designed to show my purpose in being there at that time and to show and to demonstrate the context ——

THE COURT: I am not going to permit a general discussion for or against these defendants. Prejudice will play no part in the case and in the verdict of the jurors.

DEFENDANT MANY: I take exception.

Q: How long were you on the porch?

A: I was on the porch over a period, I would say, of an hour and a half. I don't believe I was on the porch constantly all that time. I believe I was in and out, because I remember running out of staples a couple of times.

Q: And where would you have to go to get and replace the staples?

A: I would go back inside and down the cellar where — most of the time I can't find them, so I don't know where I went.

Q: Now, let's go back to March 1. Were you at home on March 1, which was ——

A: March 1, yes. That was a Sunday that Detective Ellis, who didn't identify himself — I didn't know it was Detective Ellis; in fact, I didn't realize until we saw him in court Friday that it was Detective Ellis. And I remember, there was something — a knock or a ring — the doorbell frequently doesn't work, though. I tried to repair it.

But there was a knock, and I remember that you went to the door, and I remember you were upset when you came back and you said that this person out there was a police officer who at the time had some kind of complaint but he wouldn't tell you the nature of the complaint, nor would he tell you the persons complaining. There was no suggestion, even, that the complaint was from the neighborhood. There was no suggestion that the complaint came from anywhere except from his police radio.

And I remember we discussed that at the time, and I remember advising you that we would be willing to see him and talk to him if he would make known the nature of the complaint and make known the nature of the investigation that he was conducting, but we would be willing to see and talk to him, but both in view of the light — the attitude which he conveyed, which was strongly negative, and, in a sense, brutal, and I felt he hurt you, and I felt that you didn't want him around, and I suggested that we not allow him inside the house, just as we routinely ask people who we feel are harsh or negative in their attitudes not to come inside the house. And so we rejected him as a person who we felt we wanted to have in our house.

Q: To your knowledge, have any other officials come to the house with complaints?

A: We have had other officials come to our house. In fact, we had a whole flock of officials just subsequent to the arrest. We had the Fire Department ——

THE COURT: I won't permit you to go into that, Doctor. None of it is admissible, and obviously it would be against your own interests. In any event, it is not admissible, and not before this jury.

This case involves one thing, and a very simple allegation of conduct by these defendants at a time and place on a date certain. That's all we're concerned with.

DEFENDANT MANY: I take exception.

Q: Now, I am going to show you a document; and are you familiar with this periodical?

A: Yes.

Q: Leaflet?

A: Yes. This document is *Korythalia. Korythalia* is the ——

Q: Now, before you go into it, do you subscribe to the beliefs or to some of the beliefs that — as they are set out in this document?

A: Yes. I subscribe not only to the document but to many of the beliefs as they are set out.

Q: In particular, as set out on Page 5, under "Freedom of Worship" — would you read that portion that expresses your beliefs?

A: "Because people are unique individuals, they differ in their images, conceptions and experiences of different interests and in their ways of worshipping as well. Therefore, freedom of worship is an indispensable condition of their development and fulfillment as human beings, so long as their worship imposes no undue hardship on others. Full support may be given to Article 18 of the Universal Declaration of Human Rights. Everyone has the right to freedom of thought, conscience and religion. This right includes freedom to change his religion or belief and freedom, either alone or in community with others, and in public or in private, to manifest his religion or belief in teaching, practice, worship and observance. Worship of nature and ecology ——"

THE COURT: Well, just a minute. I am going to instruct — there is no objection, but I am not going to turn this trial into something it shouldn't be.

That evidence just read by the defendant is to be put out of your minds and disregarded entirely by this jury. It has nothing to do with this case whatsoever. And I will instruct you about that more fully when we come to the end of the case.

DEFENDANT PECK: I would like to make an offer to have this marked as an exhibit in the manner that you did the others that were also rejected.

THE COURT: It may be marked as an exhibit for identification only, and that will constitute an exception to my ruling and an offer of proof.

I assume that the rest of the material in that brochure is along the same nature as that already read by the defendant?

DEFENDANT PECK: Yes, your Honor.

DEFENDANT PECK: I have no further questions.

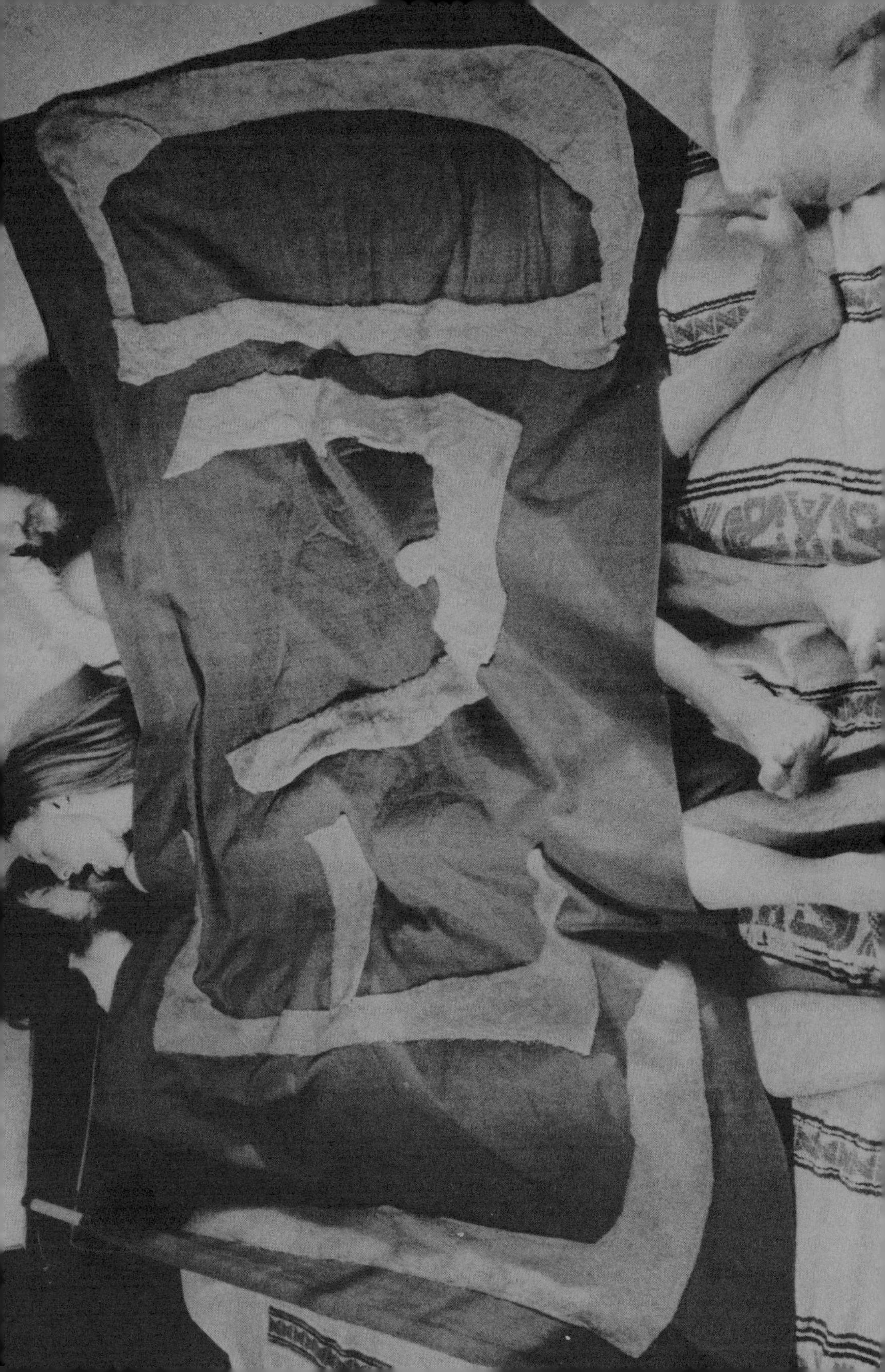

DEFENDANT MANY: I have some further questions.

EXAMINATION BY THE DEFENDANT MANY

THE WITNESS: Just a few moments ago, my co-defendant asked me what my purpose was on that porch. And because I haven't been allowed to read words which are beautiful and express that purpose ——

THE COURT: Do you want to state your purpose?

THE WITNESS: Yes, I am going to state the purpose.

THE COURT: You may do that.

THE WITNESS: As best I can, in my own words. And that purpose was to accept and to express the fact that we are part of the nature around us until we consciously, in an act of fear, decide to separate ourselves from that nature — and in this particular case, that nature, the sun, that was shining on that part of our home.

And in accord with my belief that one should be as close as one can without harming others, to peaceful nature, that one should not out of fear or shame or guilt restrict and constrict oneself with respect to that nature, my belief was that I, and my purpose was to get in and to commune, to be a part of that world around me that is expressed in the sun and in the bright light.

And so that expresses, I think, some of the feeling of a religious nature, the religious purpose, even though it was not part and is not part of any organized religion — expresses my conscious purpose to make an assertion of that universal human right to believe and to practice in a peaceful way the tenets of our conscientious understanding.

I have no further questions.

THE COURT: Mr. Mills?

CROSS-EXAMINATION BY MR. MILLS

Q: Doctor, when you were on the porch at 197 Lakeview on March 9, 1970, were you aware that persons in the neighborhood and neighboring houses or anyone outside of that area could, by looking in that direction, see you exposed and see the way you were?

A: Yes.

MR. MILLS: Thank you.

No further questions.

THE WITNESS: I would like to ask myself another question on redirect.

REEXAMINATION BY DEFENDANT MANY

THE WITNESS: I am also aware that not only persons can peek, but that they do peek into all the windows of not only our home but other homes in the neighborhood.

THE COURT: Anything further?

MR. MILLS: Nothing, thank you.

THE COURT: You may stand down.

THE COURT: Any further witnesses for the defendant?

DEFENDANT PECK: No, your Honor.

THE COURT: The defendants rest?

DEFENDANT MANY: Yes.

DEFENDANT PECK: (*Nods*)

THE COURT: Commonwealth?

MR. MILLS: No rebuttal, thank you, your Honor.

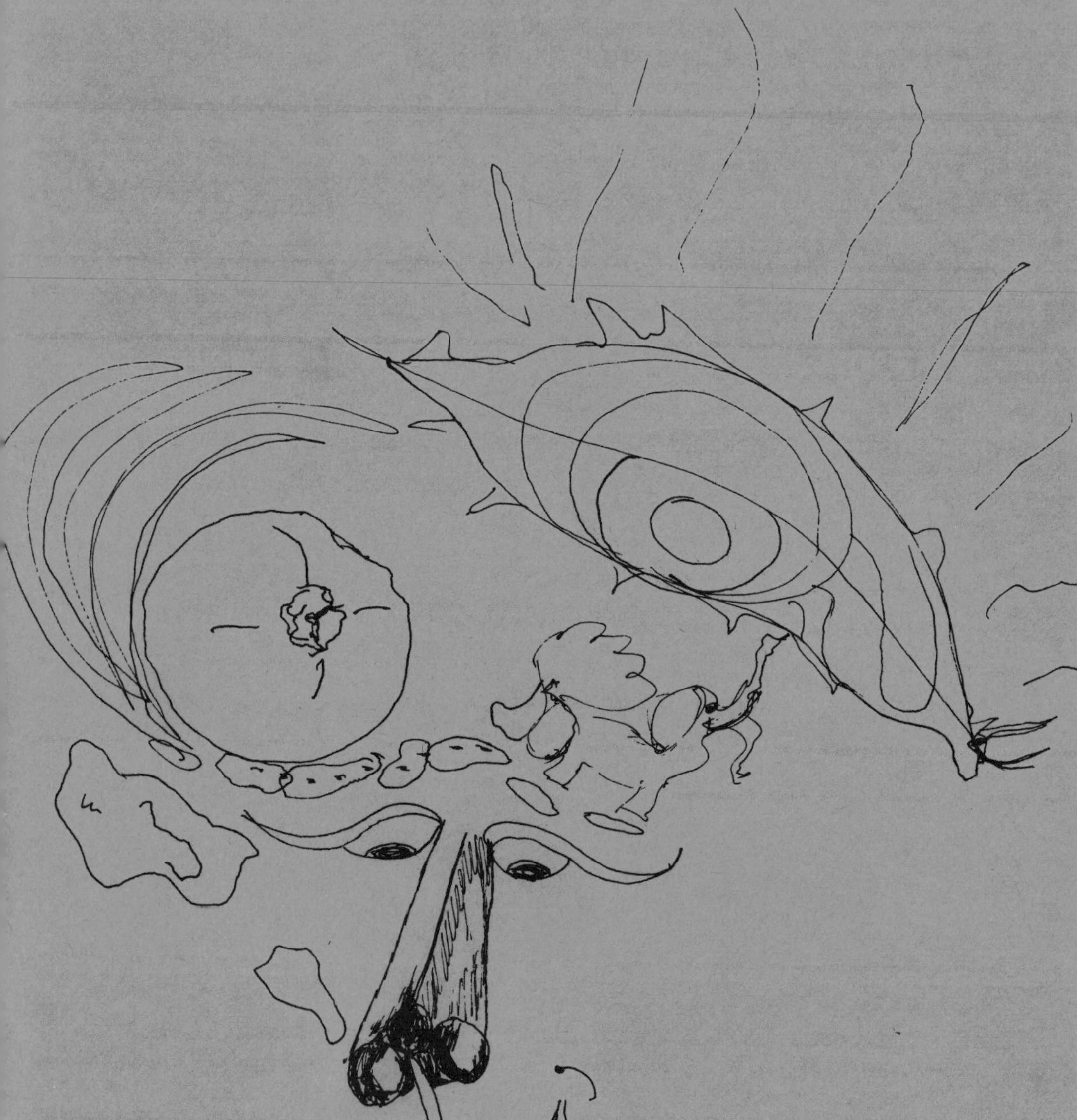

SUMMING UP

THE COURT: I will ask the Commonwealth and the defendants: Do you want to proceed with arguments and charge now or do you prefer to wait until after the noon hour?

The only question is whether you need any time to get ready for arguments and charge. I am ready any time.

MR. MILLS: The Commonwealth is ready.

DEFENDANT MANY: We are ready.

DEFENDANT PECK: We're ready.

I want to start with a brief summary of Massachusetts law which the Judge will give you in a more succinct form. After we were arrested, I looked up and read all the Massachusetts cases on open and gross lewdness, and this is as fair a statement as I can come up with.

I can give you some background for this. In the beginning, the first case is called Catlin, and there, defendants were ——

MR. MILLS: I object.

THE COURT: You are intruding on the function of the Court by reciting the law to the jury. That is my sole province.

However, in any case, you can't argue in the dark, and you may, in a very general way, if you wish, state what you think the crime alleged is, but only for the purpose of making your argument clear. You may not instruct the jury as to what the law is.

DEFENDANT PECK: Well, this was for the purpose of trying to develop what I think is lacking in the government's case against us.

THE COURT: You may state in a general way. The problem, Miss Peck, is, you are confusing — I'm sure unintentionally — the function of the lawyer and the jury and the Judge. It is my function to charge the jury as to the law. Your function now is to argue the facts of the case; but in doing so, in any case, you may in a very general way refer to what the law is, but you may not instruct the jury as to what the law is.

DEFENDANT PECK: Well, in a general way, I think that the law of open and gross lewdness is that the defendants have to intend to be open and public, and they also have to have intended to be sexually improper in some way towards the persons who are viewing them.

The cases say things like there has to be the irregular indulgence of lust; there has to be some facts that show some kind of irregularity of

sexual misconduct, of lustful indulgence, of interaction between human beings which is offensive to one human being and which is improper conduct according to some discernible standard.

I think what we are trying to develop is the problem of the standard and the problem of looking at our conduct.

Like our conduct, if you look at what I intended and what Seth intended was in terms of fixing the porch up and making it a place where we like to be and where things could grow around us and, in this case, plants.

The intention to be open, to expose ourselves to others, wasn't clearly there. I don't think the facts have been shown, developed by the Commonwealth to show that we knew a crowd, or in this case five or six people — well, seven people, gathered in one window, looking at us, and five other people outside of those who were looking at us. We had no awareness of that.

The complaint states "in the presence of." It's clearly a one-way kind of presence. They could see me, but I couldn't see them. I was in their presence, but they weren't in my presence in any meaningful sense.

This is a strange kind of law when you are being — when you might be convicted for offending someone that you don't even know is there and could have no way of knowing was there, because they did not make any effort to call attention to you, their attention that they were there to you, so that you could know and modify your conduct accordingly.

Similarly, I don't think that there is any showing of sexuality or improper sexual — nudeness alone is not sexual — need not be. There may be instances when you experience nudeness when you take a shower or perhaps in a gymnasium or, as Seth mentioned at one point, you are born nude. That isn't necessarily sexual.

Ordinarily, some other kind of conduct must be shown to create, to create an inference, to create the facts of some kind of impropriety of a sexual nature.

There wasn't. There were no other factors other than that we were nude and doing things that ordinarily a man and a woman could do in their own home. There is no showing that the place was public. It was in the back yard at the side of our house, our home, owned by us. Something traditional in the law that a man's castle is his province, and that the state and other citizens shouldn't be allowed to look in and be given the sanction of the law and say, "Yes, go ahead. Peek on your neighbors, and then tell us what you see and we'll see what we can do with it."

Again I urge you that it's not your subjective reactions to the facts that are important, just as it should not be relevant what the subjective reaction of witnesses to us, to our way of life, to what they saw, was. There has to be some objective standard, something ascertainable that you and I can both know is a standard for right and wrong conduct.

I don't think there has been any showing of what — how we have violated any objective standard.

Again, there has been no intent either to be seen or to prove that we were lewd or lascivious persons.

The statute is a felony. It's a serious offense. The result of your deliberations will be that we will be marked criminals and with the consequences therefrom which flow, which aren't just a sentence, but which are other things of which you are probably familiar with in your capacity as citizens, fellow-citizens.

And I guess — I can see that the main function of the jury is to build into the whole process the human concern, the concern with some kind — with justice that maybe can't be gotten at by the words of the statute, which are vague, or the words of the statute which don't really tell us what's involved.

So you have to look inside of yourselves and decide whether what we did was something criminal. And I know that I, too, look in my heart to decide whether I am criminal, and I know that I don't feel a criminal.

THE COURT: Dr. Many?

DEFENDANT MANY: I would like to first, in my summation, final remarks before the jury, comment on the prosecution evidence as I have seen it presented.

First, I would like to state that Detective McNulty, the first witness, by his own testimony ——

THE COURT: Doctor, excuse me, I don't think the jurors can hear you for a moment.

(*Airplane flew over*)

DEFENDANT MANY: Detective McNulty was never in our presence, nor did he make his presence known to us. Yet in this indictment of us, the terms of the indictment read that Detective McNulty was in our presence. The indictment is clearly faulty in that particular sense, and thus there was no basis for even arresting us.

Second, Detective McNulty, through the prosecution, introduced pictures which purported to be the view from the house at 187 Lakeview, a house that, I remind you, is occupied and owned by a fellow police officer.

Now, this view which was illustrated by the pictures — and it came out on cross-examination over my objections to the pictures being entered into evidence — these were taken with telephoto lenses which are designed to enlarge and magnify. And these views, further, on cross-examination were offered up not as views that would in any sense be what the eye — as the eye saw it, but as exaggerations and blow-ups of what the eye might see.

I remind you also that Detective McNulty's testimony about being in our presence was only made clear by reference to his prior testimony under oath in a district court, and it was only by drawing his attention to the conflict in such testimony that the fact that he was not in our presence nor were we in his, was made clear.

Now, with respect to Detective Ellis' testimony, a week prior to the alleged crime he came, dressed in plain clothes, and made a visit to our front porch. He said he had a complaint, but he refused to identify the nature of the complaint, or the persons who made it, until he was allowed admission into the house. This was his claim. And he was not allowed admission to the house, on the basis that we have suggested before, that he was not a person that we desired to have in our house.

The fact that he was denied admittance to our home — nor, may I remind you, did he have such a warrant for any admittance — there is nothing in the law or elsewhere that compels us, as free citizens, to admit the police to our homes — the fact that he was denied has been alleged to bear on our intention to commit the crime, the alleged crime of March 9, the fact that he was denied admittance, yet he had no legal right to press for such admittance.

Now, I maintain that the introduction of Detective Ellis and that evidence was highly prejudicial, and I think you will find my objections in the record.

Detective Amoroso, like Detective McNulty, secretly gathered in the house of a fellow police officer at 187 Lakeview to make observations of us, observations in our own home at 197 Lakeview. These observations showed only that we were naked, a fact that we have never denied — only that we were naked, not that there was any behavior tending to arouse lust or to excite interest or sexual interest. In fact, that the defendants took no notice whatsoever of the witnesses, nor did this witness, as with the other witnesses, make any personal attempt either to show his presence to us or to contact us.

Furthermore, Detective Amoroso indicated under oath that such behavior as he did observe was in our house, not out of our house. Thus, he was looking into our home through a broad window, through a solarium window. He was voluntarily and of his own will and in secret and in a private home peering into our home.

Now, Sandra Ridley and her mother, Priscilla Pentz, gathered secretly and unbeknownst to us and made observations purported to be from the house, the rear porch. They made no attempt to contact us, and they made no attempt in any way to indicate at the time of the alleged crime that they were in our presence or that we were in their presence.

Mrs. Murphy gathered secretly in her private home at the same day, in testimony with other companions, knowingly gathered there for the purpose of secretly viewing our behavior in our own home. They made no attempt to contact us, and Mrs. Murphy in her testimony indicates that we did not know of her presence.

Now, those are the facts before us as presented by the prosecution. Those are the facts that have been brought out on cross-examination and by introducing elements of testimony taken under oath in a prior court proceeding. We are not guilty of any known crime on the statute books of the Commonwealth of Massachusetts. There is no crime against nudity on those books. There is a crime against open and gross lewdness and lascivious behavior. There is such a crime on those books. We have been denied any attempt, and I cannot in conscience, in truth, assert that we have demonstrated that our behavior followed from our deeply held, conscientious beliefs, because we were not allowed to make such claims. We were not allowed to demonstrate the effects of our behavior on the neighborhood. We were not allowed to demonstrate these effects despite the fact that the Supreme Court in a decision having to do with obscenity, which governs the Federal statute —

(*Mr. Mills rises*)

THE COURT: Doctor, I'm sorry, but I must say to you that you are intruding into the province of the Judge, and you may not do that. I say that by way of instruction and not criticism, but you can't adopt that line of argument to the jury.

DEFENDANT MANY: Let me tell you that it is and was our understanding on the date of the alleged crime that acts of nudity, that observations of nudity, that pictures of nudity have all been upheld by the Supreme Court as being outside of the province of obscenity, and thus our act on that day in no way represented an act of open and gross lewdness and lascivious behavior. There was no intent to engage other persons nor to butt into their way of life.

Our acts in no sense have been demonstrated to be of great seriousness, to be flagrant, to be shameful or repulsive or to be sickening behavior. Our acts in no way accord with the sense of lewd, which has a long historical origin, dating back into the centuries, the earliest times of Judeo-Christianity, when such lewd behavior was held to be a matter of frequenting whorehouses.

Our behavior has not been prosecuted as such, nor was it in any way determined to be such type of behavior, nor, in fact, did the prosecution demonstrate any element other than the fact that we have naked bodies, any element of overt sexuality.

My own belief is that we are sexual persons. My own belief is that that is an undeniable fact, as a doctor, as a person, as a human being, in relationship to other persons. I have confronted this in so many ways I can't believe it, but it is an inescapable fact to me that we are humans and we are sexual persons. However, the prosecution did not demonstrate even the least iota of sexuality.

Furthermore, the prosecution did not demonstrate any so-called lascivious behavior. Now, if this law has meaning, the prosecution must produce evidence that each of these terms has some kind of substantial meaning in our behavior. Now, there was no evidence that there was any lascivious behavior. There was, in fact, evidence was denied as to whether there was any lust aroused in the observers, which is the basic element which is necessary to understand what lascivious behavior is.

Lascivious behavior is defined as behavior which tends to excite lust. That is what lascivious behavior means.

Now, we have been denied the right to inquire as to the effects of our behavior. Thus, we have been denied the right to defend ourselves in an open court of law. We have been denied the right to point out the terms in which this law is meaningful, through the testimony of either our witnesses or the prosecution witnesses. Instead, the prosecution has sought to impress upon us specific values, a specific way of life, specific interest with regard to the way in which they view human sexuality. Those persons have a different and perhaps an honest commitment to their way of life, and they have sought to protect it through the utilization of a law which is vague in the extreme and arbitrarily applied. They have interfered with our freedom of worship and the worship of the nature around us. They have interfered with our veneration and love of creative and open behavior. They have interfered with our ability to express ourselves openly and honestly. There is no legitimate state interest at stake here. There has been no evidence of harm of any kind introduced in this court.

The right to be let alone, which is the essence of privacy — and that can occur, I remind you, on the streets, where you have long hair or a black skin or you wear different-colored glasses — the right to be let alone, which is the essence of privacy, was denied in this case by the infringement of our neighbors' using the law as their particular mode of power, using the law to come down upon us.

Again, I remind you, there was no evidence of any harm introduced in this case. There is no readily identifiable community standard. How many times did we go through "What is the community?"

I ask each of you, today, in 1970, what is the community? Five hundred thousand people gathered at the Woodstock Nation. A half a million people gathered there and grooved. They got together and enjoyed it. And many of those persons were naked. Did they harm the persons around them? Were they open and grossly lewd and lascivious? On the contrary, these were people engaged in an expression, creative expression of love, of love of the world around them, and they were engaged, furthermore, in a peaceful expression of that love. This is not an isolated incident, and half a million people is not a small number.

But I would remind you that, today, like the Twentieth Century, the community is not our commune — I don't believe that. The community is not the area bounded by one and a half blocks. The community is not Cambridge. In fact, the legal community here is Middlesex County. But THE community, just as the community standards of medicine, spreads far beyond the particular community that we have been allowed to examine. And we have not been allowed to examine a community of interests that stretches far and wide — not across this nation, but across the world — and that's the community of love.

The acts described, furthermore, were not constitutionally — were not different from acts that are constitutionally protected as acts of free expression; that the primary difference between our behavior and the behavior of others whose acts are allowed on the stage, in the films, the primary difference is that we did not do it for money.

Finally, I can say no more to you but that the prosecution has not in the simplest element upheld their responsibility, either in the prosecution of this case or in the arrest leading to the prosecution. There was no proof, there never has been any proof of the crime of open and gross lewdness and lascivious behavior. They have not sustained their burden.

THE COURT: I hoped we might be able to finish arguments and charge before noontime, but we can't do that. We will stand in recess until 2 o'clock.

(*Court recessed at 12:55 p.m.*)

AFTERNOON SESSION

(*Court convened at 2:04 p.m.*)

MR. MILLS: May it please the Court, ladies and gentlemen of the jury, at the close of each trial — and now this trial is closing — the parties have their opportunity to comment upon the evidence.

Just prior to lunch you heard from both of the defendants, and now it is the opportunity for the Commonwealth to comment to you upon the evidence as it has been presented at the trial.

Subsequent to my comments, Mr. Justice Ford will instruct you as to the law in this case, and he will tell you, as he indicated prior to lunch, that as far as the law which is to be applied in this case, your instructions come from one source only, and that is the Judge sitting on the bench. The definition of this crime, what this crime is, and the elements of the crime, are not a matter to be presented into evidence, and any comments made by the defendants to you either during the course of the trial or in argument are not the law. The law will come from but one source.

And however singular that the Judge's authority is as to the law, we come to the role of the jury and the application of the facts. I bring this to your attention because it is the jurors' prerogative and only the jurors' prerogative — not the Court's, not mine, and not the defendants' — to tell you what facts you are to believe and which you are to disbelieve, and which you are to take in whole or in part.

It is my feeling that during the course of argument before you, there were matters which were not properly expressed as far as what the evidence was at the trial — and, as the Court will tell you, it is your recollection which is to control as to what you, the jurors, remember

about the facts in this case. That is your solemn oath as jurors, and your duty as citizens and jurors in this courtroom.

And now the law allows me to comment on the evidence as presented both in the defendants' case and the Commonwealth's case before you. And I am allowed to tell you about the testimony of Detective McNulty and Amoroso and of Special Detective Ellis and of Mrs. Crowley and Mrs. Murphy and Mrs. Ridley — and I think you've heard about that.

Perhaps the real question that has been presented by the defendants' case in this trial is the question of just who is to determine standards of behavior for members of this society. Is it going to be persons determining the norms of behavior for themselves, or is there going to be a common law to which we all, in part and to a certain degree, must adhere?

I suggest to you that the defendants' arguments have been eloquent. Their presentation to you in this courtroom at times could not be described as anything but courageous, and at the same time I think that the entire point of their presentation as it was presented to you was the question, who will determine for me how I am to act?

Now, there is a law, and the law will be defined for you by the Court, and you will apply that law to the facts as you remember them. And it is not the philosophy or the standards of life of these particular persons, no matter how sincere they may be in their convictions, which you are to apply to the law as the Judge will instruct you.

I think that the defendants will probably find it hard to believe today, or they may believe a week from now that there may be other people in this courtroom who admire them, who share some of their convictions, all of their convictions or none of their convictions.

But that is not the question before you. The question will be whether or not the Commonwealth has demonstrated to you by evidence beyond a reasonable doubt according to the law as you will be instructed by the Judge that the behavior which has been described to you, whether or not that behavior falls within the statute.

Your decision as to these matters is not to be swayed by prejudice, bias or feelings other than those of truth, and I think that when you apply the facts to the law as the Judge instructs you, you will find a violation of the law — and I say this in some respects not happily, because not liking to see anyone violate the law, I don't like to see sincere people violate the law, but sincere or otherwise, the standards of behavior for these people and for me and for you are determined from the common weal for the common good. There is one law for all of the people. We may not pick and choose which laws we are going to obey and which laws we are going to disobey.

Thank you for your kind attention.

Thank you, your Honor.

Etc.

CHARGE & VERDICT

THE COURT: Will the jurors rise, please?

(*Jurors rise*)

THE COURT: It is customary to rise at the beginning of the charge for the sole purpose nowadays to have a change of position.

You may be seated.

(*Jurors sit down*)

THE COURT: We today do that customarily in an attempt to make the jurors more comfortable. My charge will last about 20 minutes, which is normal for me. The first ten minutes will be necessarily devoted to the general rules by which you decide criminal cases.

In running a government and a country and a court of laws and not of men, you must decide this case according to the law as I give it to you. You cannot decide this case and must not decide this or any case based upon your notion of what you think is the law or what it should be or what it might be, because all of us, including Judges, are under and not above the law.

(*The Court, in great detail, describes the general rules for the jury, then continues with specific instructions relating to the case.*)

THE COURT: Now, the crime which they are alleged to have committed is found and defined in Chapter 272, Section 16, of the General Laws of Massachusetts, which reads, briefly and in material part, as follows:

A man or woman, married or unmarried, who is guilty of open and gross lewdness and lascivious behavior, shall be punished — and it goes on to state what the punishment is.

I do not read to you that section of the statute because the degree of punishment to be imposed in the event of a conviction is wholly and exclusively within the province of the Court and not within the province of the jury and should play no part whatsoever in your determination.

Now, how are these matters defined? We do not have too many cases of this, but I am going to read to you from a few cases, a few definitions.

The word, "lewdness," has been defined to be that form of immorality which has relation to sexual impurity.

"Lasciviousness" has been defined, among other things, as being lascivious desires or conduct; lustful; wantonness; lewdness; that form of immorality which has reference to sexual impurity.

As far as lascivious lewdness is concerned, the specific characterization of the offense is the openness and publicity of the act, as distinct from a secret act.

The word, "open," as used in the statute, means "public" rather than "secret."

We are dealing here basically with the condition of nakedness of these two people in an area where it is alleged that they could have been seen and were seen by their neighbors.

Now, the law as to nakedness and as to obscenity is not the easiest thing in the world to talk about. I don't mean that from a feeling of reluctance. I mean, it's difficult to define precisely.

Let me start with a basic proposition. When it comes to the criminal law, all of us are under the law and not above it. Whether we like a law or not or whether we agree with it or not, there is the duty of all of us to abide by it.

If the law is to be changed, there is a method to change it; and that is by the Legislature. The Legislature enacted the statute. If it is to be changed, they are the ones to change it. As long as it is on the books, it is our duty — your duty and my duty — to apply the law as set forth in the law books.

Now, this crime relates to nakedness. Everybody at some time walks about their house without any clothes on. But the problem is this: When is the state of nakedness, if ever, something within the purview of the criminal law?

Well, it comes down, I suppose, to a consideration of what we mean when we talk about privacy and the right to be free and the right to do what we wish to do. The whole criminal law — whether we are talking criminally or civilly — revolves around that question, as all of our court cases do.

Each one of us has the right to do anything he wants to, freely, with the utmost of liberty, up to a point; and that is the point where we start to interfere with the similar right of other people. That is the basic approach which you must use.

Now, as against the alleged right of anybody to walk around naked in his own home, you must take into consideration the rights of other people not to have the sight of naked people inflicted upon them.

In other words, it's one thing to talk about going to the theater or buying a book or seeing nakedness on the stage or seeing it portrayed in a book. It is one thing to be a willing participant or asking for that kind of information or sight. It is quite another thing if that sight is inflicted upon you without your consent.

Now, what is in issue here is not — and I repeat, "is not" — the political views, the religious views, the racial views, which were dragged out all during the trial. They have nothing whatsoever to do with this case.

If you would reflect for a moment, you would realize how utterly unfair that would be to the defendants, especially, if they were in issue. It should not make any difference — a person's religion or political views — as to whether they are guilty or not guilty, in a criminal case.

The first thing that would mean is that those defendants who were not popular would be found guilty, and that those who were popular would be acquitted.

The issue is: What was the conduct of the defendants? Did that conduct constitute a violation, a crime, as defined by the Court?

If you find upon the facts that no crime was committed, it is your duty to return a verdict of not guilty. That is, if you fail to find beyond a reasonable doubt that either or both of these two defendants committed this crime in question, it is your duty to return a verdict of not guilty, regardless of whether you like or dislike their political views or their appearance or anything about them.

On the other hand, if you find beyond a reasonable doubt that on the ninth day of March, 1970, either of these defendants or both of these defendants did something which constituted open and gross lewdness and lascivious behavior at the time and place in question, then it is your plain duty, as a matter of law, to bring back a verdict of guilty, despite your liking or disliking for their appearance, their racial or religious views, or anything else about them.

Prejudice must not play a part either by way of sympathy or by way of punishment that may be inflicted on any criminal defendant or on any party in any court of the land.

So now we have a conflict. What is the right of a person to be naked, and what is the right of a person not to have someone else's nakedness inflicted upon them?

What is in issue is the alleged conduct of the defendants or either of them, insofar as it relates to public conduct. If you were to find, for example, that the conduct of these defendants was wholly confined to their own house and that they neither knew nor had reason to believe that their openness and their nakedness would be seen by others in the area, then, of course, they are guilty of no crime.

On the other hand, was their conduct secret or open? It is not their secret intent which governs this, because all of us are judged and should be judged by what a reasonable man would expect to have happen. Was it reasonable for them not to know or, did they know or should they have known, that in walking around that back porch of theirs at the time in question, that other people in the area could or would see them?

If they knew or should have known that, then purity of heart or purity of mind is no defense to the crime alleged against them. Sincerity of purpose is not a defense to a violation of the criminal law. A sincere lawbreaker is just as much a lawbreaker as an insincere lawbreaker.

Whether they are guilty or not, whether they violated this law or not, is for you and for you alone to decide.

Now, did these people who testified as witnesses before you here see what they claim they saw, or did they not? Of course, if there is no evidence which you believe before you that actually these persons were seen in the state of nakedness together on that porch, then, of course, your verdict must be not guilty as to these defendants.

You have got to make up your mind from the evidence. First of all, what are the facts? What happened at that time, regardless of their secret intent, regardless of life-style, regardless of appearance? That neither helps them nor hurts them.

The issue is: What did they do? Not what they might have secretly intended or how sincere they may have been. But: What was the ordinary and probable result of their conduct? Should they have expected or reasonably expected to have known that other people could or would see them?

If they could have so reasonably known or expected, and you find that beyond a reasonable doubt, then their conduct was not secret but was open.

Whether or not it was grossly lewd and lascivious is for you to determine upon the facts. Now, in making that determination, I tried as best I could to avoid letting any witness testify as to his or her own feelings about that matter, whether they were shocked or not. If you think for a moment, you can't decide a case like this or any case based upon what a witness thinks about it, because then these criminal defendants would be at the mercy of any witness who wanted to come in and say, "I saw something; I was shocked."

By the same token, the defendant can't help himself by bringing in a witness who says, "I saw it and I was not shocked." That is not the issue. The issue relating to obscenity, to lewdness, and to lasciviousness is: What is the community standard?

That standard — following the statute — is something that you have to decide, you twelve jurors.

What is your opinion? What is your verdict? Taking their conduct as you find it to be, do you find that conduct to come within the meaning of this statute, or do you not?

Do you find their conduct to be open? Do you find it to be lewd? Do you find it to be lascivious? Do you find that they could or should have known that they could be seen? Was it the kind of conduct which would be susceptible to or can reasonably be supposed to inculcate lust in the eyes or the mind of the beholder?

These are things that you have to decide, not based upon any witnesses who sometimes slipped in their subjective reactions; but you must apply the standard that you think should be applied in these matters.

Now, you are required to reach a unanimous verdict. As I said before, to sustain a conviction on these cases, you must make a finding beyond a reasonable doubt as to each element necessary for a finding of guilty.

There is one further point that came up in this case which, again, as a matter of law, I should explain to you, and that is the definition of the word, "presence." The complaints allege that whatever took place, took place in the presence of Mr. McNulty.

Presence does not mean within touching distance. As a matter of law, if you find that Mr. McNulty was in that house and if you find that he saw the things that he says he saw, the fact that he did this by using long-distance vision or that he was some 100 or 200 feet removed does not make him any more less in the presence of these defendants.

Now, you are required to reach a unanimous verdict, and I know that you will take all the time that you feel is necessary to decide this case.

Now, ladies and gentlemen, I give these instructions — more often than not — without notes. I do that not in any spirit of bravado, but because I think it makes for easier communication to talk to you than to read to you. Sometimes, I am afraid more often than not, I leave something out that I should have included.

So let me ask counsel and the defendants: Is there anything about the charge that you wish to comment upon to me?

MR. MILLS: The Commonwealth is content.

THE COURT: Miss Peck?

DEFENDANT PECK: Yes.

At the Bench.

DEFENDANT PECK: This is in reference to when you talked about obscenity and lewdness. The United States Supreme Court decisions have held that viewing just people in the nude, nude males or nude females, is not lewd or obscene.

I think that that should be excluded, because in your charge it seems like there is an equation, to me, to being nude.

And, also, the part where you talked about privacy and the rights of others not to see that. It didn't seem clear that they didn't have the right not to see anything they like, but it still had to meet the standards of the statute being open, gross, lewd, and lascivious, being, like, there was an infringement.

I find that kind of prejudicial because it came before the other specifications.

THE COURT: As you know, this is not an easy subject to define, but I think I will leave it that way. I will note your exceptions to my charge.

DEFENDANT MANY: I would just like to note that I think you neglected the whole area that constitutes a gross act. In other words, an act might be open, lewd, and lascivious; yet, not be gross in its nature. "Gross" means: flagrant or highly shameful, highly inciteful.

THE COURT: I think that you are right. I will do that. Anything else?

DEFENDANT MANY: That is all.

THE COURT: All right. (*To Mr. Mills*) Is there anything that you want to say?

MR. MILLS: Nothing. Thank you, your Honor.

THE COURT: All right. I neglected that.

End of Bench Conference.

THE COURT: I am going to give you some further instructions which will be brief in nature, and I admonish you that what I now say is of no more importance or no less importance than what I have already told you.

It has been brought to my attention — and correctly so — that I did not discuss with you what the word, "gross," means. Of course, that means: extreme, flagrant, and so forth.

What I also neglected to add — and this is something that counsel and the defendants have not brought up — is that I ought to say to you that when it comes to nakedness, you must have in mind that there may be times when the condition of nakedness — even though you may be exposed to others — is brought about by some reasonable necessity or excuse.

For example, it you are in your house at night and you have a fire

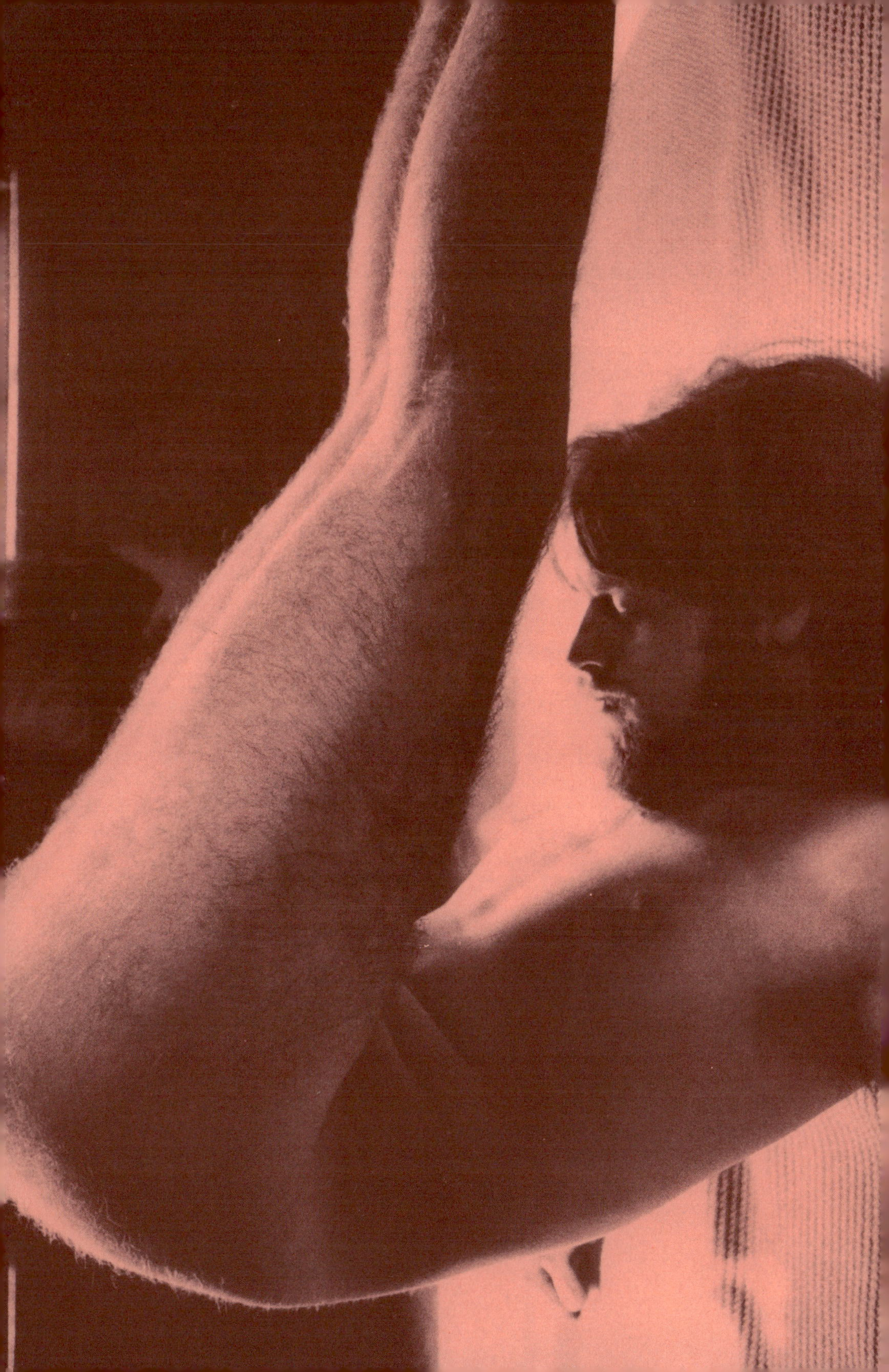

and you race through the house and you happen to run out to the yard naked, that does not mean — even if there are a thousand people there — that you have committed any crime. This is not something that you are intentionally doing by way of exposing your person. It is by way of necessity.

You will have with you in the jury room, as you begin your deliberations, the photographs that have been received in evidence.

You will have with you also excerpts from a transcript.

As I said, these complaints are not evidence, but are simply documents just to show the allegations against the defendants.

Is there anything else?

THE CLERK: No, your Honor. May the jury retire, your Honor?

THE COURT: Yes. Recess.

(*Recessed at 2:37 p.m.*)

(*Returned at 3:50 p.m.*)

THE COURT: Mr. Foreman, ladies and gentlemen, counsel, and parties. I am in receipt of a written question from the jurors, reading as follows, and I quote: "Can we find the defendants to be guilty or not guilty of the first part of the charge (open and gross lewdness) and bring in the opposite verdict for the second part of the charge (lascivious behavior)?"

Signed by "Vernon Reeves, in capacity as Foreman."

Please mark that as an exhibit.

(Jury question marked Exhibit No. 7 and received in evidence.)

THE COURT: Let me see the complaints, Mr. Clerk. I was about to read the statute, but I want to make sure that what is typed in the complaint is in conformance with the statute, which I assume it is. . . . These complaints allege that the parties were guilty of open and gross lewdness and lascivious behavior. You will note that the charge is set forth in what is known as the conjunctive, not the disjunctive. It is not "or."

In other words, for you, the short answer to your question is: no. But I want to explain the reason for it.

In any criminal case, you must find beyond a reasonable doubt as to each of the elements making up the charge. If any one of those elements should not be found by you to exist beyond a reasonable doubt, then, as a matter of law, you are required to return a verdict of not guilty. The Commonwealth has the burden of proving each element necessary to sustain a conviction of guilty.

So we will send those complaints back to you, and we trust that that answers the question, and we will ask you to return to the jury room.

Recess.

(*Recessed at 3:54 p.m.*)

(*The jury returns to the courtroom at 3:58 p.m.*)

THE CLERK: Mr. Foreman, —

THE COURT: I do not know what this verdict is going to be, and what it is, is up to the jury; but I want the spectators to remember that they are still in court and there will be no activity on their part. They are spectators and not participants. Go ahead.

THE CLERK: Jury, please rise.

(*The jury rises.*)

THE CLERK: 87990 and 1, Carolyn R. Peck, and Seth E. Many, Mr. Foreman, has your jury agreed upon its verdicts?

THE FOREMAN: Yes, it has.

THE CLERK: On 87990, on this complaint against Carolyn R. Peck, what say you, Mr. Foreman? Is the defendant guilty or not guilty?

THE FOREMAN: We find the defendant not guilty.

THE CLERK: On Complaint 87991, on this complaint against Seth E. Many, what say you, Mr. Foreman? Is the defendant guilty or not guilty?

THE FOREMAN: Not guilty.

THE CLERK: May the defendants be discharged?

THE COURT: Yes.

THE CLERK: 87990 and 1, Carolyn R. Peck, Seth E. Many, the jury having returned verdicts of not guilty on each of these complaints, it is ordered by the Court that you be discharged and go without [into the] day insofar as these complaints are concerned.

THE COURT: Recess.

(*Recessed at 4:01 p.m., Tuesday, January 12, 1971.*)

VERDICT
VICTORY DANCE